Enrique Moradiellos is Professor of Modern Spanish and European History at the University of Extremadura, Spain. He has previously taught at Queen Mary, University of London and Complutense University, Madrid and is the author of ten books on twentieth-century Spain, published in Spanish. In 2017 he was awarded the Premio Nacional de Historia (National Prize for History) by the Ministry of Education of Spain.

'Enrique Moradiellos is one of the most distinguished historians of twentieth-century Spain. For a concise and lucid account of Franco, the man and his dictatorship, it would be difficult to improve on his balanced and learned account.'

Paul Preston, author of *The Last Days of the Spanish Republic*

FRANCO

Anatomy *of a*
Dictator

———

Enrique
Moradiellos

Published in 2018 by
I.B.Tauris & Co. Ltd
London • New York
www.ibtauris.com

ISBN: 978 1 78453 942 9
eISBN: 978 1 78672 300 0
ePDF: 978 1 78673 300 9

A full CIP record for this book is available from the British Library
A full CIP record is available from the Library of Congress

Library of Congress Catalog Card Number: available

Typeset by JCS Publishing Services Ltd
Printed and bound in Sweden by ScandBook AB

MIX
Paper from
responsible sources
FSC
www.fsc.org   FSC® C007584

To Susana and Inés

CONTENTS

Illustrations

Map

The division of Spain, August 1936. The shaded areas are those held by the government.

FRANCE

Toulouse
Toulouse-
Francazal ✗ ✗ *Toulouse-Montaudran*

Marseille

Sète

Perpignan

ANDORRA

R A

Huesca

RAGON   CATALONIA

Zaragoza

Belchite

Reus ✗ Barcelona
Prat de Llobregat

Tarragona

eruel

Castellón   MALLORCA   MENORCA

V A L E N C I A

Valencia

IBIZA   B A L E A R I C   I S L A N D S

Alicante

urcia

artagena   *t   e   r   r   a   n   e   a   n*   *S   e   a*

Algiers   ⬅ Nationalist offensive

⬅ Republican offensive

ALGERIA   Airlift

✗ Air base

Orán

| 0 | 100 | 200 | 300 | 400 km |

| 0 | 50 | 100 | 150 | 200 miles |

Introduction

FRANCO
An Uncomfortable Spectre
from the Past

A little over 40 years ago, on 20 November 1975, General Francisco Franco Bahamonde died of natural causes in Madrid, just as he was about to celebrate his eighty-third birthday. For almost 40 years, from 1 October 1936, he had been the 'Caudillo', the head of the dictatorial regime of Spain. This book is an introduction to his personality, his activities as a political ruler and the nature of the institutional regime that he established and led until his death.

In the public memory of Spaniards and of European and international contemporaries, Franco was above all the 'Caudillo of Spain by the grace of God'. So read the inscription on the back of all Spanish coins minted since December 1946, approved by the unanimous decision of the Plenary of the Cortes (the Spanish Parliament). This was just one of the many honours and official tributes awarded to the soldier who had born in El Ferrol in December 1892, a man who had spent the majority of his military career in the bloody colonial war in Morocco, who later revolted against the government of the Second Republic in July 1936 and won an unconditional victory in the Civil War in April 1939. He had held the titles of head of state, head of government, generalissimo of the armies, *homo missus a Deo* (the man sent by God) and national chief of the Falange (the one-party state), 'only responsible to God and history'. He was, in short, the Caudillo, the 'supreme captain of the race', the 'Caesar undefeated', the 'saviour of the Fatherland', 'guardian of the Spanish Empire' and 'sentinel of the West'. He was an absolute dictator with full powers, deeply reactionary, ultra-nationalist and a Catholic fundamentalist who had assumed on 1 October 1936 'all the powers of the New State' and whose

authority would be 'providential and for life'.[1] He was not merely a simple
'dictator', for reasons articulated with typical hyperbole by the politicized writer
and poet born in Cádiz, José María Pemán:

> Francisco Franco: the quiet bravery, the clear purpose in the strong will and
> the smile. Franco is not a 'dictator' who presides over the triumph of a party
> or a section of the nation. He is the father that gathers under his command, as
> one big family, all the national forces of Spain. His gesture is not surly, his face
> is not, as Spaniards say, that of an unpleasant host. Franco excludes no one:
> Franco smiles and welcomes. Because under his command he has not only
> soldiers, Falangists or *requetés* [militiamen]. Under his command is the whole
> of Spain, the sum of all it is. His watchword is 'integration' – in other words,
> unity. The word of Rome and of Isabel and Ferdinand; and of Charles V and
> Philip II. The key to our history.[2]

A man who carried all that authority and received all that majestic flattery
for almost 40 years necessarily had to be present in every manifestation of the
public and social life of Spain. In the year 2000, on the occasion of the twenty-
fifth anniversary of Franco's death, the writer Antonio Muñoz Molina recalled
that Franco was 'the face that I saw everywhere'.[3] Two years later, the historian
Vicente Sánchez-Biosca corroborated that, between 1936 and 1975, Franco was
'an icon of Spanish life, reproduced everywhere that would catch the eye of
Spaniards: posters, newspapers, magazines, monuments, letters, photographs,
film, television'.[4]

The image of Franco was, of course, present on the coins, but he was also
depicted on postage stamps, in the classroom – to the right of the crucifix –
on the walls of the dependencies of all government agencies and some private
individuals, in street names in Spanish towns and cities, on the No-Do (the
official cinema newsreel) in black and white, then also on the television news
and as imposing equestrian statues (in Madrid, Barcelona, Valencia, Ferrol,
Santander, Jaén and elsewhere). His name was also present, pronounced both
in official speeches that ended with the threefold invocation ('Franco, Franco,
Franco!') and in Sunday sermons seeking divine protection for the Pope, the
bishop of the diocese and 'our head of state, Francisco'. His peculiar voice, a

high-pitched monotone, was heard by radio or television audiences on many solemn and festive occasions: on 1 October, during the national holiday for the 'Exaltation of the Caudillo'; on the corresponding Sunday in May on the occasion of the victory parade; on 18 July in commemoration of the start of the 'glorious national uprising'; on 25 July during the tribute in Santiago de Compostela to the 'patron saint of Spain' and, above all, on 31 December in the traditional 'message from His Excellency, the head of state, to the Spanish people'.

Given the omnipresence of Franco during his regime of absolute personal authority, his apparent disappearance from public discourse and almost from the memory of Spanish citizens since his death is striking. In fact, his non-existence and the citizenship's virtual forgetting of the Caudillo is one of the most significant and surprising aspects of the process of political transition from dictatorship to democracy in Spain between 1975 and 1978. The truth is that, even today, 125 years after his birth and after the widely covered fortieth anniversary of his death, the carefully named 'former head of state'[5] seems to be missing, unknown, silenced or forgotten by general public opinion in the country, especially among the younger generations born after his death and after the restoration of democracy.

The few informative surveys about him unreservedly and repeatedly confirm this impression of conscious absence or involuntary amnesia. For example, in 1981, the sociologist Juan José Linz conducted a broad national-level survey which, among other issues, offered respondents five ways to define their personal political attitude to the immediate collective past: 'pro-Franco', 'anti-Franco', 'both', 'none' and 'no answer'. It is highly indicative of the degree of genuine oblivion or deliberate silence that 32 per cent chose 'none', in spite of the fact that all respondents were of the generation that had experienced the dictatorship as fully formed and socially active adults.[6]

Four years later, in 1985, on the tenth anniversary of Franco's death, a small survey of primary and secondary school pupils conducted in the city of Madrid revealed that 'today's Spanish children barely know General Franco'.[7] If that was the situation among those who, because of their youth, had only indirect and mediated knowledge of his character, no less revealing was the situation among those who had had a direct experience of the same. Of the

1,500 people over 18 years old who were asked about their feelings at the time of the death of Franco, the results of the survey were as follows: 30 per cent said that they had felt 'hope'; 27 per cent 'indifference'; 22 per cent 'sadness'; 20 per cent 'fear'; 9 per cent 'liberation'; and 6 per cent 'don't know/no answer'. To compare the sentiments of different generations, the same survey also revealed that those over the age of 55, who had lived through the years of the Republic and the Civil War, had more feelings of sadness and fear, while young people aged 18 to 34, mostly born during the development of the 1960s, were most likely to declare feelings of hope and liberation. However, the most significant result of the survey remained the notable proportion who had felt 'indifference' at the death of Franco, a percentage that was basically concentrated among young people aged 18 to 25 and increasingly declined in older age groups.[8]

The results of a series of surveys and polls carried out in November 2000, on the twenty-fifth anniversary of Franco's death, did not vary substantially from the situation of 15 years earlier. In fact, it emphasized those trends. For example, a new survey among secondary school pupils asking for their impressions about the Caudillo demonstrated respondents' difficulty in 'placing him in a precise moment of history', with replies as peculiar as they were anachronistic: 'the king before Juan Carlos', 'Franco, in the Battle of Las Navas de Tolosa [1212]', 'Franco, in the Cortes de Cádiz [1812]'. Significantly, according to the author of that survey, this widespread ignorance among young people had a notable caveat: 'the exception is in the Basque country, where young people still detected in the Franco regime the root of their conflict [Basque separatism]'.[9]

The first of these surveys was performed and published by the Madrid centre-left newspaper *El País* on 19 November 2000.[10] The second was commissioned by centre-right Madrid paper *El Mundo* and was published on 20 November 2000.[11] Significantly, their results were very similar and revealed several contradictions and notable paradoxes on the subject.

According to the survey in *El País* (from a sample of 1,000 people), the feelings that Franco engendered amongst Spaniards were the following: 'indifferent' (42 per cent); 'negative feelings' (38 per cent); 'positive feelings' (17 per cent); 'don't know/no answer' (3 per cent). The question about the degree of presence and persistence of the Franco regime in Spain in 2000 received these replies: 'definitely something in the past' (59 per cent); 'it has some influence' (33 per cent); 'still a significant influence' (5 per cent); 'don't know/no answer' (3 per cent).

In the survey by *El Mundo* (a sample of 800 people) almost all of those asked claimed to know 'who Franco was' (99 per cent). However, this positive result appeared to be mere rhetoric because the rest of the answers revealed very vague notions about him, his regime and his historical prominence. Thus, for example, responses to the question 'Do you know how he got to power?' gave the following results: 75.2 per cent subscribed to the correct response of 'coup d'état'; 20.6 per cent replied 'don't know/no answer'; 3.2 per cent answered 'hereditary succession'; and even 1 per cent chose 'democratic elections'. Indecision and historical ignorance were also shown in the answers to two questions: 'Were human rights respected under his rule?' and 'Did the quality of life improve under his regime?' To the former, 12.8 per cent of respondents declined to answer or did not know how to, whereas in the latter, that percentage rose to 16.3 per cent. Also, compared to the 67 per cent who believed that Franco did not respect human rights, 20.2 per cent estimated that he did (inexplicably). Although 38.5 per cent of respondents recognized the improvement of the quality of life during the regime, 45.2 per cent denied it without hesitation (and against the historical evidence of the economic development that started in 1959 and continued until the crisis of 1973). This persistent division of views also manifested itself in the replies to the key question: 'What image do you have of Franco?' This 'image' was considered 'bad' or 'very bad' by 38.1 per cent of respondents, while 33.1 per cent considered it 'fair', 22.5 per cent rated it as 'good' or 'very good' and a modest 6.2 per cent chose 'don't know/no answer'. Interestingly, that balance between favourable, unfavourable and neutral perceptions (which was also reflected to a lesser extent in the survey by *El País*) set itself against the result of responses to the question about 'history's judgement' of Franco. An absolute majority of 53.7 per cent was convinced that it would be 'negative', unlike a small 19 per cent who believed it 'positive' and a notable 27.3 per cent who preferred not to respond.

The *El País* poll revealed similar (and not very disparate) percentages in the responses to its final question: 'Do you think that anything of Franco remains in the year 2000?', 55.3 per cent believed that there was 'little', 23.3 per cent argued 'nothing', 17.7 per cent maintained that 'much' remained and a mere 3.8 per cent 'don't know/no answer'.

The accuracy of these results was confirmed by another survey in December 2000 by the Centro de Investigaciones Sociológicas on a sample of 2,486 people. According to it, only 10 per cent of Spaniards believed that Francoism would go down in history as a positive period for Spain, compared to 37 per cent who thought it negative and 46 per cent who felt that it encompassed 'good and bad things'.[12]

Five years later, in November 2005, when the new socialist government of José Luis Rodríguez Zapatero was considering the introduction of what was later called the Ley de Memoria Histórica (Historical Memory Law), the newspaper *El Mundo* carried out a similar survey that corroborated something obvious: 'opinion on Franco had worsened by 13 points in the last five years'. According to the results, 51.2 per cent of the people surveyed at that time perceived the dictator's image as 'bad' or 'very bad' (compared to 38.1 per cent in 2000) and up to 86 per cent described him as 'a dictator' with the '[negative] connotations that arise from that word'.[13]

However, just one year later, on the seventieth anniversary of the start of the Civil War, another poll in the same newspaper produced more contrasting results: slightly more than 51 per cent of the respondents considered that 'the coup d'état' of July 1936 lacked 'any justification', while almost 30 per cent thought it was 'born out of an existing situation of chaos and violence' and another 19 per cent declined to answer. The division of opinion crossed partisan lines (although the majority who condemned the coup were on the left and those who justified it were on the right), but there was a clear age bias too: those who had known the Franco regime were 'more lenient towards the coup than those whose only experience of the Franco regime was through books, the mass media or oral sources'.[14]

This complex situation in 2005–6 was endorsed by a macro survey carried out by the Centro de Investigaciones Sociológicas in the spring of 2008, after the December 2007 enactment of the Ley de Memoria Histórica, which included several measures 'in favour of those who suffered persecution or violence during the Civil War and the dictatorship' (among other things, endorsing official financing of the excavation and identification of corpses in anonymous graves).[15]

Of the 3,000 Spanish respondents, 41 per cent were supporters of the law, while almost 28 per cent had qualms because it could resurrect past grudges; another 13.2 per cent regarded it 'an incomplete measure', 3.1 per cent considered it excessive and 11 per cent had no opinion. However, this division of views on that legislation did not extend to opinions on 'the preferred political regime': democracy gained more than 85 per cent of the support, while only 6 per cent favoured 'an authoritarian regime' in certain circumstances, and another 5 per cent considered them equal. In respect of the key question about the kind of 'feelings' held towards the Franco regime, respondents showed the following revealing responses: rage (23.5 per cent), sadness (16.2 per cent), indifference (11.8 per cent), lack of understanding (10.5 per cent), discomfort (9 per cent), fear (8.6 per cent), do not know (7.1 per cent), other feelings (4.7 per cent) and patriotism (3.2 per cent).

In conclusion, since 1975, Spanish citizens have maintained a predominantly negative view of Franco and his regime, albeit with many nuances and significant divisions of opinion. This sociological reality has combined with a high degree of forgetfulness, silence or ignorance about him that cannot be explained in logical terms, not least because a large part of the Spanish population was born, grew up, lived and (in some cases) suffered during the dictatorship of the Caudillo. If that direct personal experience was insufficient for those who had personal memories of the period, in addition there was and still is a diverse range of biographical studies on Franco, his regime and historical era. This literature has always been available to refresh the people's memory and to inform the ideas and knowledge of those who were then too young or were born after his death. As an analyst of the phenomenon recently recalled:

> Spanish society of the post-Franco era, in contrast to what has been said, did not want to forget but to know more of its own past, in particular about the Republic, the war and the dictatorship. It wanted to leave behind the lens of the dictatorship of imposing a single truth, which suppressed dissenting voices and debate in the public sphere.[16]

This paradox been explained as a peculiar amnesia or as evidence of a self-imposed silence and self-induced forgetfulness that became a key element of the political culture of the new Spanish democracy. The tacit political agreement, sealed during the transition, avoided mentioning in public or using as a political weapon the memory of crimes committed by both sides during the Civil War and the Francoist repression following the victory, in order to avoid the risk of destabilizing the new democratic regime. An upset of the balance might have been triggered by demands for people to be held responsible for past actions and the settling of old scores. In short, it is obvious that the long shadow of blood cast by the Civil War of 1936–9 and the general will of the people not to repeat this traumatic experience under any circumstances ('never again a civil war' was a general code of conduct) promoted the badly named 'pact of forgetfulness' about a past and a person so recent as to be uncomfortable and disturbing (however well-known and remembered *sotto voce*). The sociologist Karl Mannheim had already warned long before: 'If society wants to continue to exist, the social memory is as important as the oblivion.' The philosopher Friedrich Nietzsche, at the end of the nineteenth century, agreed without reservation: 'The knowledge of the past is only desirable if it is useful for the future and the present, not if it weakens the present or destroys a vital future.'[17]

In the recent case of Spain, the double political amnesty of the years 1976 (the legislative decree of 30 July) and 1977 (the law of 15 October) demanded, as a necessary and lesser evil, a tacit collective and selective historical amnesia that persisted for a long time before it became increasingly invalid and inoperable. The common etymological root of both 'amnesty' and 'amnesia' was acknowledged in the 1976 decree approved by the first government of Adolfo Suárez, in its supporting preamble: 'As Spain moves towards full democratic normality, the moment has arrived to finalize this process with the *forgetting* of any discriminatory legacy from the past that could affect the full fraternal coexistence of Spaniards.'[18] The urgent practical need to draw a discreet public veil over that traumatic past was recognized by *El País*, the spokesman of the anti-Franco democratic opposition, in an editorial of 17 July 1977 commemorating the anniversary of the start of the Civil War: 'It is difficult to forge an accord on the memory of the bloodshed amongst brothers.'[19] The same influential newspaper would reiterate the imperative for the adoption of the amnesty law in October 1977:

Democratic Spain should, from now on, look forwards, forget the responsibilities and the deeds of the Civil War, leave aside the 40 years of dictatorship [...]. A people neither can nor should lack historical memory, but this must serve to nourish peaceful coexistence for the future and not to nurture resentment from the past.[20]

With democracy already consolidated, there were various important recognitions of the existence of this singular 'pact of forgetfulness', as the initial caution which had driven its existence ceased to function as a new generation of Spanish society were born and grew up. One of the most notorious comments was made during the bitter election campaign of May 1993, when the leader of the right-wing opposition, José María Aznar, criticized Felipe González, the head of the socialist government, and 'accused him of repeatedly violating the pact sealed during the transition not to stir up the past'. Nearly a decade later, in 2001, with Aznar already in power, the new socialist leader, Rodríguez Zapatero, corroborated the existence of a 'tacit pact of silence' whose hours were numbered, in his view: 'The transition drew a veil over the collective memory to achieve reconciliation.'[21] To search for the origins of this equivocal 'pact of forgetfulness' merely in the political cautiousness of the defeated left-wing (or in its fear of 'settling old accounts' due to the sheer force of the tacit powers of Francoism) could perhaps be overly simplistic.[22] Another explanation could be offered for the enduring explicit or tacit agreement during recent decades: the ideological and historical anachronism of the extreme alternatives faced during the Civil War and the inability of Spanish citizens to identify with any of them personally, totally and exclusively. The writer Francisco Ayala, a lucid witness of that time who spent many years in exile, wrote on the occasion of the sixtieth anniversary of the start of the conflict:

The decision to cover the Civil War in silence was not, therefore, only due to an act of political prudence, but had been imposed by a basic reality: nobody felt solidarity with the ideological positions that had been in play during that war.[23]

It is probably the historian Santos Juliá who has followed this line of reasoning with the greatest emphasis and clarity. In his view, an examination of the complex relationship between remembrance and oblivion of the Civil War and the Franco regime in Spain has to begin with the fact that the second was a result of the first and that this, regardless of its causes and respective responsibilities, resulted in a brutal harvest of blood with no fewer than 90,000 Republican casualties (perhaps another 40,000 in the postwar period) and up to 55,000 Francoist deaths (caused only during the war).[24] The overwhelming awareness of these abominable crimes created the context for the peaceful transition from dictatorship to democracy in Spain through a cultural formula well known in many countries and in many similar transitional processes: to 'cast into oblivion' the traumatic and divisive past (as a case of *oblivione mandare*, oblivion act, *d'en renouveler la mémoire*). That formula involved a voluntary political and civic will to remain silent on (that is, not to mention or use publicly as a weapon) something that would prevent progress and could block or hamper the continued peaceful existence of a political community.[25] The result of this political choice, progressively developed between both the elites and the citizenship, was in tune with the new perception of the Civil War during the 1960s – that it was no longer the heroic and laudable myth (an anti-fascist or anti-Communist crusade) but a new tragic and deplorable myth (a criminal and shameful fratricidal war). In the words of Juliá:

> The question, therefore, is not that nothing has been spoken of (the war and the dictatorship), but what has been said and with what intention; not that the facts are ignored, but that their meaning has undergone changes imposed over the years. It forms part of the Civil War that each side treats the other as criminal, assassin and saboteur, as Carl Schmitt wrote in his article of 1947. But this representation of the other side as a killer that must be exterminated, which was overwhelming in the years of war on both sides and persisted among the Francoist circles of power until the end, increasingly gave way, first among the exiles, then among dissident groups of the dictatorship, to a representation of that past as a fratricidal war: the other was no longer a criminal or a murderer but a brother. It is not that the war was not to be written about or that it was left to fall into oblivion,

but in political speeches, reports, opposition parties and group resolutions and manifestos, its meaning was transformed with the accumulation of new experiences and the pursuit of other political goals. The exaltation of their own cause, even among those who had fought in the trenches, gave way to a representation of the war as a collective tragedy. This gave rise to a sense of shared responsibility and the demands for an amnesty as a first step to start a constitutional process that would culminate in a new regime fully accepted by the majority of Spaniards, whichever side they had fought for during the war.[26]

In short, the so-called tacit 'pact of forgetfulness' (in essence the agreement not to use the war and its crimes as an active political weapon) made possible the peaceful transition from dictatorship to democracy. But it also involved the progressive elimination of any public disruptive and vindictive reference to 'the former head of state' in order not to hamper that transition and further democratic consolidation. It should be noted that the process started just as Franco's body was buried in the retrochoir of the Basilica of the Valle de los Caídos (Valley of the Fallen) on 23 November 1975. A day earlier, on his proclamation as king of Spain, Don Juan Carlos de Borbón y Borbón had set the tone when referring to his predecessor in a neutral and generic style: 'The name of Francisco Franco is already a milestone in Spanish events, to which it will be impossible not to refer in order to understand our contemporary political life.'[27]

The consequent elimination of the public vestiges of Franco and his regime from 1975 was as slow and necessarily complex as the transitional process and the corresponding democratic consolidation, although it did not raise major public controversies or notable political or parliamentary clashes. Perhaps a paradigmatic example of this gradual disappearance by 'consensus' is the fate of the imposing equestrian statue of Franco which looked over the parade ground of the castle of Montjuïc in Barcelona. One day in May 1986, close to the fiftieth anniversary of the start of the Civil War, the horse and its illustrious rider were dismantled and moved, stealthily and without witnesses, to the library of the military museum in the interior of the castle itself (and later, in 2008, it was placed in a municipal warehouse closed to the public). A similar fate awaited another equestrian statue of the Caudillo which presided over Valencia's main square. After successive delays in the execution of a plan agreed by the city council of March 1979, in September 1983 the statue was dismantled with little incident and withdrawn to the interior of the Capitanía General (General Headquarters) de la Región Militar de Levante, in Valencia, where it still remains.[28]

But if the fate of the equestrian statues of Franco in Barcelona and Valencia denote a form of discreet removal of the Caudillo to the annals of history or the barracks of his comrades in arms, the destiny of the equestrian statue in his home town of El Ferrol exemplifies the problematic boundaries of this process of public and official elimination. Cast in bronze in 1967 in the shipyards of Empresa Nacional Bazán, this statue probably weighed more than 6 tons. Although the anti-Franco left won the municipal elections in the city, and even though there had been multiple demonstrations against the statue's presence (including two unsuccessful bombings), it continued undaunted in its location in the Plaza de España until well into 2002, when it was withdrawn to the Naval Museum (before moving in 2010 to a closed store at the Naval School). It is possible that no one had dared to remove it previously because, as acknowledged by the city's mayor, who was from a left-wing Galician nationalist party, it 'weighed a lot'. It could also have been influenced by a survey by the newspaper *La Voz de Galicia* of the inhabitants of the city in the autumn of 2000 which revealed a significant sociological reality: '46 per cent of those polled supported the elimination of such an uncomfortable relic, one the town hall did not even include in its guidebooks, but 40 per cent were against disturbing their equestrian countryman.'[29]

Nor was the equestrian statue of Franco in Madrid, located in the Plaza de San Juan de la Cruz (next to the Nuevos Ministerios) since 1956, immediately dismantled and removed. It remained at its post until the morning of 17 March 2005, when it was taken to a ministerial warehouse amidst a small flurry of nostalgia for the old regime. It was not the only physical memory of the Caudillo in the capital and province of Madrid. There was still a street, a square (in El Pardo, near the neo-classical palace which had been his official residence for 35 years) and a triumphal arch (in Moncloa, at the beginning of the Ciudad Universitaria and the exit to the road to La Coruña).[30] This was in contrast to the few honours in the capital to other heads of state such as Niceto Alcalá-Zamora Torres or Manuel Azaña Díaz, to name only his immediate predecessors between 1931 and 1936 (although there are more monuments to Alfonso XIII and Alfonso XII). In fact, one prominent analyst has recently drawn attention to the glaring imbalance in street names in Madrid when it comes to honouring the memory of general combatants on the side of Franco and those of the Republican government, for example:

If Aranda, Asensio Cabanillas, Fanjul, García Escámez, García Morato, Captain Haya, Millán Astray, Mola, Moscardó, Orgaz, Saliquet, Varela or Yagüe have their corresponding street in the capital of Spain, why not Aranguren, Asensio Torrado, Batet, Ciutat, Cordón, Escobar, Hernández Sarabia, Hidalgo de Cisneros, Lister, Miaja, Mera, Pozas, Rojo, Riquelme or Tagüeña? An unforgivable oversight, a definitive omission, perhaps?[31]

Perhaps only the city of Santander exceeded that of Madrid in this overabundance of Francoist symbols in the streets and in urban public monuments. According to a study conducted at the beginning of 2001, the Cantabrian capital had no fewer than 30 streets dedicated to personalities of the dictatorship (including José Antonio Primo de Rivera, the founder of the Falange, his sister Pilar, the lifetime national delegate of the female section) and another 12 statues and monuments relating to the regime (including an equestrian statue of the Caudillo, one of three by the sculptor José Capuz). But here also the effects of the Law of Historical Memory were inescapable: in December 2008 the statue was removed from its pedestal in the centre of the city and transferred to a municipal warehouse.[32]

In short, in the form of public statues, names of avenues, squares and streets, in plaques or commemorative monoliths of his birth, his death, his visits or his political work, the name of Franco continued to be a tangible and recurrent presence in Spanish society for a long time (and there are still some minor tributes scattered around). However, knowledge of his historical role is somewhat diffused and scant among the citizenship, in particular among the younger echelons, who are increasingly prevalent in the population pyramid. As Santos Juliá recalled in 2002:

Spaniards have an ambiguous assessment of Franco, quite unlike the Germans' demonization of Hitler. Perhaps it is because the majority of adults did not know the worst years, the 1930s and 1940s, but rather knew the 1950s, 1960s and 1970s. They recall that in the second half of Francoism although there was a lack of freedom there was also an improvement in the material quality of life.[33]

Thus, today, Franco represents the name of a spectre from the past, uncomfortable but very real and significant. A considerable part of today's political culture may have its genesis and its origins, for better or worse, in the times he presided over and moulded, and this may have given rise to, among other aspects of political life: the obsession with unanimity in political decisions, the tendency to demonize conflict and differences, the inclination to identify government with nation, the massive growth of the executive against other state powers, the liking for charismatic leadership, the complacency towards corruption and venality, etc.[34] A humorous vignette by cartoonist Max in *El País* on 28 March 2015 epitomized this with a succinct dialogue between a young man and a know-it-all. The first asks: 'Master, what remains of Francoism?' The second responds: 'Do you see this sprinkling of grey dust everywhere? It's dandruff and it is an attitude.' A similar explanation was offered that same year by the historian Julián Casanova: 'Such a prolonged authoritarian rule had profound effects on political structures, civil society, individual values and the behaviour of different social groups.'[35]

Perhaps the most common attitude of Spaniards to Franco and Francoism is that subtle indifference that conceals and eclipses the majority of negative feelings aroused by his personality and undemocratic and reactionary politics. This is borne out by the strange statement made in November 2000 by the mayor of Ávila, of the right-wing Popular Party, to justify his refusal to meet the opposition demands that he change the name of the street dedicated to General Franco and remove its corresponding plaque and effigy: 'One has to accept history with all its consequences. [...] It does not disturb me to see the squares referencing such dreadful characters from our history. Nor does it bother the people.'[36] As announced on the cover of the influential British magazine, *The Economist*, in its issue of 25 November 2000, Spain had passed in the last quarter of a century 'From Franco to Frantic', at least until the economic crisis of 2011 temporarily called a halt to that process.

Still the unwelcome shadow of Franco keeps cropping up in public life, with the corresponding media and political agitation. It appeared with the controversy of 2001 and 2002 over the official financing of the digitization of his personal archive, jealously guarded by the Fundación Nacional Francisco Franco (a private organization headed by Carmen Franco Polo, duchess of Franco, a title granted in November 1975).[37] And in a funny, nostalgic film by Albert Boadella about the last two years of Franco's life (*Buen viaje, Excelencia*), released in October 2003 to public and critical success. And even in satirical form with the release of the five CDs of *The Golden Age of Spanish Pop* in 2004, featuring a bust of the Caudillo in his later years with a blond wig, painted red lips and blue eye shadow. And in the 2010 proposal to remove Franco's body from the crypt of the Valle de los Caídos and transfer it to the cemetery of El Pardo, where his wife's remains already lay.[38] The ghosts of the past can always be banned and exorcized, but they can never be eradicated completely or assumed to have never existed. It is an old lesson that Lord Acton confirmed more than a century ago: 'If the past has been an obstacle and a burden, knowledge of the past is the safest and surest emancipation.'[39]

This work, for all its modesty and limits, aims to contribute to the emancipatory knowledge of the character of Franco and the Francoist regime. An understanding of the former requires a knowledge of the latter, for reasons well exposed by Ian Kershaw in his magisterial biography of a contemporary much admired by the Caudillo: 'We need to examine the dictatorship as well as the Dictator.'[40] For that reason this book is divided into three complementary parts, each studying a different aspect of the same historical phenomenon. Chapter 1, 'The Man: A Basic Biography', gives an insight into the human profile and life story of Franco. Chapter 2, 'The Caudillo: A Charismatic Dictator', looks at the socio-political and legal bases of his extraordinary power as absolute dictator, and Chapter 3, 'The Regime: A Complex Dictatorship', examines the character and nature of his regime of personal power.

1

THE MAN
A Basic Biography

We do not accept upon our shoulders the burden to lead Spain only to open a parenthesis of comfort, as happened with the dictatorship of Don Miguel Primo de Rivera. We accept the command and direction of Spain to stage a revolution, to make a decisive change in the life of Spain, to lead Spain and the Spaniards in the direction of greatness, restoring unity, freedom and justice.

Speech by Franco in Madrid, 18 July 1953

Biographies of Franco

As a figure of great significance in the history of Spain, General Franco has been the subject of a diverse biographical literature since the Civil War. However, until relatively recently, there have been hardly any biographies of academic rigour and historiographical quality.

Of course, 40 years of personal dictatorship generated a vast apologetic and almost hagiographic literature. In this section, five works of special importance for their impact and international market are highlighted. The first was published by the journalist Joaquín Arrarás Iribarren in 1937 and became the official version of the life of the Caudillo during the war and after. It was so well received that by October 1939 there had already been eight editions in Spain and it had been translated into English, French, German and Italian. The book would serve as a source of inspiration and information for newspaper reports and subsequent biographies due to its bombastic and obsequious style, detectable in its final paragraphs:

Ambition, of any kind, does not motivate General Franco, when he embarks on an undertaking (to save Spain). Neither does he care about command, which he does not crave, nor human vanities, which he disregards, or material advantages, which do not interest him. In his prime he has reached those peaks which rarely crown prestigious men and cap a glorious military career. [...] Franco, Caudillo of the Faith and of Honour in this solemn period of history, who accepts the most glorious and overwhelming of responsibilities. [...] Franco, Crusader of the West, elected Prince of Armies in this tremendous hour, to allow Spain to accomplish the destiny of the Latin race.[1]

After the end of World War II in 1945, with the victory of the Allied powers over the Italo-German Axis, that biography and similar works were outdated and unsuitable for modern times, at both national and international levels. For this reason, they were replaced by another work, by journalist Luis de Galinsoga and Lieutenant General Francisco Franco Salgado Araujo, cousin of the Caudillo and head of his military household.[2] These authors took care to reflect more favourably on Franco's ambiguous conduct towards the Allies during the recent world war, bypassing his identification with the German–Italian side, his anti-democratic diatribes and anti-Semitism for a more beneficial and cosmetic generic anti-communism. Indeed, as shown by the title (which translates as *Sentinel of the West*) and date of publication (1956), the work had in mind the general political situation imposed by the Cold War and Spanish military dependence on the United States following the agreements on the installation of US military bases in Spain in September 1953.

Nearly a decade later, in 1964, there appeared a new biography of the Caudillo in the form of a documentary screenplay as part of the official campaign to commemorate 'the 25 years of peace of Franco'. Its authors were the writer José María Sánchez Silva and the filmmaker José Luis Sáenz de Heredia, who had produced a very simple text: *Franco, ese hombre* (*Franco: That Man*). In keeping with the expanding economy at the time, which was generating in Spanish society an incipient material well-being and marked political apathy, Franco was portrayed above all as a 'man who gave [Spain] peace, work and prosperity'. The caudillo of victory became the caudillo of peace, less heroic and more humanized, dressed in plain clothes, with a normal family life and receiving support from a people 'united as never before with the man who won the war against communism, who miraculously preserved our neutrality and was building a better and fairer Spain'.[3]

The last great laudatory biography written in the lifetime of General Franco was the work of the prolific historian Ricardo de la Cierva and plotted his career until the start of the 1970s. It was published in the form of collectible instalments by Editora Nacional during 1972 under the title of *Francisco Franco: un siglo de España* (*Franco: A Century of Spain*). The following year it appeared in book format (in two volumes) with the same title. Certainly, with its use of primary sources, its photographic accompaniments, its length and thoroughness, and even its author's own literary capability, the work much improved on previous official biographies. And this was all with an apparent critical objectivity and political distance which in no way diminished his portrait and the favourable vision of the illustrious and humane Caudillo.[4]

With the work of La Cierva, the peak of the regime's political openness had been reached in regard to biographies of Franco. After the death of the Caudillo in November 1975, subsequent Francoist biographies (in both senses) did not surpass this achievement. However, of them all, one stands out for its documentary value: that of the medievalist Luis Suárez Fernández: *Francisco Franco y su tiempo* (*Francisco Franco and his Time*).[5] The author, a former senior education policy adviser of the regime in its time of economic development and political openness, used in the text unpublished documents from the private archive of General Franco – documents guarded by the Fundación Nacional Francisco Franco and closed to the public (and even more so to historians) until very recently. Despite the invaluable and unprecedented worth of this substantial document, the work of Suárez Fernández even surpassed La Cierva in its apologetic character and lack of criticism.

Openly confronting all the biographical literature favourable to General Franco, the divided and defeated anti-Franco opposition generated its own portraits of the Caudillo. From the time of the Civil War, these biographies were published in all sorts of formats (text, caricatures, photographs and cartoons). Varying degrees of demonology and human and political denunciation predominated, with Franco portrayed as a cunning traitor, the puppet of Hitler and Mussolini, a tool of capitalists and landowners, an ambitious, cruel and bloodthirsty dictator, an inquisitorial Catholic fanatic and so on. By way of example were the diatribes of Salvador de Madariaga in his 1959 book *General, márchese usted* (*General, Go*) against 'the cynical hypocrite who usurps power' in Spain as 'the leech of the West' (an ingenious reference to Galinsoga and Franco Salgado-Araujo's book).[6]

However, it is evident that it was not until the 1960s that a true biography from the democratic opposition came to light: the work of 'Luis Ramírez', *Francisco Franco: historia de un mesianismo.* (*Story of a Messianism*).[7] Hiding behind this pseudonym was the writer and Basque journalist Luciano Rincón Vega, who published under the imprint Ruedo Ibérico in Paris, a respected institution of Spanish exile in France founded in 1961. Ramirez/Rincón's book was a huge success in anti-Franco circles in exile and in the interior, enjoying several reissues (three by 1973) and foreign-language editions, and shaping the image of Franco among his opponents inside and outside Spain.

After the death of Franco in 1975, the process of democratic transition and the end of censorship made it possible to publish in Spain more or less critical or even hostile biographies or biographical sketches of the Caudillo. Of the many that appeared, it is worth mentioning the booklet that was mainly drawn up by the sociologist Amando de Miguel, published in 1976 under the ironic title of *Franco, Franco, Franco.*[8] It could even be argued that in this same genre belongs, with the appropriate qualifications, the well-known literary fictions of writers Francisco Umbral (*La leyenda del César visionario* (*The Legend of a Visionary Caesar*)), Manuel Vázquez Montalbán (*Autobiografía del general Franco*), José Luis de Vilallonga (*El sable del Caudillo* (*The Sword of the Caudillo*)), Albert Boadella (*Franco y yo. Buen viaje, Excelencia* (*Franco and Me: Farewell, Your Excellency*)) or Juan Luis Cebrián (*Francomoribundia*).[9]

The end of the Franco regime and the establishment of the new democratic order also created the potential for an avalanche of works and accounts by witnesses and protagonists of the political dictatorship. That flow of testimonies provided whole new insights and information on the character and private behaviour of the late Caudillo. On the basis of these new eyewitness accounts and the progressive opening of state archives to researchers, the beginning of a historiographical review of the figure of General Franco became more feasible, objective and documented – a reconsideration of events that was faithful to the canonical dictates to treat history *bona fides, sine ira et studio*, in good faith, without partisan rancour, and a thoughtful reflection on the material available.

Aside from minor and scattered contributions, the first fruit of this patient work of historiographic reconsideration was born in 1985, just ten years after Franco's death, when Professor Juan Pablo Fusi published his famed short biographical essay: *Franco. Autoritarismo y poder personal* (published in English as *Franco: A Biography*).[10] For his equanimous treatment and his use of the newly available supporting documents on the life and work of the General, Fusi's essay made a definite and decisive break with previous biographies. This historiographic review deepened in 1992 (the centenary of the birth of the General) with the appearance of two works, different in scope and perspective. On one hand was the brief biographical summary drafted by the American Hispanist Stanley G. Payne, *Franco, el perfil de la historia* (*Franco, a Profile*). On the other hand was Javier Tusell's exhaustive study of Franco during the years 1936–9, *Franco en la guerra civil* (*Franco in the Civil War*).[11]

However, despite the advances in understanding Franco represented by the contributions of Fusi, Payne and Tusell, 100 years after his birth and almost on the twentieth anniversary of his death, a general biography on his character and historical performance, based on the enormous amount of testimony and archival material that was emerging, was still missing.

This omission was amply rectified in the autumn of 1993, with the publication in England (and its translation into Spanish the following year) of a biography by the Hispanist Paul Preston, entitled simply *Franco: A Biography*. That work, the fruit of more than a decade's research, was monumental in size and in the comprehensiveness of primary documentary support. The book was 'a closed study of the man'. Its basic aim was to produce 'a more accurate and convincing picture than had hitherto been achieved', following Franco's life, both private and public, during his almost 83 years of existence from 1892 to 1975.[12] The critical and popular success and translations (in Spanish, Russian, Italian and Czech) are clear proof of its quality as a historical and biographical work.

The effort started by Fusi, deepened by Payne and Tusell and culminating in the work by Preston has subsequently been completed by a long list of authors: Alberto Reig Tapia, Bartolomé Bennassar, Fernando García de Cortázar, Andrée Bachoud, again Stanley G. Payne in cooperation with Jesús

Palacios, and so on.[13] This tradition of biographical studies has made it possible today to reveal many of the enigmas surrounding General Franco's public and private career, both before and after his conversion to Caudillo of Spain. At the same time, several myths developed by Franco's hagiographers have been crushed, particularly the three dearest to the Caudillo himself: his assumed role of providential crusader who saved Spain from communism during the Civil War; his boasted ability as a cunning and illustrious statesman who knew how to preserve the neutrality of Spain during World War II; and his conscious responsibility for the implementation of the process of economic and social modernization of the 1960s. Many of the ideas espoused by the anti-Franco opposition have also been undermined: those which portrayed him as a cruel and stupid tyrant, simply serving the interests of Spanish capitalism, as a man raised to power only thanks to the help of Hitler and Mussolini and who survived for 40 years due to a simple combination of savage internal repression and good fortune internationally. The truth about the man seems to be at some midpoint that has nothing to do with geometry: he was not as great as his apologists claimed, nor as little as his detractors argue. The following pages will try to offer a well-balanced and convincing biographical portrait.

The Forging of an Africanista

Francisco Paulino Hermenegildo Teódulo Franco Bahamonde was born in the Galician coastal town of El Ferrol on 4 December 1892 into a lower middle-class family with a long tradition of naval service. He was the second son from the marriage of Nicolás Franco Salgado-Araujo and Pilar Bahamonde Pardo de Andrade, who had three other children: the eldest, Nicolás; the third, Pilar; and the youngest, Ramón. The solitary and shy Francisco, called 'Cerillita' ('Little Matchstick') by his classmates at school because of his shortness and extreme thinness, grew up in this small provincial town (a population of 20,000) under the influence of his conservative and pious mother and distanced from a freethinking and womanizing father.

He first wanted to enter the Naval Academy to train to become an officer, like his brother Nicolás (unlike his younger brother Ramón, who would opt for service in the fledgling air force). However, Francisco's desire was frustrated because, after the colonial disaster in the Spanish–American War of 1898 the Spanish fleet had been reduced to a minimum and for years there was scarcely any call for officer candidates. As an alternative, Franco was admitted into the military school the Academia de Infantería of Toledo in August 1907, when he was 14 years old, just at the moment when his father left the family home (for which Franco would never forgive him, unlike the rest of his siblings). His time in Toledo, the old Spanish capital, fashioned much of Franco's character and basic political ideas: 'That's where I became a man.'[14]

The Spanish army, with its rigid hierarchical command structure and obedience to orders and discipline, completely fulfilled Franco's emotional needs and provided the shy boy with a new and secure identity. From then on, Franco would never hesitate over his vocation and profession: 'I am a soldier,' he claimed.[15] Thus he would also be described in later years by both his friends and his enemies. Pedro Sainz Rodríguez, a conservative intellectual who knew him in Oviedo and would later finish his life in the monarchist opposition, recalled in his memoirs: 'Franco was a man obsessed with his career; above all he was a soldier.' Tomás Garicano, a somewhat younger comrade in arms and one of Franco's last ministers of the interior, agreed: 'raised in a naval family, and naturally destined for a military life, it appears (and I think this is the truth) that the military code is his standard for living.'[16]

Indeed, with the trauma of the colonial disaster of 1898, the rising of socio-political conflicts in the country and in the heat of the new and bloody war waged in the north of Morocco, Franco adopted a good part of the political and ideological baggage of the military of that time during his years as a cadet. Above all, he endorsed a fiery, unitarian Spanish nationalism, nostalgic for past imperial glories, suspicious of the outside world that had remained impassive to the unequal confrontation with the American colossus in 1898, and extremely hostile to the emerging peripheral regionalist and nationalist movements that dared to question the unity of the fatherland. The prolific historical work of Marcelino Menéndez y Pelayo was the basic intellectual foundation of his hyper-nationalistic retrospection and identification between the fatherland and Catholic orthodoxy:

The Church nurtured us, with its martyrs and confessors, with its saints, with its admirable system of synods. Through it we were a nation and a great nation, rather than a multitude of nations, born to be the target for any greedy neighbour [...] Spain, the evangelist for half of the globe; Spain, the hammer of the heretics, the light of Trent, the sword of Rome, the cradle of San Ignatius; this is our greatness and our unity: we have no other. The day when that is lost, Spain will return to the fiefdoms of the Arevacos and the Vectones [of ancient times], or to the Kingdoms of Taifas [of the Middle Ages].[17]

Complementary to this fundamentalist nationalism was a militaristic view of political life and public order that saw the army as a praetorian institution virtually autonomous from civil authorities and sometimes, in internal or external emergencies, superior to them by its status as the 'backbone of Spain'. Thus had proclaimed King Alfonso XIII in 1902 when he ascended to the throne aged only 16:

Blessed is the sovereign who sees in you the most solid supporter of the social order, the surest foundation of public peace, the most determined defender of institutions, the strongest basis for the welfare and happiness of the fatherland.[18]

As a direct result of that doctrine of national militarism as well as the brutal personal war experiences in Morocco, much of the Spanish military (the so-called Africanistas for having served in the Army of Africa) were developing a determined authoritarian and anti-liberal mindset, blaming that liberal ideology, the parliament and the party system for the prolonged decline suffered by Spain since the War of Independence (1808–14) and throughout the nineteenth century, culminating in the disaster of 1898. As was rightly appreciated by the philosopher José Ortega y Gasset in 1922: 'Morocco made of the dispersed soul of our army a clenched fist, morally ready for the attack.'[19] Over time, and especially after the decisive three years of the Civil War, Franco would be the most genuine representative of this political worldview, prevalent among a large part of the Spanish military. In fact, at various times in his life, and throughout the 1950s, he would reiterate in public his furious criticism of liberalism as 'alien' and 'anti-Spanish' as well as his contempt for a 'decadent' and 'catastrophic' century:

> The nineteenth century, which we would have liked to erase from our history, is the negation of everything Spanish, the inconsistency of our faith, the denial of our unity, the demise of our empire, all the generations of our being, something foreign that divided us and turned brother against brother, destroying the harmonious unity that God had placed on our land. [...] The consequence of liberalism was the decline of Spain. The neglect of the needs of the Spanish soul, which kept undermining us during the nineteenth century and a large part of the twentieth century, cost us the loss of our empire and a disastrous decline. While the other global powers of those times were able to forge their might, we have buried ourselves with a dream for more than 100 years.[20]

After completing his studies in Toledo with a mediocre result (he only managed to be ranked 251 in a class of 312 cadets), Franco was assigned to the garrison of El Ferrol as a second lieutenant, where he remained in service for a year and a half. During that time, through the influence of his mother, he confirmed his religious convictions to the point of entering the Adoración Nocturna (Nocturnal Adoration Society, a Catholic lay association for nightly devotion to the Virgin). At the beginning of 1912, he was transferred to the Spanish protectorate in Morocco. The difficult conquest of this elongated, narrow region from 1904 (with the signature of the first Hispano-French Treaty for the division of Morocco) until 1926, in the face of fierce resistance offered by the native tribesmen, cost the lives of more than 17,000 soldiers, commanders and officers of the Spanish army.[21] It was, in essence, a ruthless guerrilla war over mountainous terrain where armed indigenous Moroccan tribes harassed Spanish columns and positions, who then responded by bombing their enemies and advancing inch by inch over the territory with harsh reprisals.

During his stay in Morocco, where he would remain for more than ten years (only interrupted for short periods by postings to Oviedo in 1917 and 1920), Franco proved to be a serious, meticulous, brave and effective officer obsessed with discipline and the fulfilment of duty. He was the archetype of the Africanista officer, so different from the sedentary military bureaucracy that thrived in the quiet mainland barracks and who was opposed to all forms of promotion that were not through mere seniority in the service (the so-called *junteros* for their support of the embryo of professional unions known as Juntas Militares de Defensa). These qualities and courage shown in combat (he survived a severe wound in June 1916) gained Franco rapid promotion for bravery in combat.[22] By then, his name had acquired some notoriety on the mainland due to the publication of a small work entitled *Marruecos. Diario de una bandera* (*Morocco, Diary of a Battalion*) at the end of 1922 in which he recounted directly and simply his war experiences as second-in-command of the Legion (or Tercio de Extranjeros), a newly created shock unit under the command of Lieutenant Colonel José Millán Astray, an eccentric commander repeatedly wounded in combat. The text of the book, in addition to being a proud description of a special military corps, was also a sincere reflection of the extreme brutality of the conflict:

> The campaign in Africa is the best practical school, not to say the only one for our army, due to its shaping of its values and merits, and the bravery of the officer corps that fights in Africa must one day be the heart and soul of the peninsular army. [...] At noon I get permission from the general to punish the villages from which the enemy harassed us. The work is difficult yet beautiful; to our right the terrain descends to the beach and at the foot is a long stretch of small houses. Meanwhile a section opens fire on the houses, covering the manoeuvre, lets themselves down a small steep gorge and surrounds the settlement, killing the inhabitants. Flames rise from the roofs of the houses and the legionaries chase the inhabitants.[23]

His extensive service in Morocco, in the midst of a ruthless colonial war and in command of a crack force like the Legion, reinforced Franco's hardline political convictions and contributed largely to the hardening of his character. From either fighting or negotiating with the rebel Moroccan leaders, the young officer learned well the tactics of 'divide and conquer' and the effectiveness of terror (imposed by the Legion) as the perfect military weapon to achieve the paralysis and submission of the enemy. In addition, his long experience in colonial Africa, where a de facto state of war prevailed and the military performed a wide range of administrative functions, confirmed in practice the alleged right of the army to exercise command without restrictions, superior to the distant and weak civilian authorities on the peninsula.[24] Indeed, thereafter, Franco always understood political authority in terms of military hierarchy, obedience and discipline, referring to it as 'command' and considering dissenters and adversaries as little more than 'seditious'. At the end of 1938, already virtually victorious in the Civil War, he recalled the influence of his time in Morocco on himself and his comrades in arms:

> My years in Africa live within me with an incredible force. There was born the possibility of rescuing a great Spain. There was formed the ideal that redeems us today. Without Africa, I can scarcely explain myself, nor can I explain myself to my comrades in arms.[25]

Promotion to the rank of general in 1926 and his subsequent appointment (in January 1928) as the new director general of the Military Academy of Zaragoza marked a notable shift in the trajectory of Franco's career. Thereafter, the daring and brave officer of Morocco would become an increasingly cautious and calculating military leader, aware of his own public standing, jealously guarding his professional interests and the advance of his career. Without a doubt, his marriage in Oviedo on 22 October 1923 to Carmen Polo Martínez-Valdés (1902–88), a pious and proud young woman from a wealthy, bourgeois Oviedo family, accentuated this change and his previous conservative and religious inclinations. Franco had met his wife in the summer of 1917 during his brief posting to the mainland, and he remained committed to her and their marriage until the end of his life. September 1926 saw the birth of his only child and beloved daughter 'Nenuca' (Carmen Franco Polo), who grew to be 'the only person who can understand his personality'.[26]

The remarkable change of character experienced by Franco even manifested itself physically: his adolescent appearance, small stature (1.64 metres), extreme thinness and high-pitched voice would be transformed into a military commander with a tendency to plumpness and markedly overweight at the waist. His family and daily life remained relatively austere and humdrum. He did not smoke, rarely drank and although his appetite was remarkable it was not distinguished by its culinary refinement ('he is not demanding and eats everything you give him,' subsequently declared his personal physician Vicente Gil – called 'Vicentón' in Franco's family circle – of almost 40 years). He also cultivated an unusual habit from his African years: he never took a siesta or dozed at his desk; instead he used the time to chat with his few military friends, to walk alone or in company and to do some light exercise (horse riding or tennis, at the beginning; fishing and hunting during the holidays; and in his later years, golf).[27]

At this stage of his life, Franco remained on the margins of the day-to-day politics of the liberal parliamentary system of the Bourbon Restoration (1874–1923), the pseudo-democratic wrapping for the pairing of 'oligarchy and *caciquismo* as the real form of government' angrily denounced by Joaquín Costa and the *fin-de-siècle* Spanish regenerationist writers. Presided over by King Alfonso XIII, the country had undergone a rapid economic development since the colonial crisis of 1898, generating broad social and cultural contrasts. Above all, there had been sustained demographic (24 million people in 1930) and urban growth (43 per cent of the population lived in towns in 1930) that showed the strength of the industrial and tertiary economic modernization process, which was more intense in the north and east of the country than in the centre and south (an area of predominantly stagnant agriculture). Furthermore, cultural indicators (literacy, education) revealed that for the first time most Spaniards could read and write, resulting in a vigorous and diverse publishing and journalism industry.[28]

The monarchy under Alfonso XIII was a classic socio-political liberal system similar to those prevailing in the rest of Europe and, despite its forced neutrality, had undergone hard tests in the Great War of 1914–18.[29] Since the country's crisis of the summer of 1917, Spain was subject to growing internal tensions that undermined its traditional stability: intense labour disputes over galloping inflation and unemployment amongst both agricultural and industrial workers, increasing pressure from rising Catalan and Basque nationalism to reform administrative centralism, the demands for democratization by the petty and middle bourgeoisie to give real meaning to existing legislation, and popular resistance to the bloody and endless Moroccan war. With the paralysis of the oligarchic liberal order and frightened by the revolutionary spectre of Bolshevism in Russia, in September 1923, the King took a gamble with a new solution to the prolonged crisis through the implementation of a military dictatorship headed by General Miguel Primo de Rivera and supported with unanimity by all the army.

During the entire dictatorship of General Primo de Rivera (1923–30), Franco was an enthusiastic supporter of the military regime as it succeeded in pacifying Morocco by means of a victorious joint offensive with French troops in September 1925. Franco himself led troops of the Legion who were at the forefront of the landing at Alhucemas Bay and achieved there his last and greatest military victory in Morocco. This triumph guaranteed his promotion to brigadier in February 1926, at the age of 33, thus becoming 'the youngest general in Europe', honoured with this annotation in his service record: 'He is a positive national asset and surely the country and the army will derive great benefit from making use of his remarkable skills in higher positions.'[30] In addition, the dictator rewarded him with appointment to director of the Military Academy of Zaragoza in 1928, where Franco imposed a *Decálogo del cadete* (*Cadet's Ten Commandments*) for the training and education of the students inspired directly by the text of the 'Credo legionario' ('Legionnaire's Creed') which underlined the extreme importance of always observing the 'ten commandments': Love for the Fatherland and King, Cultivation of Great Military Spirit, Fulfilment of Duties, Volunteering for Every Sacrifice, Noble Comradeship and Bravery, and others.[31] He also continued to benefit from the King's public favour, appointed a Gentleman of the Bedchamber and receiving royal patronage on the occasion of his wedding.

It was during the dictatorship that Franco started to receive and devour the anti-communist and authoritarian literature sent by the Entente Internationale contre la Troisième Internationale, an organization formed in Geneva by anti-Bolshevik Russian and far-right Swiss forces in order to alert leaders across Europe to the danger of the universal communist conspiracy. This reactionary and Manichaean literature would be key in the formation and evolution of the fantastic, obsessive ideas of Franco on the hidden and divisive power of Freemasonry and the existence of a universal Judaeo–Masonic–Bolshevik conspiracy against Spain and the Catholic faith.[32] His firm conviction of anti-Freemasonry (a case of so-called 'conspiracy obsession' and 'paranoid style in political perception') very soon became 'second nature' to Franco and would transform his life into 'an anti-Freemason crusade' on which he did not allow 'any discussion'.[33] In all likelihood, that same literature encouraged his instinctive suspicion of intellectuals and the subtleties of contemporary socio-political thinking, for which he always showed a clear lack of interest and open contempt (a much-used phrase of his was: 'with the characteristic arrogance of intellectuals'). As recognized by one of his favourite ministers, economist and military lawyer Mariano Navarro Rubio: 'Franco was not exactly an intellectual. He never tried nor presumed to be one. His political doctrine consisted of a few ideas, basic, clear and rich, but he stuck rigidly to them.'[34]

Given his background, Franco felt concern at the removal of Primo de Rivera in January 1930 and the subsequent fall of the monarchy after the municipal elections of April 1931. The consequent peaceful proclamation of the Second Republic would essentially result from the monarchical regime's inability to adapt to the rapid modernizing changes experienced by the Spanish economy and society in the first third of the twentieth century. Those changes had demanded permanent and innovative solutions to enhance the political integration of the liberal-democratic new bourgeoisie and the working classes organized in trade unions and mostly reformist parties, whose numbers grew in line with economic, urban and cultural modernization. The consecutive failure of parliamentary liberalism (until 1923) and executive militarism (until 1931) had allowed the growth of interclass republicanism as an alternative formula for the democratization of Spain, based on the cooperation of bourgeois republican parties and the powerful, reformist socialist movement.

Prudence and Patience during the Second Republic

The Republican democracy was established on 14 April 1931 and evolved through several phases as rapid as they were convulsive: first a reformist two-year period (1931–3), then a second rightist/moderate stage (1934–5) and the government of the Popular Front in the first half of 1936. In essence, over those years, the socio-political dynamics were determined by a triangular struggle between mutually exclusive models which reproduced on a small scale the existing Europe-wide struggle: crude competition between democratic reformism, authoritarian reaction and social revolution to take power and reshape society. Ultimately, the transcendental peculiarity of the Spanish case would mean that, unlike in the rest of Europe, none of those projects would be strong enough to impose itself decisively on the others. In fact, between 1931 and 1936, Spain reached an unstable equilibrium, a virtual stalemate between the fragmented forces of reformism and their reactionary counterpart, with the presence of a third revolutionary force able to undermine and undercut the others. In these circumstances, the political dynamics of the Second Republic seemed to appear as a kind of pincer with two arms and one goal: reaction and revolution against reform. To make matters worse, with the passing of the years, the forces for reform saw their strength undermined as the economic crisis deepened and precipitated the political polarization that was favourable to both extremes.[35]

The arrival of democracy in April 1931 marked a noticeable blip in the hitherto brilliant career of Alfonso XIII's favourite general. In some personal notes written for unknown reasons in 1962, Franco recorded his critical judgement on the unexpected political transition, without excluding from criticism a king who had abandoned his dictator or the civilian politicians and military commanders who had 'surrendered' power without resistance:

It is necessary to recognize the illusion with which large sectors of the Spanish nation received the Republic, one that no one expected, and that was a direct result of the political mistakes of the monarchist political parties in recent years. The ingratitude of the monarchy to General Primo de Rivera, who had served so effectively for seven years, had managed to pacify Morocco and raise the level of the nation in all aspects, and the spectacle offered by the monarchist political parties, liberals, constitutionalists, revanchists at the core, that did not forgive the sovereign his collaboration with the dictatorship – all these factors had sickened and separated the people from the institutions. They created the crisis of prestige which influenced the vote of major provincial capitals.[36]

In any case, during the Republican–Socialist government of 1931–3, with Manuel Azaña at the head of the Cabinet and the War Office, the caution and

Galician shrewdness of General Franco meant he managed to avoid any open
conflict with the new authorities while keeping his distance from the established
regime: 'I never cheered for the Republic,' he recalled proudly in 1964 to his
cousin and military aide since 1927, Francisco Franco Salgado-Araujo, known
as 'Pacón'.[37] The closing of the Military Academy of Zaragoza, the review of the
promotions he had gained during the dictatorship, the campaign for political
responsibilities during the dictatorship, and the progressive and anti-clerical
leanings of the government reinforced Franco's alienation. But they did not
lead him to reckless conspiracy, which had been the reaction of his superior in
the Protectorate, General José Sanjurjo, head of the frustrated military coup
in August 1932 that sought to block parliament's approval of the Estatuto de
Cataluña (Statute of Catalonian Autonomy) and of the Ley para la Reforma
Agraria (Law for Agrarian Reform). In fact, when required by Sanjurjo to act as
his advocate in the subsequent court martial, Franco refused to accept the order
with a resounding argument: 'I don't defend you because you deserve death;
not for having rebelled but for having lost.'[38] That prudence and cold caution
that was already beginning to be proverbial (his own sister acknowledged
that 'cunning and caution define his character') motivated Sanjurjo's caustic
comment on his former subordinate: 'Little Franco is a crafty so-and-so who
only looks out for himself.' This did not stop him from considering Franco one
of the best Spanish military leaders of the time: 'He is not Napoleon, but given
what there is …' Perhaps for that reason Azaña believed by then that 'Franco
is the most fearsome' of the potential military conspirators that the Republican
regime would have to face.[39]

   Franco's fears of the socio-political drift during the two years of the
Republican–Socialist government would only last a short time. The global
economic crisis hit Spain with full force during those years, causing industrial
production rates to plummet, restricting Spain's commercial exports, increasing
its budgetary difficulties and generating huge unemployment, concentrated
mostly in the agricultural sector (in December 1933, of the more than 600,000
unemployed, more than 400,000 were agricultural labourers from southern
provinces).[40] The Republican–Socialist Cabinet was almost powerless before
the challenge and its own internal divisions accentuated the weariness of the
coalition, which suffered a serious defeat in the general elections of November

1933. The victory went to the conservatives of Alejandro Lerroux's Radical Party and the powerful and generally pro-authoritarian Confederación Española de Derechas Autónomas (CEDA – Spanish Confederation of the Autonomous Right), the new Catholic mass party led by José María Gil-Robles.

Franco had voted for the CEDA in the general election as he identified with its Catholic and conservative ideology and its pragmatic political strategy that sought to reform the Republic from within. He welcomed political change that would advance his professional expectations and reduce his instinctive repugnance towards the Republican regime. In fact, under both the Radical and Radical–CEDA governments of 1934 and 1935, Franco became the most distinguished Spanish army officer and the favourite general of the authorities: he was promoted to major general in March 1934 (just a month after the death of his beloved mother in Madrid, from where she was about to start a pilgrimage to Rome).

For these reasons of professional prestige, in October 1934, when the Socialists called for a general strike against the entry of the CEDA into the government and revolution broke out in Asturias (a revolution expoited by the Catalan autonomous government for its own ends), the Lerroux government tasked Franco with crushing both challenges with all military forces under his command, including the transfer and use of his beloved Legion to the Asturian front. This critical juncture provided an already clearly ambitious Franco with his first, satisfying, taste of quasi-omnipotent state power. For about 15 days, following the declaration of a state of war and the delegation of governmental functions, Franco was a genuine emergency dictator, controlling all the military and police forces in what he perceived to be a struggle against the revolution planned by Moscow and executed by its undercover agents and Spanish traitors. As he declared to the press in Oviedo after successfully quelling the last pockets of resistance: 'This is a frontier war against socialism, Communism and whatever attacks civilization in order to replace it with barbarism.'[41]

The overwhelming victory he won in Asturias not only made him the hero of conservative public opinion but also reinforced his moral leadership among the army chiefs and officers, far above his recognized rank and seniority. His appointment as chief of central general staff in May 1935 by Gil-Robles, the new minister of war, cemented that leadership almost unassailably. As a result of this renewed public and professional prestige, Franco was repeatedly courted by nearly all parties of the political right. Apart from his good connections with Lerroux's conservative Republicanism, his contacts with the CEDA were excellent, given the friendship shown to him by Gil-Robles and the membership of his brother-in-law, Ramón Serrano Suñer (married to Franco's wife's younger sister), a prominent CEDA deputy for Zaragoza since 1933.[42] His relationship with Alfonsist monarchism remained fluid through Pedro Sainz Rodríguez, one of the ideologists of the journal *Acción Española*, whom Franco had met when Sainz was professor of literature at the University of Oviedo.[43] With regard to the Spanish Falange, the new and small fascist party founded in 1933 by the son of the former dictator, José Antonio Primo de Rivera, contact was scarce but revealing. The Falangist leader had sent a personal letter to Franco (through a mutual friend, Serrano Suñer) on the eve of October 1934 to alert him to the danger of revolution. Franco gave him a verbal response asking him to 'keep faith in the military and give them support if a crisis broke out'.[44]

Given the circumstances, Franco's concern at the prolonged governmental crisis that undermined collaboration between the Radicals (defenders of a democratic regime) and the *cedistas* (supporters of authoritarian reform that called into question the persistence of the regime) during 1935 is not surprising. In the end, tensions led to the breakdown of the coalition and forced the president of the Republic, the Catholic and conservative Niceto Alcalá-Zamora, to call new elections for 16 February 1936, against a backdrop of severe economic depression, strong political bipolarization and acute social antagonism. To the surprise of many observers, the elections gave victory to a new coalition of the left (the so-called Popular Front) over right-wing candidates by a slight majority (no more than 200,000 popular votes) and brought to power a left Republican government headed again by Azaña and supported by the Socialist and Communist parties.

The narrow victory of the Popular Front on 16 February 1936 tempted Franco to take part in his first serious coup. Over the following two days he sought to obtain the backing of the government and the president of the Republic in order to declare a state of war and prevent the transfer of power. The attempt was thwarted by the resistance of the civil authorities to taking that crucial step, the lack of material resources to execute it and by the decision of the cautious chief of staff not to act until almost fully certain of success. When the head of government suggested to him on the 18th that the military act on their own initiative, Franco replied with full sincerity: 'The army does not yet have the moral unity necessary to undertake this task.'[45]

Consequently, Franco had to resign himself to the return to power of Azaña, who, as a precautionary measure, ordered, on 21 February, Franco's transfer from Madrid to the important but distant military headquarters of the Canary Islands. It was a very considerable professional and political setback and affected him deeply. Before leaving, he officially met the new prime minister and forcefully reproached him on his decision to dispense with his services: 'You are making a mistake in sending me away because in Madrid I could be more useful to the army and to the peace of Spain.' Azaña's response only accentuated his fears: 'I don't fear uprisings. I knew about Sanjurjo's plot and I could have avoided it but preferred to see it defeated.'[46]

Franco's concerns continued to be exacerbated by the persistent political crises experienced during the first half of 1936; the decidedly reformist actions of the government of the Popular Front again had to face a two-pronged attack. On one side were the revolutionary demands of anarcho-syndicalism, seconded by the radical faction of the socialists, which undermined the crucial cooperation between bourgeois republicanism and reformist socialism as pillars of the ruling coalition and its interclass supporters. On the other side was the convergence of the right-wing parties around a reactionary strategy which put all its hopes in military intervention to tackle the crisis and overthrow democratic reformism and the perceived revolutionary spectre behind it.

By virtue of his rank and influence, Franco was from the outset – although with his usual caution – in contact with the broad anti-republican conspiracy that was brewing within the army under the technical direction of General Emilio Mola from Pamplona (he was the former chief of security and police forces for Alfonso XIII). Finalized through the months of April and May, Mola's plan consisted of orchestrating a simultaneous uprising of all military garrisons to seize power within a few days, after crushing any possible resistance in the larger cities and manufacturing centres. Franco's hesitation to commit himself definitively to the uprising (which exasperated the rest of the plotters) came from both his fear of the consequences of failure ('We can't

count on all of the army') and his tenuous hope that the deterioration of the
situation could be tackled legally with reduced risk and cost. Many years later
he confessed with the utmost sincerity to his cousin and aide the reasons for
his caution:

> I was always in favour of the military movement, because I understood that
> the time had come to save Spain from the chaos as the socialists and all the
> forces of the left together marched resolutely to establish a dictatorship of
> the proletariat, as was proclaimed unreservedly by Largo Caballero [Union
> leader of the Socialist left] at his rallies and in the press, and especially in
> Parliament. What I always feared was that the lack of concerted action
> by the majority of the army would be a repeat of 10 August [1932]. [...] I
> realized that the military movement would be resisted with great energy, and
> therefore rejected the widespread opinion, as stated by General Orgaz, which
> you also heard in Tenerife, 'that it would be an easy job, and if I decided not
> to do it, another would'.[47]

Despite his initial scepticism, Franco persuaded his comrades in arms to
accept that the hypothetical uprising would have no defined political profile
(monarchist or otherwise) and was 'only for God and for Spain'. He also insisted
repeatedly that the operation was exclusively military, without reliance on any
right-wing party: 'No consideration was given by the movement to political
forces.'[48] He met with no opposition as all the conspirators shared his opinions,
as General Mola, 'technical director' of the conspiracy, proclaimed very soon
afterwards:

> In this formidable undertaking [the reconstruction of Spain] we, the military,
> have to lay its foundations; we have to launch it; it is our right, because that is
> the nation's wish, because we have a clear idea of our power and only we can
> consolidate the union of the people with the army.[49]

Finally, already deeply concerned by the powerful strike movements of May–
June 1936, Franco's vacillations that had unnerved the rest of the conspirators
were swept away following the murder of the monarchist leader, José Calvo

Sotelo, on 13 July 1936. The crime had been perpetrated by a group of assault guards (urban police) seeking revenge for the death of one of their commanders, a socialist sympathizer, in a Falange attack the day before in Madrid. Assuming that the assassination showed that the Republican government had no real authority and that state power lay in the gutter, Franco was prepared to fulfil his role in the coup: to conquer the Canary Islands and to proceed immediately to Morocco to take charge of the best and most hardened Spanish troops, the Army of Africa.

Divine Providence and Civil War

On 17 July 1936, as the military uprising began in Morocco, Franco fulfilled expectations and assumed command of the insurgents in the Canary Islands shortly before moving to the Protectorate to be at the forefront of the rebel troops. In keeping with the old praetorian and militaristic tradition, in his declaration of martial law he stated that 'the situation of Spain is every day more critical' because 'anarchy reigns in most of the countryside and cities' and 'revolutionary strikes of all orders that paralyse the life of the nation' proliferate, with the 'complicity and negligence of weak civil authorities'. Accordingly, 'the army, the navy and the forces of public order rush to defend the fatherland' and to restore 'peace, brotherhood and justice in all regions'. The final warning was not empty: 'the energy required to maintain order shall be in proportion to the magnitude of the resistance that is offered.'[50]

With the same mixture of caution and determination that he had shown during his years as an officer, Franco managed to overcome problems. In case things went badly, he had already shipped his wife and daughter to France (they did not return until September). He also procured a diplomatic passport and shaved off his moustache in order to go unnoticed on the flight from the Canary Islands to Tetuán. Once he arrived in Morocco (after having stayed incognito in the French Zone), he installed himself in the high commissioner's office and took over the direction of the insurrection with a strong nerve and infectious energy. He had an immediate chance to show his commitment to the cause in a difficult personal matter: it was reported that his cousin and childhood friend,

Flight Commander Ricardo de la Puente Bahamonde, had been sentenced to death for trying to resist the coup at the airfield in Tetuán. Franco did nothing to save him and temporarily ceded command to General Luis Orgaz to allow the cautionary execution.[51]

Much to the dismay of the military rebels, the insurrection launched on 17 July 1936 initially succeeded in only half of the country (the most agrarian and rural) and was crushed in the other half (the most developed and urbanized) by a combination of armed forces loyal to the government and swiftly armed trade union militias. In fact, the uprising had been strongest in a wide area of the west and centre of the peninsula (from Aragón to Galicia and the north of Extremadura, including almost all of Castile) and in a small zone of Andalusia (around Seville and Granada). The battle had been lost in two large separate zones: the east-central area (including Madrid, Barcelona and Valencia) and a northern strip (between the Basque country and Asturias). In military terms, the rebels had achieved control of most of the armed forces, including the crucial troops in Morocco (especially the Legion and indigenous regular forces, the Moors). However, they had also suffered the defection of most of the navy, air force and a good part of the forces of law and order (which had been key to saving the government in the capital and in Barcelona). As a result, in a few days the inconclusive military coup became a long and bloody civil war which pitted a military reaction, on one side of the trenches, against an unstable, forced alliance of reformists and revolutionaries on the other.[52]

In any case, the outbreak of hostilities also meant the beginning of the meteoric career of Franco to become supreme commander of the revolt and the leader of a purported 'new state' where Falangism would serve as the modernizing garb for a socio-political regime that was at heart reactionary and ultra-conservative. The Civil War waged between 18 July 1936 and 1 April 1939 laid the foundations of what would become the Francoist state, while at the same time providing an excellent political and diplomatic school for Franco. To his astounding good fortune – which he took as a sign of Divine Providence – the majority of politicians and generals who could have disputed his prominence in the insurgent camp were eliminated from the scene one after another: the charismatic Calvo Sotelo had been murdered previously; Sanjurjo was killed in a plane crash shortly after the uprising; General Fanjul and General Goded failed to succeed in their rebellion in Madrid and Barcelona respectively and were shot by Republicans; so too, the Falange leader, José Antonio Primo de Rivera, who had been in a Republican prison since March, was shot in November 1936. Meanwhile, other generals with effective commands of troops, Mola and Queipo de Llano, were limited in their aspirations by their lower seniority (the former), their previous Republican inclinations (the latter) and their shared difficulties in holding their respective war fronts (Madrid in the case of Mola, Andalusia for Queipo).

It was Franco who got timely and vital military and diplomatic support from Germany and Italy through his own personal efforts and sending direct emissaries to Rome and Berlin. It was also Franco who had been recognized as the de facto insurgent leader by Hitler and Mussolini, despite the formal existence of the Junta de Defensa Nacional (National Defence Council) established in Burgos on 24 July with General Miguel Cabanellas, the oldest rebel commander, as president.[53] Franco also attracted the strongest personal support from the Catholic hierarchy and led the victorious rebel troops who, once airlifted from Morocco, advanced unchecked from Seville to Madrid (the official capital whose occupation would lead to international legal recognition). In addition, given his reputed political neutrality, Franco enjoyed tacit and preferential support from all the right-wing groups that were confident of influencing his future political plans in their favour. This neutrality would prove to be a useful personal quality that he would use with great skill and notorious cynicism until the end of his days: 'I am here because I neither understand nor do politics. That is the secret.'[54]

At the end of September 1936, those military, political and diplomatic successes by Franco and the expectation of a final assault on Madrid raised the need to concentrate strategic and political direction under a single command to increase the effectiveness of the war effort. The show of strength by the military junta could not be sustained without very serious domestic and diplomatic difficulties. Accordingly, in two meetings at an airfield close to Salamanca, on 21 and 28 September, the generals decided to elect Franco as Generalissimo of the army, navy and air force and head of government of the Spanish state, specifically giving him 'all the powers of the new state'.[55] On 1 October, after the transfer of power from the hands of the junta in Burgos, in his first political decision signed as 'head of state', Franco created a Junta Técnica del Estado (State Technical Council) responsible for administrative functions until 'domination throughout the national territory', subject to 'the approval of the head of state'. A propaganda campaign began shortly afterwards with the first public reference to the head of state as 'Caudillo of Spain' with inevitable similar slogans in the press: 'a fatherland, a state, a caudillo'; 'the Caesars were the victorious generals'.[56]

The political rise of Franco meant the conversion of the collegiate military junta into a personal dictatorship, with an individual chosen by his comrades in arms as the absolute representative of the only power in insurgent Spain: the military. Significantly, Franco said after his election, 'This is the most important moment of my life.'[57] In his first public speech in Burgos after accepting office, on 1 October 1936, he announced emphatically both his style and political purpose: 'You place Spain in my hands. My hand will be firm, it will not tremble and I will try to raise Spain to its rightful place according to its history and its past.'[58]

Soon after becoming leader, Franco prepared the expected final offensive on Madrid, which would begin on 8 November 1936. His troops, close to 25,000 men, very weary after their long march from Seville, faced some 40,000 militiamen, ill-equipped and incapable of tactical manoeuvring, but willing to fight in an urban environment more suitable for resistance than the open countryside of Andalusia or Extremadura. In any case, Franco planned a frontal assault from the south-west flank of the city, disregarding the changes brought about by the enemy: the militarization of the militias and their adaptability to the urban battleground; the effective defensive system designed by Colonel Vicente Rojo (which earned him his title of general and leading Republican strategist); and the arrival of the first contingent of International Brigades and weapons sent from the Soviet Union. As a result, Franco's assault barely managed to open a wedge in the Madrid defences of the Ciudad Universitaria and had to be suspended on 23 November because the attackers were exhausted.[59] The first phase of the Battle of Madrid ended in triumph for the defenders. Although the capital remained under siege, it had not been occupied. The brief war that everyone had expected, inside and outside Spain, almost imperceptibly became a protracted conflict.

After the failure of the frontal assault on Madrid, Franco's strategy focused on trying to besiege the city through surrounding offensives in order to cut its communication with the rest of the Republican zone. At the beginning of January 1937, his troops had tried to penetrate the north-west area (in the Battle of La Coruña Road). Throughout the month of February he had continued the attacks in the south (the Battle of Jarama). Finally, in March, an offensive took place in the north-east sector (the Battle of Guadalajara) with an appalling intervention by the Italian contingent. Largely thanks to renewed Soviet military aid and the formation of the Popular Army of the Republic, these operations again failed: Madrid resisted the siege and maintained an eastern corridor of communication with the rest of the government territory (along the road to Valencia) until the end of the war.

The failure of repeated offensives to take Madrid from November 1936 to March 1937 forced Franco to focus on the political issues raised by the consolidation of his absolute personal authority. He had the good fortune to have the political and legal support of Ramón Serrano Suñer, who had escaped from Madrid and arrived in Salamanca (the headquarters of the Generalissimo) in February 1937. The so-called 'Cuñadísimo' (supreme brother-in-law) would soon become a dominant figure. He had evolved politically into a fervent Falangist, settled down to live in the episcopal palace in Salamanca and rapidly displaced Nicolás Franco as chief political adviser (until, a year later, he was sent to Lisbon as ambassador to Salazar).

With Serrano Suñer as mentor, Franco proceeded to take a crucial step in the institutionalization of his new state: on 19 April 1937, without consultation or negotiation with those concerned, the Caudillo decreed the forced unification of all right-wing parties, 'under my leadership, into a single national political entity, which will be named Falange Española Tradicionalista y de las Juntas de Ofensiva Nacional-Sindicalista' (FET-JONS). The purpose of this 'great party of the state' was, 'as in other totalitarian regimes', to serve as a link 'between society and the state' and promote 'the political virtues of service, hierarchy and brotherhood'.[60] The measure was dutifully accepted by monarchists, Catholics and Carlists (supporters of a rival dynastic faction led by Don Carlos since 1833) and was only subject to reservations, soon silenced, from a reduced faction within the Falange that was badly weakened by the disappearance of José Antonio Primo de Rivera and the failure to appoint a successor acceptable to all. The measure was beneficial to both parties, as the German ambassador appreciated: 'Franco is a leader without a party, the Falange a party without a leader.'[61]

From then on, the new unified party, rigidly controlled by the General Head-quarters of the Generalissimo, would become the second institutional pillar (after the army) of a personal dictatorship properly qualifying as Franquismo – Francoism. Serrano Suñer was the architect of this transformation from 'a military camp state' into a 'regime of single command and party that assumed some of the universal external features of other modern regimes'. Inspired by him and the political fascistization of the times, FET had much more of the ancient Falange than of old Carlism, the CEDA or monarchism: 'the choice of symbols, terminology and doctrine, gave preference to the Falange.'[62] The official greeting became a Roman salute with arm raised, the emblem a 'yoke and arrows', the anthem the Falange's 'Cara al Sol', the uniform that of the Falange's blue shirt (with the Carlist red beret), and the official programme the Falange's '26 points'. The process of fascistization prevailed in the selection of new leaders too: Franco named six Falangists and four Carlists on the first political executive of the FET (whose secretary was Serrano Suñer) and 'only in nine provinces was the leadership of the party given to a former Carlist, compared to the 22 provinces where it was held by a Falangist.'[63] Despite the modern trappings, the incipient Franco regime always reflected the simple political philosophy of its leader: anti-communist, anti-liberal, anti-Masonic and determined to protect national unity and the existing social order through a military dictatorship. In 1937, Manuel Azaña had already noted the lack of modernizing forces within the Spanish right:

> There are or might be in Spain all the fascists you want. But there will not be a fascist regime. If force triumphs against the Republic, we would fall back under the power of a traditional ecclesiastical and military dictatorship. No matter how many slogans are translated and how many mottos are used. Swords, cassocks, military parades and homages to the Virgin of Pilar. The country can offer nothing else, as can already be seen.[64]

This reactionary and traditionalist orientation of the regime was firmly underpinned by its third institutional pillar, the Catholic Church. The military uprising had very soon been able to count on the crucial assistance of the Spanish episcopal hierarchy and the masses of faithful Catholics. In line with its previous hostility to the secular programme of the Republic, and terrified by the anti-clerical fury unleashed in the government zone (with nearly 7,000 victims), the Spanish Church resolutely sided with the military. As reported privately to the Vatican at the beginning of August 1936 by Cardinal Gomá: 'It can be said that it is a fight between Spain and Anti-Spain, religion and atheism, Christian civilization and barbarism.' Only a month later the bishop of Salamanca would openly apply the Augustinian image of 'the two cities' to defend the cause of Franco, 'the celestial city' for the 'love of God', facing a Republic of an 'earthly city' in 'contempt of God'. Catholicism rose to become one of the main national and international supporters of the rebel war effort, exalting it as a crusade in the faith of Christ and the salvation of Spain from communist atheism and Anti-Spain.[65]

Its resolute support transformed the Catholic Church into a social and institutional force of great influence, second only to the army and ahead of the Falange, in shaping the political structures which sprouted in insurgent Spain under Franco. The recompense for this vital support could not have been more enthusiastic or generous. A flood of legislative measures revoked Republican reforms (secular education, the elimination of state funding, secular cemeteries, etc.) and gave back to the clergy control of civil society and the intellectual and cultural life of the country. For its part, given Franco's fervent Catholicism, the Spanish episcopacy did not take long to bless him as *homo missus a Deo cui nomen erat Franciscus* (the man sent by God whose name is Francisco), responsible for the triumph of the crusade 'for God and Spain', 'Caudillo of Spain by the grace of God'. This would be no mere formality used by Franco for public consumption (despite the domestic and diplomatic benefits it brought him), but a deeply rooted conviction that led him to consider himself a new 'hammer of the heretics' in the style of Felipe II, and he would later try to replicate the royal residence El Escorial with his own pharaonic temple, the Valle de los Caídos.

This conviction was fully revealed by the transfer of the Generalissimo's headquarters to the city of Salamanca. With the blessing of Bishop Pla y Deniel,

Franco settled himself into the episcopal palace in the shadow of the cathedral and recruited Father José María Bulart, the cardinal's private secretary, as his confessor and chaplain (a post he filled until 1975). He also took Mass often and performed the Rosary every day with his family, if duties allowed.[66] It is revealing of his Tridentine Catholic devotion that from February 1937 and throughout the rest of his life, Franco had in his bedroom the relic of the incorruptible hand of Santa Teresa de Jesús (the 'saint of the Race'), which he never left behind even during his travels throughout the country.[67]

This conversion of the military dictatorship into a personal regime in the process of fascistization occurred in the spring of 1937 when the course of the war suffered a noticeable change. With the confirmation of the failure of the direct assault on Madrid, from April 1937 Franco gave a crucial twist to the war strategy: he abandoned the idea of a quick victory with the conquest of the capital and opted to fight a long war of attrition on other fronts, with the objective of gradually defeating a badly supplied enemy through the systematic destruction of its capacity to resist, given the material and offensive superiority guaranteed by Italo-German supplies. Convinced of the effective resistance of the enemy in the Spanish capital, the new military strategy represented a gamble on what his advisers called 'the clash of rams': massive attacks on the weakest front, taking advantage of the fact that 'Republicans lack sufficient reserves of men and material to feed the fight'.[68]

The immediate effect of this strategic shift was the beginning of a powerful offensive against the northern Republican zone, which was gradually conquered between June (the fall of Bilbao on the 19th) and October 1937 (the occupation of Gijon on the 21st), with episodes of huge international impact – such as the destruction of Guernica by the German air force on 26 April, in the first example of the bombing of targets without military value for the purpose of demoralizing the civilian rear.[69] To better direct operations, Franco decided to move his headquarters (whose code name was 'Términus') from Salamanca to Burgos, where he installed himself at the Palacio de la Isla for the remainder of the war. Among other reasons, the death of General Mola in a plane crash on 3 June imposed a visible change in Franco's travel arrangements: he cancelled all flights and only made journeys by road or railway.

The new strategy of a long war of attrition waged by Franco reactivated the previous doubts of his German and Italian allies about the military capabilities of the Spanish leader and his strategic and tactical skills. In December 1936, following the failure of the offensive against Madrid, General Wilhelm Faupel, newly appointed German ambassador to Franco, confidentially informed the authorities in Berlin:

General Franco personally is a ruthlessly brave soldier, with a strong sense of responsibility, a man who is likable from the very first because of his open and decent character, but whose military training and experience do not fit him for the direction of operations on their present scale. [...] Franco owes the successes of the first few weeks to the fact that his Moroccan troops were not opposed by anything of equal quality, and also to the fact that there was no systematic military command on the Red side.[70]

In Rome, there were also serious doubts about the military capability of the Generalissimo to conduct the nationalist war effort effectively, according to modern military strategies. Count Ciano, Mussolini's son-in-law and his foreign minister, noted in his journal on 20 December 1937:

Our generals [in Spain] are restless, quite rightly. Franco has no idea of synthesis in war. His operations are those of a magnificent battalion commander. His objective is always ground, never the enemy. And he does not realize that it is by the destruction of the enemy that you win a war. After that it is a simple enough matter to occupy territory.[71]

However, on this controversial topic, a crucial aspect must be remembered: the exultant Caudillo was not acting under mere military considerations, nor did he want a quick victory in the style of *blitzkrieg* (lightning war) or *guerra celere* (fast war), as sought by the German and Italian leaders and strategists. His aim was wider and more profound; he wanted military operations to achieve the total physical removal of an enemy considered the Anti-Spain and as racially despicable as the rebel tribesmen in Morocco. In the telling words of Franco in

February 1937 to Lieutenant Colonel Emilio Faldella, deputy head of the Italian military forces serving under his command:

> This is a war of a special kind, which has to be fought with exceptional methods so that such a numerous mass cannot be used all at once, but would be more useful spread out over several fronts. [...] In a civil war, a systematic occupation of territory accompanied by the necessary purge and cleansing (*limpieza*) is preferable to a rapid rout of the enemy armies which leaves the country still infested with enemies.[72]

Just two months later, at the insistence of Mussolini to speed things up and streamline operations, Franco repeated to the Fascist ambassador, Roberto Cantalupo, the reasons for his new military strategy, subordinated to the political purpose of 'cleansing' and 'redemption' of enemies and the disaffected:

> We must carry out the necessarily slow task of redemption and pacification, without which the military occupation will be largely useless. The moral redemption of the occupied zones will be long and difficult because in Spain the roots of anarchism are old and deep. [...] I limit myself to partial offensives with certain success. I will occupy Spain town by town, village by village, railway by railway [...] Nothing will make me abandon this gradual programme. It will bring me less glory but greater internal peace. That being the case, this civil war could still last another year, two, perhaps three. Dear ambassador, I can assure you that I am not interested in territory but in inhabitants. The reconquest of the territory is the means, the redemption of the inhabitants the end. [...] I cannot shorten the war by even one day [...] It could even be dangerous for me to reach Madrid with a stylish military operation. I will take the capital not an hour before it is necessary; first I must have the certainty of being able to found a regime.[73]

For these reasons he insisted on waging, with tenacity and perseverance, a slow war of attrition that literally decimated the ranks of a more poorly equipped enemy and approved a ruthless crackdown on the disaffected rearguard, which stifled resistance and paralysed all opposition among the vanquished for many years to come. At the beginning of the insurrection, the intention of such repressive violence had been the physical elimination of the most prominent enemies and the creation of an atmosphere of paralysing terror that prevented active resistance among the disaffected. Franco later confessed an unusual personal distance from the phenomenon: 'the authorities had to anticipate any backlash against the Movement by leftist elements. For this reason they shot the most prominent.'[74] However, with the extension of the war and the rise of Franco, the initial repression became a persistent policy of purification, 'redemption' and 'cleansing', so the informal executions and the less organized early murders were replaced by summary trials in severe military courts. The 'redeeming' social and political purpose of this repression was responsible for a high number of deaths, which probably reached a figure close to 90,000 during the war (with another 40,000 after the victory and in the immediate postwar period), compared to 55,000 victims of repression in the Republican zone.[75]

By giving his full consent and legitimization to such ruthless repression, Franco received a huge political benefit: 'a pact of blood' which would permanently secure the blind allegiance of his supporters to the Caudillo of the Victory for fear of the possible vengeful return of the bereaved and vanquished. That same bloodletting also represented a useful political 'insurance' against the defeated Republicans; those who had not died in the process were silenced and paralysed with terror for a long time.

With the army as an instrument for victory, with National Catholicism as the supreme and all-pervading ideology and the Falange as a means to organize supporters and discipline civil society, Franco built his own dictatorial regime between 1936 and 1939 and victoriously waged a war against liberal democratic reformism and subversive social revolution.

At the end of January 1938, on the eve of the great military offensive on the eastern front that would divide the Republican territory into two, Franco confirmed his status as supreme and final arbiter of the anti-Republican coalition through the formation of its first regular government. It was a balanced executive of 11 members, with representatives from all the 'political families' prior to unification: four ministers from the military (in defence, public order, industry and foreign affairs), three from the Falange in 'social' portfolios (including Serrano Suñer at the Home Office), two monarchists, a Carlist and a right-wing technician with no clear political allegiance.[76] In tandem with the formation of the government, Franco adopted the Ley de Administración Central del Estado (Law of the Central Administration of the State), linking the government president to the head of state and ratifying his status as dictator with full executive and legislative powers with no limits. According to Article 17: 'The head of state, who assumed all powers by virtue of the decree of the Junta de Defensa Nacional on 29 September 1936, has the supreme authority to instigate and enact legal rules of a general nature.'[77]

By then, it was already evident that the Caudillo did not conceive of his dictatorship as an interim measure but for life and that he had no intention of restoring the monarchy. On 17 July 1937 he gave the first public indication of this in an interview published by the Seville newspaper *Abc*: 'If the time for the restoration came, the new monarchy would be, of course, very different from that which fell on 14 April 1931.'[78] Thus began the long journey towards the 'establishment' of a Francoist monarchy as an alternative to the mere 'restoration' of the previous overthrown and exiled dynasty.

The process of fascistization, which took decisive steps during 1938, was a fundamental part of Franco's determined attempt to cling onto power for life. On 9 March the Fuero del Trabajo (Labour Law) was approved, the first 'fundamental law' of the Franco regime and a perfect example of Italian influence (the 'Carta del Lavoro' of 1927). The text, which considered strike action and disruption to the 'normality of production' as 'crimes against the state' and 'subject to appropriate sanctions', included a resolutely quasi-fascist declaration of principles:

> As a result of the renewal of the Catholic tradition of social justice and heightened human consciousness that informed our law of the empire, the state, a national instrument for the object of unity, and a Syndicalist one as it represents a totalitarian action against liberal capitalism and Marxist materialism, undertakes the task of channelling – with military, constructive and religious zeal – Spain's pending revolution which will grant to the Spanish, once and for always, fatherland, bread and justice.[79]

Franco's political orientation was not to the liking of all the groups that made up the Nationalist coalition, given their obvious rivalry with the Falange (whose leader was already Serrano Suñer, to the detriment of 'legitimistas' Pilar and Miguel Primo de Rivera, siblings of the 'Absent', and Raimundo Fernández Cuesta, his executor). Military chiefs feared their declining influence over the Caudillo and the Falangist appropriation of powers of public order and security. The Carlists resented their loss of power in the new party and their isolation in the fiefs of Navarre and the Basque provinces. The monarchists noted the declared anti-monarchism of the Falange (aware of the difficult coexistence between Mussolini and King Victor Emmanuel in Italy) and its growing influence on Franco. The Catholics were wary of what Vatican circles called the danger of the panstatism (the totalitarian character of fascism and Nazism that threatened the autonomy of the Church).

However, all of these groups saw the need to toe the line in the final stages of the military assault against an isolated, weakened and harassed Republic. As a result, there was no serious opposition to the political leeway granted to Serrano Suñer by Franco, even during the difficult month of September 1938, when the tension between Germany and the Franco-British entente over the integrity of Czechoslovakia looked to be about to lead to the outbreak of a world war. The Anglo-French retreat enshrined in the Munich Agreement of 29 September 1938 avoided that contingency in exchange for the fall of the Spanish Republic and the break-up of Czechoslovakia. But, before achieving his most precious military target, Franco had to pay his own share of family blood: on 28 October a plane crash over the Mediterranean killed Ramón Franco, the black sheep of the family who had made amends for his previous failings by joining the insurrection in the first weeks as a fighter pilot.

After the internal collapse of the Republic, on 1 April 1939, Franco managed to end the Civil War with an absolute and unconditional victory. He did so through a final military communiqué which he drew up in bed, suffering from flu after not having missed a single day of the war: 'Today, with a captive and disarmed Red Army, the Nationalist troops have gained their last military objectives. The war is over.'[80] From that point, the legitimacy of the victory (the right of conquest sublimated) became the ultimate and supreme source of Franco's undisputed authority and of his right to exercise his power for life. The triumphant end to the bloody Civil War was the foundation of his long dictatorship. The immediate legacy would also have a lasting impact: a suffering population with at least 300,000 killed in military combat, another 200,000 dead in repressive activities, around 300,000 permanent exiles, more than 270,000 political prisoners (officially counted in 1940) and a death toll from disease or starvation that would add more than 330,000 during the war and in subsequent years. In addition there was the material destruction which would lead to severe shortages of food, services and industrial goods in the coming years. According to the most reliable estimates, at the end of the war the economic indices had fallen from their 1935 levels: industrial production had dropped by 30 per cent; agricultural production by more than 20 per cent; national income by more than 25 per cent and transport was at around 22 per cent less than prewar capacity.[81]

In any case, the total victory of April 1939 left the way clear for the consolidation of what was already without doubt the comprehensive personal dictatorship of Franco himself. His invulnerable political position was reflected by his ceremonial entrance into Madrid, the so-called 'Victory Parade' on 19 May 1939. There he presided over a march-past of over 100,000 armed men and received the Gran Cruz Laureada de San Fernando, the highest military decoration of Spain, 'in the name of the fatherland'. The next day, he went to the basilica of Santa Bárbara in Madrid to celebrate the Te Deum to give thanks to God for the victory. He delivered to the cardinal primate of the Spanish Church, Cardinal Gomá, his 'sword of victory' and received the following blessing as the envoy of Providence:

> The Lord be always with you. Let him, the source of all right and power and under whose rule are all things, bless you and with loving Providence continue to protect you, as well as the people with whose regime you have been entrusted.[82]

As a result of a systematic policy of adulation and exaltation, the Caudillo's character had become markedly colder, imperturbable, calculating and reserved, surprising even his closest friends. It had also increased his tendency to succumb to a *folie de grandeur* and to surround himself with sycophants at court. Even though he chose not to occupy the Palacio Real in Madrid, avoiding openly alienating his monarchist supporters, he decided to settle in the nearby palace of El Pardo with all the pomp and ceremony worthy of royalty (including the exotic Moorish Guard, a faithful reminder of his Africanist past). He also began occasionally to speak of himself in the third person and insisted that his wife be treated like a 'lady', accompanied by the Marcha Real (the official Spanish anthem) whenever on an official engagement, as had happened with the queens of Spain. The signs of his willingness to continue in office for life were already unambiguous, as was his determination not to proceed with the restoration of the monarchy in the person of Alfonso XIII (who died in 1941) or his son and heir, Don Juan de Borbón.

Temptation and Opportunism in World War II

Despite the profound process of fascistization that Franco's dictatorship had undergone during the Spanish Civil War and the regime's political and diplomatic proclivity towards the Italo-German Axis, the Caudillo was forced to stay out of the European war which began on 1 September 1939 with the German invasion of Poland. The exhaustion of men and the material destruction caused by the Civil War, along with the state's deep economic difficulties and growing famine, left the Spanish regime at the mercy of an Anglo-French fleet which controlled Spanish maritime access to oil and food supplies vital to its postwar recovery. The situation was a strategic certainty already assumed by Franco and his civilian and military advisers during the Civil War, as made clear in this confidential report submitted to the minister of foreign affairs in May 1938:

One only need open an atlas for any doubt to disappear. In a war against Franco-British forces, one can safely say, without the slightest exaggeration, that we would be totally surrounded by enemies. From the word go we would find them on every perimeter of our territory, on all the coasts and all the borders. We could hold them back in the Pyrenees; but it seems little short of impossible to prevent an invasion at the same time along the Portuguese

border [...] Germany and Italy could only lend us help that was insufficient for
the defence of a weak Spain, and nothing they may offer us could compensate
for the risk involved in fighting by their side.[83]

Even though the repudiation of the democracies was combined with
irredentist aspirations, both anti-British (Gibraltar in the Strait) and anti-
French (Tangier in northern Morocco), on 4 September the Caudillo decreed
Spain's 'strictest neutrality' in the conflict. Ultimately Mussolini also opted for
'non-belligerence', limiting himself to lending concealed support to his German
ally while preparing Italy's future military readiness. Indeed, as Spanish
neutrality was a pure necessity and not a free choice, it was accompanied by
official public identification with Germany's cause and limited covert military
and economic support to its war effort (in the form of logistic facilities for its
fleet, aviation and secret service).[84]

In addition to the strategic and economic reasons which had forced neutrality,
from the beginning of 1940 the internal political situation became less stable
because of the growing dominance of the Falange at the heart of the regime and
the resistance offered to this drift by other institutions and groups of the Francoist
coalition. This tension within the regime resulted in different ideas of foreign
policy, even if everyone understood the compelling need for neutrality under
the watchful and arbitral eye of Franco. Right-wing conservatives, monarchists
and Catholics (dominant in the high military command, the aristocracy, the
clergy and senior civil service) were much more cautious in their pro-German
attitude and favoured appeasing the Allied powers. In contrast, the Falangist
sector led by Serrano Suñer (well represented amongst young military officers
and new political staff recruited during the war) were fervent supporters of the
Axis, willing to risk a clash with the Allies. Assuming the ambiguous neutrality
of Franco as a tolerable, lesser evil, the Anglo-French Entente agreed to finance
a postwar reconstruction programme and supply the country with the urgently
needed wheat, fuel and industrial products. They reserved their overwhelming
naval power to patrol the Spanish coasts and measure out shipments in order to
prevent the re-export of goods to Germany via Italy.

Stunning German victories during the spring and summer of 1940, with the
defeat of France and the imminent attack on Britain, as well as the entry of

Italy into the war, allowed for a remarkable change in the Spanish position. Sure enough, the strategic situation had altered radically since September 1939: the German occupation of the French Atlantic coastline and the formation of the collaborative Vichy regime under Marshal Pétain eliminated any danger to Spain from that direction; and the Italian intervention extended the war to the Mediterranean and limited the capacity of the British fleet, which could no longer use the metropolitan and North African ports belonging to France. Under these conditions, from June 1940 Franco was seriously tempted to enter the war on the side of the Axis in order to carry out the imperial dreams of his regime – the recovery of Gibraltar from British hands and the creation of a large North African empire at the expense of France (occupying Morocco, Tangier and Oran in western Algeria). However, the problem remained the same: Spain could not sustain a prolonged war effort, given its enormous economic and military weakness and the British naval control of its oil and food supplies. A report in March 1940 to the High Council of the Army submitted by General Kindelán (then captain general of the Balearic Islands) had reiterated the strict limitations imposed by military vulnerability and economic distress:

> We regret to report that we are in no way prepared for such contingency [entry into the war]: the air force and navy have lost efficiency over the year since the [Civil War] victory and on land the reorganization has only just begun: our borders are still defenceless and the essential problems of fuel and explosives are yet to be resolved.[85]

For this reason, the cautious Caudillo tried to reconcile his expansionist goals with Spain's plight through a last-minute military intervention on the side of the Axis, at the moment of an Italo-German victory, in order to participate as a belligerent in the subsequent division of imperial spoils. Needless to say, the overwhelming German victories and Italian intervention had reinforced public inclination and covert help for the Axis. The day that Italy entered the war, Franco wrote a revealing private letter to the Duce:

> Our moral solidarity will fervently accompany you on your mission, and as for economic help you can be sure that as much as we are able (as you know our

situation well) we will willingly offer it to you. You already know the reasons
for our current position [...] I emphasize the cordiality with which we will
take advantage of any opportunity to help you with the means at our disposal.[86]

Franco was well aware that this hidden support would not be enough to
allow him to carry out his expansionist programme. Therefore, he hoped to
take part in the war on the side of the Axis powers, but only when the worst
of the combat was over and the British defeat was imminent, with a view to
participating in the sharing-out of colonial booty at the expense of France and
Britain. In the later words of Serrano Suñer, with Franco the main architect of
this diplomatic strategy, the 'intention was to enter the war at the moment of the
German victory, when the last shots were being fired' and 'always starting from
the basis of the belief that the entry of Spain in the short, almost concluded war,
would be more formal than real and would not cause us any real sacrifice'.[87] In
short, Franco was ready to take advantage of the certain Axis victory over the
Franco-British alliance to achieve Spanish territorial aspirations at a limited
cost, one which was acceptable given the conditions.

Following this tempting strategy, on 13 June 1940 Spain abandoned
'strict neutrality' and officially declared its 'non-belligerence'. To the British
government, just in case the situation altered, the change was justified as a
precautionary measure due to the spread of hostilities to the Mediterranean.
The next day, as German troops were occupying Paris, Spanish military forces
'provisionally' occupied the city of Tangier under the pretext of preserving order
and neutrality. It constituted the first step, still a cautious and reversible one, of
a more ambitious imperial programme.

The next Francoist move took place on 16 June 1940. It was a Spanish
initiative and did not respond to any German request (let alone pressure). That
day, a special envoy of the Caudillo, General Vigón, the chief of the general
staff, had an interview with Hitler and his foreign minister, Ribbentrop.
On behalf of Franco, from whom he brought a private letter for the Führer
(dated 3 June), Vigón offered Hitler Spanish belligerency in return for certain
conditions: specifically the cession to Spain, after the victory, of Gibraltar,
French Morocco, Oran in Algeria and the expansion of Spanish possessions
in the Sahara and Equatorial Guinea. The offer was also made conditional on

the prior supply of sufficient food, fuel, arms and heavy artillery from Germany to alleviate the critical economic and military shortages in Spain. While these personal negotiations were taking place, Franco informed Rome by telegraph of the Spanish conditions of joining the Axis.[88]

Fortunately for Franco, although Hitler congratulated Vigón on the occupation of Tangier and expressed his desire that Gibraltar soon become part of Spain, he refused to commit himself on the other demands and claims, alleging the need to consult Italy over any modifications in the Mediterranean. In fact, the Nazi leaders looked down on the costly Spanish offer, considering it unnecessary at a time when France was falling and Britain's defeat seemed assured. Mussolini made no effort to satisfy what he considered to be excessive demands, which moreover could give rise to a competitor in the Mediterranean and North Africa.[89]

The bilateral negotiations on the Spanish entry in the war continued during the summer of 1940, without any German or Italian pressure and with a repeated Spanish insistence on its conditions. This attitude of official reserve was emphasized by the reports on the Spanish situation sent by the German ambassador in Madrid and the Abwehr (German military intelligence). According to the ambassador, 'Spain is economically unfit to carry through to the end a war lasting more than a few months' and 'the economic assistance requested of us could represent a great burden (especially with respect to nutrition).' Admiral Wilhelm Canaris, the head of the Abwehr, accurately summarized the nature and dangers of Franco's offer for the German general staff:

> Franco's policy from the start was not to come in until Britain was defeated, for he is afraid of her might (ports, food situation, etc.). Spain has a very bad internal situation. They are short of food and have no coal. The generals and the clergy are against Franco. His only support is Suñer, who is more pro-Italian than pro-German [...] The consequences of having this unpredictable nation as a partner cannot be calculated. We shall get an ally who will cost us dearly.[90]

Spain's disappointment over the failure of its offer of belligerency was accompanied by a sudden worsening of the internal economic situation which intensified the country's dependence on Allied supplies. The new British government headed by Winston Churchill had understood from the start of the German victories the new importance of Spain in the context of the war and had hastened to take precautionary steps with respect to any possible change in Spain's position. To contain Franco's temptation to join the conflict, the British authorities put into practice two complementary operations. On the one hand, foreseeing the worst, various strategic plans were drawn up for the eventuality of Spain declaring war against Great Britain or being invaded by Germany (the occupation of Ceuta, the hinterland of Gibraltar or the Canary Islands).[91] The second line of action consisted of tightening the maritime blockade on the Spanish coasts and strictly rationing, with US help, the imports of food and fuel supplies to prevent the build-up of stocks in preparation for war or their re-export to Germany. Together these policies 'proved a vital factor in convincing Spain where her interests lay' because the evidence showed that Spain was entering 'a period of intense internal hardship, verging on famine'.[92]

The deterioration of the situation in Spain from September 1940 coincided with the crucial moment of the Battle of Britain and the first German doubts as to the feasibility of the projected invasion of the British Isles. It was in this context that German strategists started to turn their attention to Gibraltar, the conquest of which could help to break British resistance and would limit the activity of the Royal Navy in the Mediterranean. The result of this change in strategy was the invitation by Hitler for Franco to send a representative to Germany to negotiate the conditions for the entry of Spain in the war. Franco decided to send the man whom he trusted most: Serrano Suñer. Between 16 and 27 September 1940, he had several interviews with Hitler and Ribbentrop. During the conversations the disparity between the criteria of the two sides and their differing perception of the importance of Spain in the conflict and the future New Order in Europe became clear.[93] Not surprisingly, the uncertainty created by the Battle of Britain, together with the relative freedom of the Royal Navy in the Mediterranean, had heightened Franco's caution and his wish to take only limited risks in exchange for large compensation. In view of these differences, the discussions were suspended pending a future personal meeting between Hitler and Franco. Serrano Suñer left Berlin without having agreed any protocol for entry in the war and after attending the signing of the Tripartite Pact between Germany, Italy and Japan as a mere spectator.

The interview between the Caudillo and the Führer took place on 23 October 1940 at Hendaye (on the Spanish–French border), taking advantage of a visit by Hitler to the south of France for a meeting with Marshal Pétain (on 24 October). However, in the interval between the conversations in Berlin and the interview in Hendaye, the course of the war reaffirmed both sides in their positions and reduced the already narrow margin for agreement.

Franco's enthusiasm for the war began to fade for two reasons: the British victory over the Luftwaffe (which ruled out a collapse of the British resistance and led to the cancellation of the planned invasion of Britain on 12 October) and the determination of the Royal Navy to maintain its hegemony against Italy in the Mediterranean (which convinced him that an occupation of the Suez Canal was an essential precondition before any attack on Gibraltar). Furthermore, the Spanish general staff, with the support of the monarchists and the Church hierarchy, was increasingly opposed to the interventionist policy of the Falange for good reasons: Spain's extreme vulnerability, the famine in the country (the winter of 1940/1 was very harsh) and the dependence on Anglo-American food and fuel supplies. In these conditions, in Franco's opinion, the implicit risks made the complete fulfilment of all his demands essential before Spain would join the Axis.

As for Hitler, he was finding it more and more difficult to incorporate Francoist demands into his overall strategy. A few days after receiving Serrano Suñer, the Führer had a meeting in Berlin with Count Ciano, Italian foreign minister, and confessed to him that Spanish belligerency 'would cost more than it is worth'. Ciano was also of the opinion that the Spanish 'have been asking for a lot and giving nothing in return'. Moreover, a crucial new event had taken place when on 25 September 1940 the French colonial army, remaining faithful to the Vichy government, had beaten back an attack on Dakar by the forces of General De Gaulle with British support. Its leaders had guaranteed the neutrality of its army provided Germany respected the integrity of the French North African empire. Faced with these events, Hitler and Mussolini met at the Brenner on 4 October to discuss their response to Franco's demands in Morocco. Hitler emphasized that the intervention of Spain 'was of strategic importance only in connection with the conquest of Gibraltar; her military help was absolutely nil'. However, the acceptance of Spanish demands would provoke two adverse phenomena for the Axis: 'firstly, English occupation of the Spanish bases in the Canaries, and secondly, the adhesion of [French] North Africa to the Gaullist movement'. As a result, Hitler considered that, 'at all events, it would be more favourable for Germany if the French remained in Morocco and defended it against the English.' Mussolini expressed his agreement and his desire to reach a compromise between the French hopes and the Spanish wishes.[94]

Under these conditions, during the interview in Hendaye on 23 October 1940, the possibility of a Hispano-German agreement had been considerably reduced.[95] Franco refused to commit himself to a definite date for entering the war, as Hitler requested, unless the colonial Spanish claims were accepted. However, the Führer neither wished to nor was able to agree to them. Looking towards his next meeting with Pétain, Hitler had concluded that the priority was to keep Vichy France on his side to guarantee the benevolent neutrality of the French North African empire and even its anti-British belligerency, as had been demonstrated in Dakar. As a result, he refused to dismember the French territories, as such an act would push the authorities there into the arms of De Gaulle and Britain. He could not risk losing the advantages of French collaboration in the interests of the costly and doubtful belligerency of a country such as Spain, that was hungry, defenceless and half-destroyed. Despite the absence of agreement, in order to secure rights over the distribution of the postwar booty, Franco agreed to sign a 'secret protocol' in Hendaye which prescribed Spain's accession to the German–Italian–Japanese Tripartite Pact and obliged it to 'intervene in the present war of the Axis Powers against England after they have provided it with the military support necessary for its preparedness', at a time to be set by common agreement of the three powers. In this way, Spain became an as-yet non-belligerent associate of the Axis. Mussolini accurately described the significance of the above document in his meeting with Hitler on 28 October: 'That Protocol represents the secret accession of Spain to the Tripartite Pact.'[96]

The subsequent course of the war, with Italian defeats in Greece and North Africa, convinced Franco that this was going to be a prolonged and exhausting conflict. As a result, he continued to postpone *sine die* Spanish belligerency, in spite of German demands that he fulfil the terms of the protocol and fix a date for the start of the joint attack on Gibraltar. At the end of 1940 these demands were particularly intense to ensure Spanish collaboration in 'Operation Felix' (a German attack on Gibraltar, planned for 10 January 1941). Canaris had a meeting with Franco on 7 December to obtain his final approval. However, the Caudillo refused because Spain 'was not prepared for this. The difficulties in the way were not so much military as economic; food and all other necessities were lacking.' According to Franco, military weakness was so great that 'Spain would lose the Canary Islands and her overseas possessions upon entry into the war'. He therefore concluded that 'Spain could enter the war only when England was about to collapse.'[97]

From then on, Franco's regime maintained its alignment with the Axis without passing, due to simple incapacity, the threshold of war. Anti-British campaigns continued in the press; the covert help to German and Italian secret services was maintained; logistics support continued to be given to the navy and air force of both countries; the export of products useful to the Axis war effort was encouraged, including tungsten, iron ore and pyrites.

The pinnacle of Spanish identification with the Axis occurred after 22 June 1941, following the German invasion of the Soviet Union and the shift of the war to the east. Franco congratulated the Nazi government on its initiative and offered as a 'gesture of solidarity' the dispatch of Spanish volunteers to fight alongside the German army against communism. On 2 July, Serrano Suñer defined the position adopted by Franco as 'the most resolute moral belligerency at the side of our friends'. Immediately, under the slogan 'Russia is responsible for our civil war', the recruitment of volunteers began. On 14 July 1941 the first contingent of the so-called Blue Division (because of the colour of the Falangist uniform) set off for the Russian front, consisting of 18,694 men under professional military commanders. Until the final withdrawal (in February 1944), a total of 47,000 Spaniards fought with the German army in Russia (approximately 10 per cent of whom lost their lives).[98]

The political intention of the dispatch of the Blue Division was clear. With the contribution of Spanish blood to the war effort, the Axis would have to recognize future territorial claims. In the words of Serrano Suñer: 'Their sacrifice would give us a title of legitimacy to participate one day in the dreamed-of victory and exempted us from the general and terrible sacrifices of the war.'[99] Nor can one dismiss the idea that it constituted a first tentative step (there was no formal declaration of war against the Soviet Union) towards a larger intervention in the conflict at an opportune moment.

The moral belligerency reflected by the Blue Division was completed in a resounding speech given by Franco before the National Council of the Falange on 17 July 1941. Carried away by his emotions, the Caudillo abandoned his proverbial caution and showed himself more favourable towards the Axis and more scornful of the Allies than ever before:

> The die is already cast. The first battles were joined and won on our soil. [...] The war has taken a bad turn for the Allies and they have lost it. [...] At this moment, when the German armies lead the battle for which Europe and Christianity have for so many years longed, and in which the blood of our youth goes to join that of our comrades of the Axis as a warm expression of our solidarity, let us renew our faith in the destinies of our country under the watchful protection of our closely united army and the Falange.[100]

However, as on previous occasions, public alignment with the Axis did not mean a complete rupture with the Allies. To face up to British protests about the Blue Division, Franco elaborated a 'theory of the two wars' which would excuse his policy of 'moral belligerency'. According to this theory, Spain, continuing the crusade started in the Civil War, was belligerent in the fight against communism in the east. Yet it continued to be non-belligerent in the conflict between the Axis and Britain in Western Europe. From then on, and almost until the end of the war, in spite of Anglo-American reservations, Francoist diplomacy would follow the principle that 'the struggle against the Bolsheviks was something quite distinct from the battle being fought in the west between civilized nations.'[101] The instrumental character of this theory is made clear in a report by the newly appointed secretary of the presidency, later Admiral Carrero Blanco, who would become the most influential adviser to the Caudillo. On 12 December 1941 he wrote to Franco: 'The Anglo-Saxon Soviet front [...] is really the front of Jewish power where the whole complex of democracies, Freemasonry, liberalism, plutocracy and communism raise their flags [...] the Axis is fighting today against everything that is fundamentally Anti-Spain.'[102]

The entry of the United States in the war after the Japanese attack on Pearl Harbor on 7 December 1941, together with serious Italian defeats in Libya and the difficulties of the German offensive in Russia, gradually eroded Franco's belief in a final Axis victory. From then on, the Caudillo, and his advisers, understood that the war was going to be very long and that the strategic position of Spain had become more vulnerable due to American military presence in the Atlantic, the continuing presence of the British in Suez and the forced withholding of German troops on the Eastern Front. In these circumstances, to insure himself against possible hostile Allied action, Franco resorted to the trump card he had been holding: his close relation with the dictatorial regime of Salazar in Portugal, the traditional British ally in the peninsula who had supported him in the Civil War. On Spanish initiative, on 12 February 1942 a meeting between Franco and Salazar took place in Seville. In the course of this meeting the former agreements were ratified with a view to safeguarding the peace and territorial inviolability of the peninsula. Hence the Iberian Bloc took shape, conceived by Franco as a tacit offer of neutrality towards the Allies and as a guarantee of Anglo-American respect towards the Spanish regime.[103]

On 8 November 1942 Franco had to face up to a decisive event: Allied troops landed in the French Zone in Morocco and Algeria and thereby opened a successful second front against the Axis in the Mediterranean. The presence of Allied troops on the other side of the Strait of Gibraltar and along the Spanish Moroccan border was sufficient to put an end to Franco's interventionist airs. Apart from the inability of Spain to react militarily, the US ambassador, Carlton J. Hayes, handed over a personal letter from Roosevelt to Franco in which the former assured that 'these moves are in no shape, manner or form directed against the Government or people of Spain. [...] Spain has nothing to fear from the United Nations.'[104] As news arrived of the Allied victories in North Africa, Spanish diplomacy started to regain a neutralist stance thanks to the previous dismissal of Serrano Suñer (whose conflicts with the military commanders had reached a turning point in August). Progressively, public identification with the Axis and abuse of the democracies gave way to a generic anti-communist denunciation and the alignment of Spain with the Vatican's position. As the new foreign minister, General Gómez-Jordana, recalled at the end of November 1942: 'It is not exactly that we are in favour of the Axis but rather against communism.'[105] In April 1943, a little before the Allied invasion of Sicily caused the fall of Mussolini, the Caudillo reiterated to the Italian ambassador the cause of his inactivity: 'My heart is with you and I want an Axis victory. It is in my interest and in that of my country, but you cannot forget the difficulties that I have to face both internationally and in domestic politics.'[106]

The invasion of Sicily and the fall of Mussolini in July 1943 hastened Spain's return to neutrality. Conscious of their powerful position, the Allies (particularly the United States) began to put pressure on Madrid to cease all forms of covert aid to Germany. At the end of September, Franco announced the disbanding of the Blue Division. On 1 October 1943, Franco restated the 'strict neutrality' of Spain in the war. Seven days later he had to accept without protest the Portuguese decision to allow the Allies to use military bases in the Azores. Anglo-American pressure intensified at the beginning of 1944. On 28 January, the United States imposed an embargo on fuel until Franco's regime met the Allied demands. Shortly afterwards, the same measure was applied to the export of wool, causing a crisis in the textile industry. Confronted with the prospect of a total economic collapse, Franco gave way because 'Spain was in no condition to be intransigent.' By virtue of the agreement signed on 2 May 1944, the Spanish government promised to expel from its territory all German agents reported for espionage or sabotage, to prevent all logistic support to German military forces in ports and airfields, and to suspend virtually all tungsten exports to Germany.[107]

In short, at the close of the war, Franco bent to Anglo-American demands, determined to survive the collapse of the Axis. And to this end he called on the anti-communism and Catholicism of his regime and began a propaganda operation designed to portray himself as the 'sentry of the West' and 'the man who with skilful prudence had stood up to Hitler and preserved Spanish neutrality'. Simultaneously, the press began demonizing Serrano Suñer, attributing to him sole responsibility for Spanish identification with the Axis during his ministerial term. By then, Western diplomatic analysts had realized Franco's desire for political survival at any price. In mid-December 1944, after an interview with Franco in the El Pardo Palace to convey Allied protests at his past conduct, the British ambassador in Madrid informed the British government of the degree of self-confidence and self-assurance exuded by the Caudillo:

> Franco seemed entirely complacent and unruffled. He has made no counter-attack and showed no resentment at my criticism. [...] He showed no signs of being worried about the future of Spain and had evidently convinced himself that the present régime is in the forefront of human progress and the best that Spain has ever possessed. Whether this appearance of complete complacency is a pose or not, it is impossible to say. My own view is that he is genuinely convinced that he is the chosen instrument of Heaven to save Spain, and any suggestions to the contrary he regards as either ignorant or blasphemous. [...] It was only when I was leaving that I noticed a sign that the wind had begun to blow in this unventilated shrine of self-complacency. Photographs of the Pope and President Carmona [of Portugal] had taken the place of honour previously held on his writing table by Hitler and Mussolini.[108]

Resistance and Survival in the Postwar World

The end of the war, with the total victory of the Allied coalition, marked the beginning of a period of ostracization of the Franco regime. This critical juncture allowed the Caudillo to again show his political skills to resist and survive in a difficult situation, both domestically and abroad.[109] On 19 March 1945, Don Juan de Borbón, son and heir of the late Alfonso XIII, published his *Manifiesto de Lausana* requesting that Franco retire in favour of a monarchy open to national reconciliation and democratic transition. Shortly thereafter, on 2 August, the conference of the victorious Allies at Potsdam issued a statement vetoing the entry of Franco's Spain into the United Nations (UN) 'in view of its origins, its nature, its record and its close association with the aggressor States'.[110]

Beset by both international condemnation and internal pressure in favour of the restoration of the monarch, Franco fought his last great battle for survival by rekindling the hatred and memories of the Civil War and the spectre of a Masonic–Bolshevik plot against Catholic Spain (it was no longer appropriate to make anti-Semitic references in view of the Holocaust). Franco was convinced that very soon there would be a confrontation in Europe because of the antagonism between the Soviet Union and the United States and that the latter would turn to Spain for its invaluable strategic importance and its anti-communist policy. Until this rupture occurred, there was no option but to follow the confidential recommendations of his political alter ego since the ousting of Serrano Suñer, Admiral Carrero Blanco. In mid-April 1945, the faithful secretary reminded the Caudillo that it was essential to 'preach among the Spanish the holy war of anti-communist and anti-liberal intransigence' and 'take advantage' of the three 'weapons' of the regime to convince 'England and the United States' that 'we need to jointly fight against Russian imperialism': 'our Catholicism, our anti-communism and our geographical position'.[111] Three months later, evaluating the Potsdam Conference, Carrero Blanco underlined the tensions between the West and the Soviet Union and sought to define what would be Franco's attitude in the future:

> In short, with the last shot in the Pacific, the diplomatic war between the Anglo-Saxon powers and Russia has begun. England and the United States are united against Russian imperialism [...]. In this obvious case of cold self-interest, the Anglo-Saxons (despite what they say on the radio, in the media and even the politicians, great and small) not only do not support, but oppose everything that could create a situation of Soviet hegemony in the Iberian Peninsula. They are interested in order and anti-communism but would prefer to achieve this with a different regime to the current one. [...] The pressures of the Anglo-Saxons for a change in Spanish politics that breaks the normal development of the current regime will be much lower, the more palpable is our order, our unity and our impassivity to threats and impertinences. There can be no other formula for us than: order, unity and endurance.[112]

Franco responded to the monarchist challenge by emphasizing the process of defascistization of the regime, already developing into a 'Catholic and organic democracy' which dignified humanity and was more perfect than 'the formal and garrulous democracy that exploits it'.[113] The purpose of this declared campaign of 'constitutional cosmetics' and 'apparent change of façade' was to improve the public image of the regime and minimally meet the democratic sensibilities of the victorious Allies. It was, according to the private testimony of Franco before his ministers, a 'cleansing of the imitation' of the Axis without 'yoking us to the democratic cart'. And all this without substantial changes: 'To cede would be taken for weakness.'[114]

The conversion of the national syndicalist regime into a National Catholic regime was formalized with the enactment by Franco, on 13 July 1945, of the third of the 'fundamental laws' of Francoism (after the Fuero del Trabajo in 1938 and the Ley de Cortes adopted in 1942) – the so-called Fuero de los Españoles, a substitute for a real charter of civil rights and democratic freedoms. Just a week later, Franco formed a new government; most notable (aside from the inclusion of six military men who continued in key portfolios) was the promotion of a leading Catholic politician as minister of foreign affairs: Alberto Martín Artajo, president of Acción Católica, who had accepted the position on the advice of the cardinal primate, Pla y Deniel, to collaborate in 'the evolution of the regime towards a Catholic and monarchist formula'. In any case, the new Cabinet was a demonstration of the juggling skills of the Caudillo to form balanced, useful and submissive governments. The final act of this conversion to organic and Catholic democracy was the adoption, on 22 October 1945, of the Ley de Referéndum, intended to open to Spaniards a consultation mechanism on proposed bills that the Caudillo believed suitable for plebiscite.

Measures taken by Franco in 1945 and afterwards gradually reduced the pressure from the monarchists and military in favour of Don Juan de Borbón. Before them all, the Caudillo made clear his determination to remain in power without surrendering the state headship to the pretender, although he would be prepared to offer apparent concessions. Introducing the new Fuero de los Españoles at the Falange National Council, on 17 July 1945, he pointed out: 'It is not a question of replacing or changing the commander unless it is in the national interest, but defining the regime and ensuring its succession faced with the hazards of mortality.'[115] He was even more clear and explicit in his statements to General Kindelán: 'As long as I live, I shall never be a queen mother'; 'I will not make the same mistake as Primo de Rivera. I do not resign; from here to the cemetery.'[116] To the most influential of the monarchist officers,

General José Enrique Varela, then high commissioner in Morocco, Franco coldly warned at the end of 1945 of the risks of breaking the unity of the victors of the Civil War: 'If they succeed in toppling the goalkeeper, we would all fall; if they find us united they will not dare to attack to the bitter end.'[117] Very soon the British ambassador in Madrid clearly appreciated that Franco's die-hard resistance strategy was achieving its objectives:

> All those who fought on Franco's side in the Civil War are once more giving rein to their fears of renewed strife and are inclined to cling to Franco rather than risk a change while French Communists are still dominant in Paris. [...] Franco is playing upon the general dread of a renewal of the civil war and even those former adherents who are sick of him, notably Army leaders, prefer his régime which at least maintains order to the risk of chaotic conditions or worse if French and Moscow are allowed to have their way. Franco feels moreover in a strong position as long as his opponents both Monarchist and Republican are still divided and poorly led and he argues that there is no alternative between him and the Communists.[118]

Indeed, faced with the dilemma of either enduring him indefinitely or trying to overthrow him by force and risking a war with the hypothetical return of the Republic, the monarchists mostly resigned themselves to Franco's pompous reign without a crown. In fact, Franco began to make unlimited use of all the royal prerogatives, including the right to approve new bishops, the entry into cathedrals under a canopy and the granting of titles of nobility (which he exercised on 39 occasions throughout his life). A few years later, he dared to confess to his status as de facto regent with constituent powers: 'We are indeed a monarchy without royalty, but we are a monarchy.'[119]

To a large extent, the failure of the anti-Franco opposition, whether it be monarchical or Republican, lay in its limited active social backing (with a hungry population fearful of a new war) and the patent lack of encouragement and firm support it received from abroad. Franco knew that he had only one real enemy: 'Only the Allied armies could throw him from power and they do not seem very inclined to do so.'[120] In fact, from the beginning of 1945, both the United States and Britain had launched a policy of 'cold reserve' and occasional 'pinpricks' against the Spanish regime to force the voluntary withdrawal of Franco on behalf of Don Juan, with the support of the military high command and without risking a recommencement of civil war. The geo-strategic interest of the Iberian Peninsula for the defence of Western Europe, accentuated by the first signs of dissension between the Soviet Union and its former allies against Nazism, reinforced the will to preserve the principle of non-intervention in the internal affairs of third countries and to prevent any danger of political destabilization in Spain. Both Washington and London agreed with that analysis for shared and powerful reasons: 'If we are too stiff with Franco we may give undue encouragement to Communist elements. In the present mood of Moscow they might well turn out to be as inimical to our long-term interests as the Falange itself.'[121] Therefore, rejecting Soviet demands to apply effective sanctions (diplomatic, economic or military), the victors of World War II were limited to imposing a toothless international ostracism within whose ambiguous framework – the disintegration of the great Western–Soviet alliance and its replacement by a climate of cold war – was forged the survival of the Franco dictatorship in the postwar world.

In these circumstances, just like the monarchists, the victorious democratic powers ended up resigned and yielding to the Caudillo: the alternative to supporting a harmless Franco was provoking political destabilization in Spain with an uncertain outcome. The new British Labour government, like the US Democratic administration, resolved to endure his presence as a tolerable lesser evil preferable to a new civil war or a communist regime on the Iberian Peninsula, despite the profound personal and political displeasure it caused in official and governmental circles. In August 1945, after a tense audience with the Caudillo, the new British ambassador in Madrid confidentially described him to his superiors with the following words: 'He is certainly a smiling villain – rather absurdly unlike the popular idea of a dictator with his Pekingese goggle eyes and fat tummy and short legs.' In London, the diplomatic analysts for the Foreign Office added to that description a few very revealing notes: 'And I fear he is a shameless liar. The captured German documents in our possession prove that', 'He has a skin like a rhinoceros.' However, despite these reservations and antipathies, almost a year later, another senior official from the same ministry privately summed up the reasons that precluded all effective Allied pressure, economic or military, to achieve the fall or retirement of Franco:

> The fact remains that Franco is not a threat to anybody outside Spain, odious though his régime is. But a civil war in Spain would bring trouble to all the Western Democracies, which is what the Soviet Government and their satellites want.[122]

This rather weak diplomatic cold shouldering had begun in March 1946 with a tripartite British–French–American declaration (without the USSR) expressing those nations' repudiation of the Franco regime and their wish to see democracy restored in Spain. At the end of the year, the UN General Assembly recommended the withdrawal of ambassadors from Spain to force the democratic transition (a measure not taken by the embassies of the Vatican, Portugal, Ireland or Argentina). Franco's imperturbable resistance to these measures revealed the bankruptcy of Western policy to oust him peacefully and without violence. In his speech before the Cortes in May 1946 he warned the Allied powers of the danger of undermining the stability of a regime that had only one enemy ('Communism, which has been working for universal Bolshevism for more than 25 years') and a legitimacy of origin ('Our victory saved a society on the point of dying'). It was, he claimed, a regime that was not a mere 'dictatorship' but a 'Catholic state' and 'organic democracy' tailored to the 'individual character of the Spaniards' and their tendency 'to selfishness and anarchy', as had been shown during the Republic (a product of 'all changes, revolutions anarchy from all previous periods'). It was a regime that had not entered the world war ('He did not allow himself to be carried away by the temptations for his own benefit'), nor had it seconded the policies of the Axis despite the gratitude that was due for their assistance in the Civil War, nor could he be considered alien to the Western world:

> Others try to present ourselves to the world as Nazi-fascists and anti-democratic. Once, we did not mind that confusion given the prestige enjoyed by this kind of regime in the world; today when the cruelty and ignominy of the vanquished has been revealed, it is fair to highlight the very different

characteristics of our state. [...] The perfect state for us is the Catholic state. [...] Spain has set an example of how to practise the Catholic doctrine. With it, Spain has survived the biggest crisis in its history and achieved, without the least outside help, its reconstruction.[123]

Following the same policy of essential resistance and formal flexibility, in March 1947 Franco passed the Ley de Sucesión a la Jefatura del Estado (Law of Succession to the Head of State), which defined Spain as 'a Catholic, social and representative state in accordance with that tradition, declaring itself to be a kingdom'. It bestowed sovereignty and a lifetime regency upon the figure of the 'Caudillo of Spain and of the Crusade', which conferred on him the right to designate a successor 'to the title of king or regent' at any time and revocably.[124] Franco submitted the Ley de Sucesión to a referendum in July 1947, just when the international outlook began to clear (four months before, President Truman had made public his doctrine of containment of Communism in Greece, Turkey and the rest of the 'free world'). The result of the poll, which had been orchestrated by the regime from start to end, could not have been more satisfying for Franco. The law was adopted by such an overwhelming majority (93 per cent of the voters, with an 82 per cent turn-out) as to be suspicious: of the 17,178,812 adults with the right to vote, 15,219,565 went to the polls, 14,145,163 voted in favour, 722,656 voted against and 336,592 votes were invalid or void.[125]

In any case, the passage of the law substantially reduced any room for monarchical manoeuvres and accentuated the divide between the collaborationist majority and the minority opposition. The intensity of the blow sustained by the monarchist cause was very well appreciated by a disillusioned General Kindelán in a private letter to Don Juan:

Franco is these days, as I say, in a state of total euphoria. He is a man in the enviable position of believing everything that pleases him and forgetting or denying that which is disagreeable. He is also puffed up with pride, intoxicated by adulation and drunk on applause. He is dizzy from the heights; he is sick with power, determined to hold on to it, sacrificing whatever is necessary and defending it with tooth and claw. Many see him as perverse and evil; I do not. He is crafty and shrewd, but I think that his work has convinced him that his destiny and that of Spain are intrinsically linked and that God has put him in this position for some grand design. Dizzy from his unwarranted elevation and lacking any cultural awareness, he does not appreciate the risks of an excessive extension of his dictatorship that every day is more difficult to end. [...] In summary: I do not think Franco, in his current egotistical state, will restore the monarchy, when at his feet are 12 million submissive slaves.[126]

The triumph of this last-ditch strategy by the Caudillo was evident at the beginning of 1948, when the French government ordered the reopening of the Spanish border which had closed two years earlier. Shortly thereafter, in August, Don Juan met with Franco on a yacht in the Bay of Biscay and yielded to Franco's demand that his son and heir, Prince Juan Carlos, was educated in Spain under Franco's tutelage. The Caudillo already had very serious doubts about the qualities of Don Juan to succeed him and had begun to outline the idea of cultivating as a potential and fortunately distant successor the prince (then only ten years old), in which the Francoist doctrine of the monarchist 'appointment' and the principle of the dynastic 'restoration' could be reconciled.[127]

From the end of 1948, with Prince Juan Carlos in Spain and at the height of the Cold War abroad, Franco already knew that no essential danger would call into question his 'command' or his diplomatic recognition in the West. The young Prince would remember later (when king) that his predecessor as head of state was a 'cold and mysterious man' who 'did not speak much and hated to explain himself', whose main political lesson consisted of 'look, listen and keep quiet'.[128] One of the maxims that Franco most liked to repeat was, 'One is a slave to what one says but the owner of one's silence.'[129] His messianic belief that he was providential for Spain had also deepened, as noted by the writer José María Pemán, a supporter of Don Juan but still a collaborator with the regime: 'It is no joke; it is a sincere conviction, created by 100 limitations of military training and 200 adulatory mirages.'[130] The proof of the complacency exhibited by Franco at the time was the marriage of his only daughter to the son of the count of Argillo, the doctor and Madrid playboy Cristóbal Martínez Bordiú (Marquis of Villaverde). The splendid wedding ceremony, with more than 800 guests and officiated by the archbishop of Toledo and cardinal primate of the Spanish Church was held in El Pardo on 10 April 1950 and was worthy of a king's daughter. The sermon delivered by Cardinal Pla y Deniel reached the pinnacles of National Catholicism when, while talking to the bride and groom, he compared the Franco family to the Holy family: 'You have an exemplary model in the family of Nazareth and another more recently in the Christian home of the head of state.'[131]

'Nenuca's' wedding would change the life and family of Franco considerably. Firstly, the couple would give him, between 1951 and 1964, seven grandchildren who he would shower with affection and attention both in private and in public. Secondly, the numerous Villaverde clan displaced in El Pardo the families of Franco's brothers and exerted a remarkable aristocratic influence on Carmen Polo (especially evident in her fondness for antiques and jewellery). In any case, although he never criticized his son-in-law, Franco 'finished by ignoring him altogether'. His cousin and aide considered the son-in-law 'lightweight in the extreme', while his personal confessor showed on several occasions his concern 'for his frivolous conduct and lack of consideration to his in-laws'.[132]

The marriage of his daughter took place during the final stage of the international rehabilitation of the Franco regime, which would be formally completed in June 1950 when Soviet–US tension triggered a real 'hot' war in Korea. The conflict would eliminate all reservations amongst Western leaders because it underlined a pressing need: 'Spain as a people and Spain as a geographic entity should be a part of the Western community.' And that meant negotiating with a Caudillo who was not particularly wanted but essential. In the words of the American chargé d'affaires in Spain in June 1950:

Franco is a Gallegan. This is in a sense a synonym for stubbornness. He certainly holds the whip hand in Spain today. He thinks he knows better than anyone else what is best for Spain and the Spaniards today. He listens to what he wants to hear, shuts his mind and ear to all other. [...] Franco is the kind of Spaniard who likes to get into the movie without buying a ticket. He has certainly given no evidence of willingness to pay any price for admission to the West. [...] As a result, Franco leans back with complacency and anticipates the world will come to him on his terms. Franco's vision stops at the borders of Spain.[133]

Under the impact of the Korean War, in November 1950 the General Assembly of the United Nations decided to revoke by a large majority (with strong US support and French and British abstention) the 1946 condemnatory resolution towards Spain. This opened the way in successive months for Western ambassadors to return to Madrid and the approval of the entry of Spain into specialized international agencies (the Food and Agriculture Organization, UNESCO, the World Health Organization, the International Labour Organization, etc.). The eventual entry of Spain to the UN would have to wait until the General Assembly of December 1955.

Even so, the rehabilitation of the Franco regime in the West was partial, limited and entailed a tremendous economic and political cost for Spain itself. The survival of the Franco dictatorship, still associated with the Axis in Western public opinion, excluded Spanish participation in the crucial US economic aid for European reconstruction (the Marshall Plan, launched in June 1947). It also barred Spain from the Western joint defence talks started in March 1948 that would give rise to the North Atlantic Treaty and the creation of NATO in April 1949.

In any case, Franco achieved his greatest diplomatic triumphs in 1953. In August of that year, the long-awaited Concordat with the Vatican, which endorsed the incontestable Catholic and confessional nature of the regime, was signed in Madrid. A month later, in September, Franco signed bilateral agreements with the United States that reintegrated Spain into the Western defence system with the installation of several US military bases on Spanish soil.[134] As Franco rightly said on 1 October 1953, in his speech at the Fiesta del Caudillo, it was 'a time of plenty for our foreign policy'.[135] In private he was no less sparing in giving full rein to his satisfaction. After signing the agreements for the bases, he was heard to comment, 'At last I have won the Civil War.'[136] He had sound reason to celebrate because, from then on, no fundamental danger called into question his command and comprehensive authority in Spain nor his diplomatic recognition in the West, albeit as a minor partner and despised for his political structure and recent past.

Regardless, by then, his official life was already strictly regulated except on rare occasions: on Tuesdays he held military audiences; on Wednesdays, civil hearings; on Thursdays he worked with Admiral Carrero Blanco and his military and private secretaries in addition to receiving credentials from ambassadors; on Fridays he presided over the regular meeting of the Council of Ministers. The rest of the week he rested and devoted time to his hobbies and family life.[137]

A Long Reign Without a Crown

From the mid-1950s, Franco, firm in his position and recognized as supreme and final arbitrator for all the Francoist political 'families' (Falangists, Carlists, Catholics, monarchists and the military), lived perhaps the happiest and calmest stage of his long life as Caudillo. A palpable demonstration of the security of Franco both domestically and internationally was the increase in the amount of time he devoted to leisure and the enjoyment of his favourite sports. These pastimes did not include (nor for Doña Carmen) either music (light or classical), literature, dance, theatre, opera, poetry or the visual arts in general (except for a brief flirtation with oil painting: still life, landscapes and some family portraits). The complete absence of a personal library in the private apartments of the Franco family in the palace of El Pardo gives an idea of the dominant cultural hobbies and the insular, almost provincial atmosphere prevailing there. Pilar Franco Bahamonde, who was invited to El Pardo for lunch once a week or fortnightly, would remember that her brother allowed himself 'very few distractions: golf, fishing, hunting. He is very fond of bullfighting, but I think he likes football the most.'[138]

Aside from these sports, Franco regularly played tennis (until prevented by old age) and golf. He continued with his long discussions with friends, preferably those from the military, who also served as companions and opponents in card games (mus and tresillo) and dominoes.[139] Franco also maintained his fondness (shared by his wife) for watching movies in the lounge of El Pardo (normally on Saturday and Sunday afternoons) and listening to daily radio programmes (and later television once it started broadcasting in 1956).

Around the early 1950s, as a result of internal institutional changes and international rehabilitation, Franco's regime was fully consolidated. However, the economic situation was still terrible due to the failure of autarky, a policy that he still stubbornly followed. In 1950 all economic indicators remained below or at the same levels as those prior to the Civil War. In that year, the income per capita in Spain ($694 in 1970) was even lower than it had been in 1940 ($746) and had still not exceeded that of 1930 ($798).[140] Consequently, Spain was one of the poorest and most underdeveloped countries in Europe (together with Greece and Portugal) and remained in a state of economic prostration that the devastated Western combatants of World War II (including Italy and Germany) had already overcome. Its social welfare and public consumption levels were even lower than some Latin American countries. At the beginning of 1951, a civil governor of the regime (the supreme authority in a province) witnessed this with regret, 'We must recognize clearly that there is hunger, unrest and discontent.'[141]

Seeing the end of Spain's isolationism and the need to alter the course of the autarky policy, Franco changed his government in July 1951. The ministerial reshuffle was very broad, although the character of the 'coalition team' was still predominantly military and Catholic (apart from Martín Artajo, Joaquín Ruiz-Giménez, former ambassador to Rome, as education minister, and Gabriel Arias Salgado as minister of information and tourism).

The most notable feature of the new cabinet was the promotion to the post of Cabinet secretary of Carrero Blanco, who was already 'the *eminence gris* of the regime', an action justified to him by Franco on the basis that it would avoid Franco 'having to repeat [to him] the proceedings of the Council [of Ministers] afterwards'.[142] The renewed National Catholic majority at the heart of the regime, along with the monarchist institutionalization *sui generis*, increased the frustration of the Falangist 'family' and led to growing friction between it and the remaining political forces. The Falangists were particularly critical of the policy of controlled cultural and university 'liberalization' that Ruiz-Giménez would undertake. The rivalry between the Falange and political Catholicism in the 1950s replaced the previous rivalry between Falangists and the military-monarchist bloc.

Although aware of the intensity of the internal friction in his Cabinet, Franco always refused to relegate the Falange entirely (and even less to dissolve it), as the Catholics – with the support of other political forces and sectors of the army – wanted. On the contrary, the Falange was kept in power because it served as a counterweight to monarchist and Catholic demands, provided 'service

personnel' for the public administration and trade union bureaucracy and was
the most faithful of the available forces since it had no basis for its existence
other than its loyalty to the Caudillo. As Franco said to Martín Artajo in the
critical moments of 1945 when asked for the 'displacement of the Falange', it
was 'an effective tool' ('They warn me of dangers'), that 'educated opinion and
organized forces' ('I see it on my travels'), and served as a shield from criticism
('They are blamed for the mistakes of the government').[143] For that reason, in
October 1953, just after having signed the Concordat and agreements with the
United States, and in one of his Solomon-like judgements of political balance,
Franco allowed in Madrid the first (and only) National Congress of FET and
the JONS, despite criticism from some ministers who regarded it as 'madness to
give this sense of revitalization of the Falange'.[144]

The tension that grew between Falangists and Catholic *aperturistas* (who were
open to change) culminated in February 1956 with serious riots at the University
of Madrid. Their origin was in the new generation of university students'
growing dissatisfaction with rigid official control and the overwhelming lack of
critical intellectual freedom in higher education. Clashes between students and
Falangists precipitated a political and ministerial crisis of great significance. On
10 February, for the first time, Franco ordered the suspension of several articles
of the Fuero de los Españoles, the closure of the University of Madrid and the
arrest of several student and intellectual leaders. The Caudillo considered that
'the university is now like a regiment without sergeants' and it was necessary to
impose discipline urgently.[145] The apparent bankruptcy of public order resulted
in the sacking of Ruiz-Giménez, considered 'guilty' of the disturbances, and the
secretary general of the Falange, accused of being unable to control its members.
However, the Caudillo could not settle the internal tensions in his regime that
the crisis of February 1956 had brought to light.

Indeed, as a result of the relaxation of autarky measures and US financial
aid, the 1951–7 period was 'the first time in the Spanish postwar period when
there was significant growth' of economic activity, together with 'a rapid
advance of the industrial sector compared to agriculture'.[146] In just a decade,
the income per capita of the country grew from $694 in 1950 to $1,042 in 1960,
while the industrial production index (base 100 in 1929) jumped from 106.8 to
203.6 between 1950 and 1960.[147] This renewed economic activity had allowed

an exultant Franco to end the much-hated rationing in June 1952. However, the worrying reversal of that process of growth, for which US aid could never compensate, was brought about by a growing inflationary trend, aggravated by a worsening of the balance of trade and a lack of means of international payments that would reach distressing conclusion in 1957. By then, the expectation of financial bankruptcy meant it was essential to make profound economic changes that would bring a definitive end to autarky and fully open the Spanish economy to the outside world.

The quick Cabinet reshuffle approved by Franco in February 1956 was an emergency solution to a major crisis, due both to its impact on public order and its institutional implications. In turn, the failure of successive attempts to choose between a Catholic and Falangist profile created the need to initiate a third institutional and political-economic alternative. The change was made in a progressively worsening international context due to the process of decolonization that was underway. Just a month after the resolution of the ministerial crisis, Franco had to bury his Africanista dreams after the unexpected decision of France to grant independence to Morocco. On 7 April 1956 Franco recognized Mohammed V as king and without conditions ceded him the Spanish Protectorate.

The abandonment of Morocco coincided with a serious deterioration of the economic situation that called into question the precarious political balance between autarky and liberalization which had hardly managed to reach the macroeconomic prewar levels. By the middle of 1957 the Spanish economy was at an impasse. Inflation had risen by 11 per cent in that year, and would rise another 11 per cent the next and another 5.5 per cent by June 1959. At the same time, financial strangulation led to an accelerated reduction of currency so that by the end of 1957 there were hardly any reserves left. As a result, the spectre of the suspension of foreign payments was obvious and the risk of financial bankruptcy a very real possibility.[148]

Faced with the dual crisis of political paralysis and economic bankruptcy, Franco was forced to carry out profound ministerial changes postponed from the previous reshuffle. At the end of February 1957, he appointed a new government which saw the final decline of the Falange and a commitment to the alternative political-economic programme sponsored by Carrero Blanco. Despite the presence of the usual military, Catholic and Falangist quotas, the new stars of the Cabinet were economists belonging to the Catholic Opus Dei who formed a team of so-called 'technocrats'.[149] Their spectacular rise was due to the strong support of Carrero Blanco, who largely shared their religious fundamentalism and had them implement his programme of institutionalization, economic liberalization and international openness. Indeed, the new government in February 1957, under the direction of Carrero Blanco and with the encouragement of the technocrats, thus embarked on a three-part programme to improve the effectiveness of state administration, complete the institutional profile of the regime under the formula of a traditional monarchy (with a successor included *in pectore*), and promote economic reform to put an end to the vestiges of interventionist autarky, instead opting for growth based on an opening to the outside world and the primacy of free private enterprise.

The administrative reform measures were to overcome the traditional lack of coordination and the fragmentation of the state bureaucratic apparatus in Spain. Although Franco was extremely reluctant (delaying the completion of the reform until the approval of the Ley Orgánica del Estado (the Organic Law of the State or constitution) in 1967), the set of measures taken meant, with all its flaws, the implementation of a state network across the whole of Spain, a uniform extension of general functions and the emergence of a bureaucracy recruited exclusively on merit and not politics.

In its political dimension, Carrero Blanco's programme was to continue the institutionalization of Francoism in a traditional, monarchist and Catholic sense with the succession issue resolved in favour of Prince Juan Carlos. Things were slower than expected because the Caudillo delayed the monarchical succession as much as he could, although he had already ruled out Don Juan and set his sights on the young Prince. As he confessed to his cousin and assistant at that time: 'I have already said on different occasions and political events that while I have health and physical and mental faculties I will not give up the leadership of the state.'[150]

The third aspect of the political programme hosted by Carrero Blanco and profiled by the technocrat ministers was to undertake economic reform which exceeded the exhausted autarky-interventionist model, avoided financial bankruptcy and laid the foundations for productive growth at least similar to what was starting to happen in Western Europe (evident from March 1957, following the establishment of the European Economic Community). The genesis of the subsequent Plan de Estabilización y Liberalización (Plan for Stabilization and Liberalization) approved on 21 July 1959 was haphazard and not without political complications. In particular, Franco was very reluctant to recognize the failure of autarky ('things were not so bad') and harboured serious doubts about the potential political effects of the recommended economic openness. As Carrero Blanco noted, the Caudillo was 'suspicious' of the new direction in economic policy, which he probably did not understand in all its complexity: 'I'm turning into a communist.'[151] Franco finally accepted the urgent need for change when his technocrat ministers explained to him, not the origins, but the hypothetical outcome of his obstinate hesitancy: 'General, if we have to return to ration cards, what will we do if the orange harvest is hit by frost?' Faced with that frightening possibility, the Caudillo relented and approved the stabilizing and liberalizing measures. He did not do so willingly, but out of forced pragmatism: 'He is not happy; he is deeply suspicious,' confessed Carrero Blanco to his main technocrat adviser, the lawyer Laureano López Rodó.[152]

The implementation of the Plan de Estabilización of 1959 meant a profound change of economic course in the evolution of the Franco regime. Several measures (budgetary rigour, credit restrictions, devaluation of the peseta, an end to state interventionism, a salary freeze and the opening of the Spanish economy abroad) laid the foundations for spectacular economic growth from 1960 which would radically transform Spanish society. Thus, paradoxically, the political regime that had for 20 years interrupted the process of economic and social modernization which had been initiated in Spain at the end of the nineteenth century, became its new advocate and sponsor. Consequently, the new phase of productive modernization and socio-professional diversification would be developed and credit taken for it by a static political system, alien and unaffected by such profound evolution. Very soon, that increasing dysfunction between static political structures and dynamic socio-economic realities would create serious internal tensions in the country. Economic development would not only give new strength and legitimacy to the Franco regime in the short term – it would also generate deeply discordant social and cultural conditions within an anachronistic political system unprepared for its own socio-economic reality and success.

Indeed, after a brief initial recession, the implementation of the Plan de Estabilización achieved its basic objectives – avoidance of the danger of financial bankruptcy and recovery of foreign-exchange reserves. After that, in line with the expansion in the rest of the Western economies, Spain's economy entered a stage of unprecedented development, the so-called 'Spanish economic miracle', with annual growth of over 7 per cent between 1960 and 1970 that was only interrupted by the international economic crisis of 1973. As a result of the sustained expansion, the Spanish economic structure underwent a remarkable change between 1960 and 1970: Spain ceased to be a predominantly agrarian country and became fully industrialized with a diversified and buoyant service sector.[153] The intense process of development was the combined result of the new economic policy of liberalization and three concurrent exogenous factors: the large investments of foreign capital (whose volume multiplied by 15 between 1960 and 1972, with the US as the main investor); substantial revenues from mass tourism (between 1960 and 1973 the number of tourists went from 6 to 34.5 million, a figure equal to that the population of Spain); and the capital transfers from waves of emigrants which alleviated domestic unemployment and eased the balance of payments (between 1960 and 1972 emigration abroad exceeded 100,000 people per year, with a total of at least 843,000 permanent emigrants and a similar number of semi-permanent or temporary emigrants).[154]

The social effects caused by the rapid economic growth soon became apparent. The Spanish population grew during the 1960s at the fastest rate in its history, from 30.4 million in 1960 to 35.4 in 1975. The composition of the active population underwent a similarly radical change: the percentage of the population employed in agriculture decreased from 42 per cent in 1960 to 22.8 per cent in 1970, while during this decade the industrial population rose from 31 per cent to 38.4 per cent and those occupied in the service sector from 27 per cent to 34.1 per cent.[155] The Spain of the industrial and services boom was also the Spain of intense urbanization through a massive depopulation of the countryside. In a decade the country had more than half of its inhabitants residing in cities (with Madrid exceeding 3 million inhabitants and Barcelona close to 2 million). The corollary was the growth of an industrial and services working class and its gradual transformation during the decade into an increasingly qualified and specialized workforce. While economic development precipitated this change at the heart of the working class, it also reinforced and consolidated a much-diversified middle class that swelled and renewed the intermediate sections of Spanish society. Even the upper classes were affected by economic change; the loss of important agriculture meant the collapse of the hegemony of the landowning oligarchy within the ruling elite and its replacement by new dominant forces from the expanding financial capital sector and the industrial and commercial bourgeoisies.[156]

In short, during the 1960s, at a time of intense economic development, a society was being created that was increasingly closer to its counterparts in Western Europe in structure, composition, characteristics and degree of development and diversification (including a massive incorporation of women into the workplace). This was a society in which the average life expectancy rose from 69.9 years in 1960 to 73.3 in 1975, while the literacy rate grew between these years until it encompassed virtually all of the population. It was a society that was progressively immersing itself in the culture of mass consumption, and began to enjoy unknown levels of well-being: in 1960, only 1 per cent of households had a TV, only 4 per cent a refrigerator and only 12 per cent a phone, while in 1971 56 per cent of households had a TV, 66 per cent a refrigerator and 39 per cent a phone.[157]

After giving the go-ahead to the implementation of the Plan de Estabilización, an ageing Franco (he would be 70 in December 1962) gradually withdrew from active and everyday politics in favour of formal ceremonies, the company of his grandchildren and the cultivation of his leisure and recreational interests (in particular, watching television, a hobby he shared with his wife). The deep social and economic transformations during the decade of technocratic development emphasized his withdrawal because, quite simply, the Caudillo could not fully understand the complexity of the new situation and its demands. This was apparent, for example, in his increasingly silent presence at the head of the weekly meetings of the Council of Ministers. In addition, his alter ego, Admiral Carrero Blanco, continued dealing with the effective work of the presidency of the government in a manner as colourless and loyal as it was efficient and satisfactory.

This progressive retreat of the Caudillo from the political front line was accentuated by the serious hunting accident he suffered on 24 December 1961 in the mountains of El Pardo, an accident which could well have cost him his life. The explosion of a faulty cartridge in his shotgun fractured several bones in his left hand and his index finger, forcing him to undergo a painful operation in a Madrid military hospital, requiring a general anaesthetic and a long period of rehabilitation therapy. It was the first setback in a medical history that had been almost clear of incident, according to the testimony of his personal doctor, 'Vicentón': 'his illnesses have been scarce and commonplace. Two or three cases of flu, oral infections, minor food poisoning.' Not long after the accident and more obviously from 1964 onwards, Franco began to show symptoms of Parkinson's disease, with its corresponding trembling of hands, progressive facial and body rigidity and a gradual weakening of his already thin voice.[158]

The incipient physical decline of Franco reinforced the political ascendance of Carrero Blanco, evident in the ministerial reshuffles of July 1962 and July 1965. It was the political triumph of a technocratic programme that sought to promote the growth of the economy as the generator of prosperity for the population, in the hope that from such well-being social peace would thrive, replacing the lack of free democratic participation and giving 'legitimacy of office' to a regime that was still authoritarian but acting as an agent of modernization. The sustained economic expansion of the 1960s meant that the ideological discourse of the dictatorship replaced the old 'legitimacy of victory' with the new 'legitimacy of achievement' delivered in office.[159] The Caudillo himself joined that campaign for ideological renovation, attributing to himself conscious paternity of the 'Spanish economic miracle' and its benevolent effects on popular consumption. In tune with this campaign, on 1 April 1964, on Victory Day, Franco declared to the press that he was very satisfied:

Economic development, which needs and demands peace, continuity and internal order, is a direct consequence of political development. Without our political movement it would not have been possible to reach the base from which we start today; the nation had superior resources in the past and could not undertake it. On the other hand, economic development simultaneously values, lends it prestige and affirms the political movement and drives its evolution and improvement.[160]

Despite the new official rhetoric, the Caudillo remained immersed in the doctrine bequeathed by the Civil War, impervious to the calls for tolerance, openness and political developments that began to emerge in Spain. In fact, the only limit he imposed on the experiments of the technocratic government lay in the political sphere: nothing should diminish his supreme decision-making power because 'it is unimaginable that the victors of a war cede power to the vanquished, saying nothing has happened and everything should go back to the starting point, or when the disastrous Republic was installed.'[161] In public he was even clearer: 'Liberalism is one of the main gates through which Communism enters', and 'we have not gone from totalitarianism to Liberalism because we are neither of these things.'[162] On the contrary, as he stated before the Cortes in June 1961, the Spanish regime was a compromise 'between the world of Soviet slavery and that of inorganic democracy' with a brilliant future founded on 'an armed plebiscite':

> A state like ours, born out of a truly national movement, could not live with its back to the people, could not let anybody beat it in a clean and true democracy. [...] A nation on a war footing is a final referendum, a vote that cannot be bought, a membership that is sealed with the offering of one's life. So I believe that never in the history of Spain was a state more legitimate, more popular and most representative than that we began to forge almost a quarter of a century ago.[163]

The government programme of modernization as a promoter of well-being culminated in the declaration of the Ley Orgánica del Estado, which Franco, with his usual parsimony, did not approve until the end of 1966. Subjected to a national referendum in December that year (gaining 95.9 per cent of the vote in support), it would be the last of Franco's fundamental laws and was a remarkable rationalization of the Francoist political regime. The Caudillo himself participated in the controlled propaganda campaign with an emotive speech on radio and television two days before the vote. He adopted the endearing role of grandfather of the nation and called for popular support to continue his strenuous efforts on behalf of the common good and the progress of the fatherland:

I want you to meditate on what we were and what we are. You should always bear in mind the comparison of the misfortunes of a sad past and the adventurous fruits of our present. [...] You all know me: those who are now the older generation have known me since the days of Africa, when we fought for the pacification of Morocco; those who were already mature, when, in the midst of the disasters of the Second Republic, you placed your hopes in my leadership for the defence of the endangered peace; the combatants of the crusade, because you will never be able to forget the emotional times of those shared efforts in the victory over communism; those who suffered under the yoke of red domination, because you will always evoke the infinite joy of your liberation; those who since then have stayed loyal to my leadership, because you are part of that victory over all the conspiracies and sieges that were laid against Spain; those who have lived the incomparable peace of these 27 years, encouraging our people with your songs of faith and hope, because you all know only too well how I always kept my word. I was never motivated by ambition for power. From a young age, responsibilities were cast on my shoulders, greater than my age or rank. I would have liked to enjoy life like so many Spaniards, but the service of the fatherland has occupied my hours and filled my life. I've been ruling the ship of the state for 30 years, saving the nation from the storms of the world today; but despite everything, here I stand, still at the helm, with the same sense of duty as in my youth, using what remains of my life in your service. Is it too much to ask that you give support to laws for your exclusive benefit and for that of the nation which are about to be submitted for referendum?[164]

The propaganda triumph of the success of the second referendum of the Franco era gave further impetus to the efforts of Carrero Blanco to continue the programme of institutionalization of the regime through the designation of a successor to the title of king. By then, Franco had already ruled out the possibility of appointing Don Juan as a successor and increased signs of preference for his son, who in May 1962 had married Princess Sofia of Greece and taken up official residence on the outskirts of Madrid, a short distance from the palace of El Pardo. In October 1968 Carrero Blanco submitted to the Caudillo a memorandum on the subject of 'succession' in which he reiterated his opinion: 'What the Spanish people want, my General, is that his Excellency, in the fullness of his powers, designates who will succeed him in his day, and that God would make that day the furthest possible.' Franco responded tersely: 'I agree with everything.'[165]

Finally, on 12 July 1969, aged 77, Franco invited Juan Carlos to El Pardo to announce his decision to appoint him successor 'to the title of king' and asked him to accept or reject the offer, 'there and then' without consulting his father (who was head of the House of Bourbon and holder of the dynastic rights). Arriving at the moment he most feared, the Prince chose to put the monarchy ahead of the principles of dynastic legitimacy and said: 'Of course, my General, I accept.'[166] He had the certain conviction that, once on the throne, thanks to the executive powers of the head of state, he might start the process of transition towards democracy in a legal and peaceful manner – and all this without committing perjury or ignoring the difficulties implicit in the process. His main tutor and adviser, Torcuato Fernández-Miranda, professor of political law and a monarchist from the Falange ranks, had calmed his fears with solid legal arguments: 'Your Highness should not worry. Swear to the principles of the movement, which can be changed later legally, one after another. We must go from law to law.'[167] Less than a month before the interview with Franco, Juan Carlos had consulted with his father at his Portuguese residence in Estoril about a hypothetical offer of the crown:

If you forbid me to accept, I will pack my bags, take Sofi and the children, and leave. I cannot stay in the Zarzuela [his official residence in Madrid] if he [Franco] calls me and I don't accept. I have not plotted so that the appointment falls on me. I agree that it would be better that you were king, but if the decision is taken, what can we do? [...] And if, as I believe, he invites me to accept, what will you do? Is there another decision other than that of Franco? Are you capable of carrying the monarchy?[168]

Consequently, on 22 July 1969 Franco proposed to the Cortes the appointment of Juan Carlos as 'my successor' at the forefront of a 'national monarchist movement, a permanent continuity with the principles and institutions' and guarantor that, 'when by natural law my leadership will end, which inexorably has to arrive, [...] everything is tied up and secured for the future'. The vote, nominal and public by express request of the Caudillo, received 491 affirmative votes, 19 negative, 9 abstentions and 13 absences. Don Juan tacitly accepted the decision and openly refused to overrule his son, although he published a new manifesto reaffirming his status as 'head of the Spanish royal family' and his commitment to 'the peaceful evolution of the current system towards these directions of openness and democratic coexistence'.[169]

The appointment in the summer of 1969 of Juan Carlos as successor was the culmination of the institutionalization of the Franco regime sponsored by Carrero and his technocratic team. However, it also meant a worsening of the growing fractures at the heart of the government. With the new social conditions generated by intense economic growth, the various Francoist 'families' had to define themselves politically in respect of this transformation. The consequent dividing lines created two broad groups defined by their willingness to continue unchanged (the *inmovilistas*) or to accept evolution (the *aperturistas*).[170] It was an internal fracture that tore apart the different 'families', setting the younger members against the most senior in each 'family' (the latter having lived through the war as adult combatants, the former being only young children during the same period). The *aperturista* adversaries of Carrero were the government representatives of those 'families' who had lost out to the technocrats, whose hopes of return were based on fostering a timid political openness that went hand in hand with economic liberalization. This approach was assumed by the Falangist youth, led by ministers José Solís Ruiz (trade unions) and Manuel Fraga Iribarne (information and tourism), and political Catholic ministers Fernando María Castiella (foreign affairs) and Federico Silva Muñoz (public works). The openness of the latter two derived from the new democratizing directive of the Second Vatican Council and the Magisterium of popes John XXIII (1958–63) and Paul VI (1963–78). The neo-Falangist pro-reform sentiment was above all the result of generational renewal in its leadership and of acute consciousness of the anachronism of a near-totalitarian party in the contemporary Western context.

Carrero Blanco took advantage of the political triumph of the summer of 1969 to ask the Caudillo for a total reshuffle of the Cabinet, accusing Solis of trying to use the unions to 'seize power' with the support of Fraga (whose press law had opened 'an escalation against the Spanish way of being and public morality') and Castiella (whose 'stubbornness' on the issue of the decolonization of Gibraltar was putting in danger the support of the United States, one of the 'fundamental axes of our foreign policy'). Weakened by the powerful medication he was taking for his Parkinson's, and demoralized by the intensity of the crisis, Franco bowed to demands for 'a fresh and united government' and authorized Carrero to form a 'monochrome' executive in which he remained formal vice president but with the functions of a real president.[171] In consequence, the new government, announced on 29 October 1969, broke the tradition of equilibrium between the Francoist 'families' and revealed the hegemony of Carrero Blanco and the technocratic team at the heart of the regime.[172]

Both the origins and outcome of the October 1969 ministerial crisis definitively accentuated the general schism between the Francoist 'families' and within them, at the time of the Caudillo's perceptibly weakening health and mental agility. Fraga detected this physical decline just a month after his removal from office, during a hunting excursion: 'I found him old and distant, sad and lonely.' López Rodó would remember that, in view of Franco's health, from October 1969, Councils of Ministers in El Pardo were limited to the morning (in the past they could last for 12 hours) thanks to the preparatory meetings chaired by Carrero Blanco.[173] From then, not only Franco but also the regime entered its final stage of terminal crisis and agony.

End of a Reign, End of an Era

The perceptible physical decline of Franco in 1969 changed the fearsome dictator of previous times into a weak and trembling old man, officiating as a symbolic and strict father figure to a Spain that would have been unrecognizable to his generation. The growing uncertainty created by this situation was aggravated by deep public disagreements between the senior leaders of the regime revealed by the government reshuffle of October 1969.

Both phenomena showed that the regime had entered a terminal phase of structural crisis, partly caused by its increasing anachronism compared to the social and cultural change generated by the intense economic development of the 1960s. In 1970 Spanish society was only different from its European counterparts by the peculiar and outdated authoritarian nature of its political system, which showed clearly its increasing inadequacy and patent dysfunction in respect of Spain's new society (urbanized, industrialized, diversified and secularized), with ideology and culture epitomized by consumption, tolerance and the will for political participation and democratic approval. In the face of this progression, the regime could offer no answers. In fact, the regime itself was the problem.

The difficulties of the split between Carrero's ruling team and the *aperturistas* were insignificant in comparison with the problems confronted by the regime in broader political and social spheres. Between 1970 and 1973, the 'peace of Franco' definitively broke and the government was nearly impotent before a quartet of serious internal challenges: (1) a high level of labour disputes, with the number of strikes jumping from 491 in 1969 to 1,595 in 1970, and the reappearance of free trade unions, well established and led by socialist and communist activists; (2) protest in the universities, where, for around half a million students, opposition to the dictatorship became a mark of generational and collective identity; (3) ecclesiastical defection which, in keeping with the doctrine of the Second Vatican Council, rejected National Catholicism, advocated a peaceful evolution towards democracy and was viewed by Franco as a bitter 'stab in the back'; and (4) the reappearance of terrorist activity, in the first killing by the Basque independence organization ETA in the summer of 1968, which would lead to an escalation of repression of enormous intensity and harshness.[174]

The patent political failure of the government of Carrero Blanco on these four fronts was exacerbated by the increasing paralysis of decision-making due to Franco's age and ill-health, which aggravated the internal crisis of the regime and made obvious the political bankruptcy of any idea of a continuation of the Francoist dictatorship. The government crisis was finally exposed in May 1973 with the explosive resignation of the interior minister, General Tomás Garicano Goñi. The ex-minister sent Franco an explanatory letter that was an open denunciation of the dead-end that had resulted from the unchanging path followed by Carrero Blanco:

> The political problem of hardliners or *inmovilistas* and *aperturistas* survives and is fundamental; I understand [...] that the triumph of the first would be fatal for Spain and the sad reality is that every time they are becoming stronger. The approaching day of the succession frightens them [...]. I think that a genuine openness is necessary, although I understand that it has its risks, but the country wants it and wants it during the Caudillo's lifetime, because all the loose ends can be better tied. It seems clear that the power, even moral, which today resides in the head of state, will not pass in any way to his successor. Hence all the measures, like the laws concerning local government, elections and political openness, all fundamental for the future, should be completed soon, in the lifetime of the Caudillo; the sooner we do it, the safer we will be.[175]

The shocking resignation of this military minister served as a pretext for Franco to appoint a new Cabinet in June 1973, in which, for the first time, Carrero Blanco took the official role of prime minister. The rest of the ministers responded to the preferences of the Admiral and there was no great change from the political orientation of the previous Cabinet. The most notable appointment was that of Torcuato Fernández-Miranda – adviser to the Prince and successor, as well as being the secretary general of the Falangist movement – who was promoted to deputy prime minister. The only imposition of Franco, influenced by his family circle, was the new minister of the interior, considered a 'hardliner' and very different to his reformist predecessor: Carlos Arias Navarro, the former military prosecutor during the Civil War, former head of security and 'dear friend of Doña Carmen Polo de Franco'.[176]

According to the intention of its president, the political work of the new government was to prepare for the future continuity of the regime once its founder had gone. It was fraught with difficulties, an almost insurmountable task. Spain was a devoutly Catholic state, where the Church itself condemned the regime and demanded its reform; it was a state which banned strikes but where labour disputes proliferated in their thousands despite fierce repression;

an authoritarian state opposed to liberalism yet looking anxiously for some similar form of democratic legitimacy; a state which guaranteed morality and traditional customs where the most modern and avant-garde social attitudes and ideas were spreading. Moreover, since the beginning of 1973, the old formula of exchanging prosperity for democracy was increasingly unworkable in view of the severe energy crisis that precipitated the international economic downturn.

In any case, the Cabinet chaired by Carrero Blanco would only be effective for six months. In the early hours of the morning of 20 December 1973, its president was brutally murdered when a bomb planted by ETA exploded in the heart of Madrid. It was the work of a cell active in the capital; it did not involve any of the implausible conspiracy theories that saw the hidden hand of the American CIA, the Soviet KGB or other foreign espionage organizations. The success of the operation was instead the result of a combination of successful moves by ETA and patent errors by the Francoist security services: the secrecy and novelty of the terrorist unit (ETA had not acted outside the Basque country until then and its attacks had been limited to those on local police officers) and the token protection measures around Carrero Blanco (a person of fixed daily movements, routine habits and with a minimal security escort).[177]

The unexpected death of Carrero Blanco led to the most serious political crisis of all for the Francoist dictatorship and spread fear among the civilian population and the opposition forces. With Franco stunned by the great personal and political loss (until the afternoon of 20 December he did not acknowledge that it had been a deliberate assassination and continued to believe that it had been an accident), Fernández-Miranda took immediate charge of the presidency and was able to maintain official calm and public order. In any case, Carrero's murder eliminated the loyal, designated guarantor of the survival of the Franco regime after the death of the Caudillo: 'It was a tremendous trauma. Politically, I realized that his death put an end to Franco's regime,' wrote López Rodó. Indeed, the effect of that assassination was well noted by Luis Suárez Fernández: 'On 20 December 1973 Franco's era ended and a little later what would be called the "transition" began.'[178]

Following his long-standing practice, Franco did not attend the funeral of the Admiral, which was held on 21 December. However, he attended the memorial Mass that was held the next day and this revealed the intensity of the crisis of the regime in some detail: the aged Franco, weak and hesitant, wept profusely in front of the television cameras on greeting Carrero's widow; a 'hardline' minister was allowed to offend Cardinal Tarancón, archbishop of Madrid and officiant of the ceremony, publicly by refusing to shake hands with him. The Cardinal had to withstand the hostile shouts of far-right demonstrators in the street.[179] Undoubtedly, by then the terminal crisis of the Franco regime had entered its decisive and dying phase.

Franco felt the moral and political coup which meant the loss of his most loyal collaborator deeply, but he took the decision to dispense with Carrero's partners and, in particular, Fernández-Miranda (whom the *inmovilistas* feared due to his pragmatism and his closeness to the Prince). Instead, he decided to appoint a new prime minister, Carlos Arias Navarro, by virtue of his reputation as a hardliner, despite his undeniable responsibility for the failures of the security services. Arias Navarro formed his Cabinet in January 1974, again with representatives of all the Francoist 'families' and, surprisingly, of all political persuasions, whether *inmovilistas* or *reformistas*.[180] However, very soon the reformism of Arias Navarro showed its internal and external limitations.

The president of the last Franco government, perhaps because of his age, character and training, while recognizing the inviability of the Francoist regime without Franco, was not able or willing to endorse the necessary democratic change requested by reformers and other moderate opposition forces. Ultimately, Arias Navarro, like the majority of the Francoist political elite, was aware that any in-depth reform would have to wait for the death of Franco and the coronation of Don Juan Carlos. In the words of a minister of the last Franco government: 'While the protagonist of an era in the history of Spain lived, it was impossible to consider substantial changes.'[181]

The government's disarray was immediately exacerbated by a crucial international event: on 25 April 1974, the Portuguese dictatorship (presided over by Caetano since the death of Salazar in 1970) collapsed in a coup staged by an army tired of fighting an endless colonial war in Africa. The sudden Revolución de los Claveles (Revolution of the Carnations) across the border (and the almost immediate fall of the military regime in Greece) greatly deepened internal differences within the Francoist political elite, fuelling a siege mentality in some, while others became more aware of the patent anachronism of the dictatorship.[182]

The situation worsened at the beginning of the summer of 1974 with Franco's first serious illness. Due to an attack of thrombophlebitis (precipitated by the many hours spent watching television, especially the World Cup), the Caudillo had to be admitted to a Madrid hospital on the morning of 9 July on the decision of his personal physician and despite the reservations of Franco himself ('This will be a political bomb'). Anticipating a possible loss of consciousness, Franco told doctors that his care and treatment was entrusted to the person most near and dear to him: 'If I am not in a fit condition, look to my daughter.' Although the medication for the phlebitis proved a success, complications from the long medical treatment of Parkinson's caused gastrointestinal bleeding that provoked severe despondency and almost cost Franco his life. He even received the last rites from the hands of his confessor, Father Bulart, against the advice of the Marquis of Villaverde, who felt that 'the presence of a priest makes one nervous'. Given the seriousness of the disease, on 19 July, Arias Navarro urged the Caudillo to sign the decree provisionally delegating his powers into the hands of a reluctant Don Juan Carlos.[183] Despite the hopes raised in reformist sectors and that of the opposition by the temporary disability of Franco, the interim period of the Prince as head of state emphasized throughout the summer the sense of institutional paralysis and the expected end of Franco's reign. Even though the Caudillo was discharged and on 30 July returned to El Pardo, his situation continued to be very serious, as his new personal physician, Dr Pozuelo, remembered: 'Franco's voice was then extinguished, with virtually no timbre; the voice of a Parkinson's sufferer, with an inclination to bronchial failure. He remained quiet but his eyes still had that peculiar vividness.'[184]

To combat this physical decline and the signs of misery in an 82-year-old (Franco confessed that he only wanted to retire to a Carthusian convent), Dr Pozuelo launched an intensive programme of diet, therapeutic exercises and rehabilitation. Among other things, in order to alleviate anxiety and the depression of his patient, he made Franco perform exercises to the sound of military music (amongst others, the march 'Soy valiente y leal legionario') and urged him to speak of his youth and glory days (his talks were recorded on audio tapes).[185] Thanks to the effectiveness of this medical programme, Franco continued to recover from his illness. On 2 September 1974, without previously warning anyone apart from his family, the Caudillo decided to resume his office, thus extinguishing the possibility of a final retirement from power within his lifetime.

From then on, Franco's regime continued under the shadow of total uncertainty and impermanence, with a much weakened octogenarian head of state, recovering from a recent serious illness and undergoing constant medical attention and rehabilitation exercises (for walking and even speaking). To make matters worse, despite being the protagonist in a chronicle of a death foretold, the Caudillo decided to put an end to the reformist inclinations of his government. His instinctive rigidity was endorsed on 13 September 1974 by a brutal attack by ETA in the centre of Madrid which resulted in 12 dead and 80 injured (including several policemen). Apart from the consistently repressive reaction against the whole of the opposition, Franco demanded and obtained from Arias Navarro a Cabinet reshuffle that eliminated his own reformist members.[186] With their departure from the government, the sacked reformist elite opted to open negotiations with the anti-Francoist forces for a democratic reform that only waited for the succession of Don Juan Carlos to make it viable and effective. Ex-minister Manuel Fraga Iribarne would shortly afterwards utter an emphatic pronouncement: 'Democratic legitimacy is to be recognized in an election of a representative chamber by universal suffrage.'[187]

Throughout 1975, the government of Arias Navarro used repressive measures to face the deterioration of the economic situation (with galloping inflation) and an escalation of labour disputes that tripled in number over previous years. In fact, the 931 strikes recorded in 1973 became 3,156 in 1975. The number of strikers grew from 357,523 to 647,100 and the number of hours lost rose from 8,649,265 to 14,521,000.[188] There was a parallel increase in the terrorist activity of ETA (which killed 14 people in 1975) and the FRAP (the Revolutionary Anti-Fascist Patriotic Front), a new radical Marxist-Leninist group which commenced activity in 1973. The ineffectiveness of the government's attempts at repressing these movements and its potential political and diplomatic danger was clear in September 1975, when military courts sentenced to death three ETA militants and eight FRAP activists (including two pregnant women). In the midst of serious internal tension (on 11 September there was a massive general strike in the Basque country in solidarity with those condemned) and multiple requests for clemency from abroad (from, amongst others, the Pope, Don Juan, and the queen of Great Britain), the Caudillo decided to exercise the prerogative of mercy on six of the condemned and approve the death sentences of the five others. As a result, on 27 September 1975 two ETA members and three of the FRAP were executed. Strong international condemnation was expressed in the form of massive demonstrations at Spanish embassies in European capitals and the withdrawal of several ambassadors from Madrid.

The regime's response was a show of support for Franco, celebrating 1 October in the Plaza de Oriente in Madrid, with banners from hardline sectors that read 'ETA, to the firing squad' and 'We don't want openness, we want heavy-handedness'.[189] Moved to tears, trembling and visibly haggard, the Caudillo gave his version of the facts to protesters in a very weak and plaintive voice:

Spaniards: thank you for your devotion and for the serene and strong public demonstration that you offer me in reparation [...]. Everything is due to a Masonic–leftist conspiracy among the political class in collusion with the communist-terrorist subversion in society, which if we honour ourselves, they degrades themselves. [...] The unity of the forces of the army, navy and air force supports the will of the nation and lets the Spanish people rest easy.[190]

In fact, no other event of the late Franco period revealed more clearly the gap between a society and economy that had modernized dramatically and a political system archaic in its *caudillismo*, ossified at the head and notoriously lacking popular legitimacy and any prospect for the future. Proof of these last shortcomings was the result of a survey of the Spanish citizenship in 1974 about their 'attitudes to authoritarian and democratic principles of government'. Of the respondents, 60 per cent expressed their agreement with the principle that they should be governed by 'people chosen by the electorate', while 18 per cent favoured 'an outstanding man to decide for us' and another 22 per cent declined to answer.[191] This obvious sociological and cultural reality in favour of a democratic political system was the incentive and spur for the reformist sectors of the regime which had put their hopes in Franco's successor.

The executions of September and the speech of 1 October 1975 were virtually the last governmental acts of an exhausted Franco on the verge of death. The strong emotional tension caused by this crisis, along with the serious news about the situation in the Spanish Sahara generated by Morocco's annexation policy, irreversibly affected the fragile health of an old man, nearly 83 years old. According to his personal doctor, thereafter, 'Franco was another man, he lost weight daily, was constantly nervous and could hardly sleep normally.'[192] In this condition, a slight case of flu, starting on 12 October, was followed by a heart attack three days later. On the evening of the 20th Franco suffered another heart attack and said to his aide de camp and his personal physician: 'It is finished.'[193] The next morning, a reassuring official note charted the progress of the 'influenza' of Franco and an episode of 'acute coronary weakness'. Neither public opinion nor the political elite were deceived: Franco was dying.[194] On 24 October he suffered another heart attack, complicated by intestinal paralysis and continual gastric haemorrhage (the product of his medication against Parkinson's).

On 30 October 1975, aware of his fragility, Franco ordered the execution of Article 11 of the Ley Orgánica del Estado, transferring his powers to the Prince. Four days later, suffering from peritonitis, he had to be operated upon in a makeshift theatre in the palace of El Pardo. He barely survived and needed to be admitted to hospital in Madrid to receive dialysis treatment for kidney failure. On 5 November Franco underwent further surgery that removed two-thirds of his stomach. Kept alive by a wide range of technology and constant transfusions of blood (50 litres by the 13th), he suffered a long and painful agony and while semiconscious mumbled, 'Dear God, how long it takes to die!'[195] Finally, given his irreversible state, his daughter insisted he be allowed to die peacefully. The agony probably ended on the night of 19 November although the exact time of his death was set at 5:25 in the morning of 20 November 1975 by the large medical team that attended him.

Franco's death was a symbol of the contradictions existing in Spain in his later years: a dying Caudillo was helped by all kinds of modern medical devices, yet on his deathbed he was holding the cloak of the Virgin of El Pilar and to his side was the relic of the hand of St Teresa of Avila. By coincidence, on 19 November, on the eve of the death of the most significant Spanish

Africanista, the Francoist Cortes approved the Pacto Tripartito signed five days earlier in Madrid, under which Spain withdrew from its colony of the Sahara and gave the administration to Morocco and Mauritania, who committed themselves to respect the views of the Saharan population and to communicate its results to the United Nations. An even greater symbol of the closure of one era and the opening of another were two immediate consecutive ceremonies. As a sign of condemnation of the last executions he had authorized, no significant head of state attended Franco's funeral or his burial in the retrochoir of the Basílica of the Valle de los Caídos on 23 November 1975, with the notable exception of the Chilean General Augusto Pinochet, Prince Rainier of Monaco and King Hussein of Jordan. In dramatic contrast, on 27 November – with the noticeable absence of Pinochet, who was not invited – the French President Giscard d'Estaing, the Duke of Edinburgh, the Vice President of the United States and the President of the Federal Republic of Germany attended the Mass to commemorate the proclamation of Don Juan Carlos as king of Spain by the Cortes.

With the death of Franco and the proclamation of Juan Carlos as king, the political alternative to the regime ceased to be a dialectic between the continuity advocated by the *inmovilistas* and reform encouraged by the heirs of *aperturistas*. The Franco regime was so associated with its founder that it was impossible to prolong its existence beyond the death of the Caudillo. From then on, the crucial political dilemma would be to restore democracy either by reform from within under the auspices of post-Franco elites or by the total break from the regime favoured by opposition forces. In the end, and largely due to the omnipresent memory of the Civil War and the tacit will not to repeat it, the process of political transition contained elements of both: an agreed and gradual reform that would lead in the end to a break in form and substance from the previous regime. In fact, as was lamented by one of the most distinguished Francoist critics of reform, General Iniesta Cano, the small and inevitable changes that everyone expected after Franco's death became a 'brutal rupture with all that had gone before'.[196] In effect, the speed of this transitional process and its own formal characteristics are an irrefutable proof of the marked anachronism of the Franco regime and of its noticeable lagging behind the peculiarities and dominant values of mid-1970s Spanish society. It also offers us an understanding of the rapid cloak of silence and voluntary amnesia surrounding the figure of Franco in the years after his death, an integral part of the durable and peculiar so-called 'Pact of Forgetfulness' that made possible the peaceful transition and consolidation of democracy.

2

THE CAUDILLO
A Charismatic Dictator

Charismatic rule has long been neglected and ridiculed, but apparently it has deep roots and becomes a powerful stimulus once the proper psychological and social conditions are set. The Leader's charismatic power is not a mere phantasm – none can doubt that millions believe in it.

Franz Neumann, *Behemoth* (1942)

The Conversion of Franco to Caudillo:
A Complex Process in the Context of Civil War

'Francisco Franco, Caudillo of Spain by the grace of God.' As noted in the introduction to this book, these words formed the inscription that encircled a very recognizable image on the back of Spanish coins minted after December 1946, unanimously approved by the Cortes and published in the *Boletín Oficial del Estado* as the 'Law of 18 December on the Establishment of a New Monetary System'.[1]

It was not the first time, nor the last, that General Francisco Franco Bahamonde received an official and public honour of the kind normally reserved for Spanish royalty; 'the currency is an expression of sovereignty', as Franco himself pronounced on 20 January 1939, a few months before his definitive victory in the Civil War.[2] Nor was it the only time that a state agency and an official document accorded him the title 'Caudillo of Spain' to define the supreme political authority and the main institutional office he had held since his 'exaltation' to the head of state on 1 October 1936.

At that crucial time for the regime, in the Capitanía General (General Headquarters) in Burgos, Franco had been transferred 'all the powers of the state' which had been assumed on 24 July 1936 by the Junta de Defensa Nacional, the collegiate body of command created by the rebel generals to transform an only partly successful military insurrection in half of Spain into a civil war. The dictatorial nature of the interim political solution had been undisputed and recognized as the only model known and appreciated by the rebel leaders: the dictatorship of General Miguel Primo de Rivera (1923–30). Franco himself, in statements to the Portuguese press on 13 August 1936, had used the concept and technocratic formulas of that political example:

> The Military Directorate will call together those elements presumed necessary to achieve the projected enterprise in the shortest time. Its administration will be in charge of technical and not political elements, as we try, and succeed, in completely transforming the structure of Spain. [...] The military dictatorship will seek to promote those who deserve it by their ability and [because] their technical preparation offers the most promise.[3]

The explanatory statement of the decree that transformed Franco into the personal and individual representative of the only effective and dictatorial power prevailing in insurgent Spain highlighted 'the desirability of concentrating everything in a single power which will lead the final victory and the establishment, consolidation and development of the new state'. For this reason, his comrades in arms agreed to his appointment as 'head of the government of the Spanish state' (a political-administrative function) and 'Generalissimo of the national forces of land, sea and air' and 'general chief of army operations' (a strategic military role), with the addition of the full personal assumption of 'all the powers of the new state'.[4] The words of Franco on receiving this transfer of powers from the military junta left no doubt that he was well aware of the immense authority that he received and of its original military provenance:

> My general, general chiefs of the junta: You can be proud; you received a shattered Spain and you deliver to me a Spain united in a grand and

unanimous ideal. Victory is on our side. You put Spain in my hands and I will not tremble, my hand will always remain steady. I will raise the country to its highest or die trying. I want your cooperation. The Junta de Defensa Nacional will remain at my side.[5]

It should be emphasized that the first legal provisions that served as a basis for the wide political authority assumed by Franco did not include any mention of 'caudillo', but only his status as 'head of state', 'head of the government of the state', 'supreme commander (Generalissimo)' and 'general chief of the armies'. In fact, the first formal and legal public use of that title of leadership came almost a year later, when the *Boletín Oficial del Estado* of 28 September 1937 published a crucial order by the president of the Junta Técnica del Estado (the civil administration that Franco had created to assume the powers of the junta of Burgos). In it, official status was granted to the 'Fiesta Nacional del Caudillo', which became a compulsory commemoration for the duration of the Francoist regime:

The next 1 October will be the first anniversary of the historic moment on which by the grace of God and true will of Spain, assuming the highest powers, was solemnly proclaimed Head of State and Supreme Commander of the National Armies of land, sea and air, His Excellency, Sr. General D. Francisco Franco Bahamonde, National Head of the Falange Española Tradicionalista y de las JONS and Caudillo of the Movement to save Spain.

Subsequently, a second chance to endorse the legal status of 'caudillo' was offered by the publication of the decree of 31 July 1939 which contained the 'Estatutos de Falange Española Tradicionalista y de las JONS' (Statutes of the Falange Party). In this text, which sanctioned the single party formed in April 1937 by the compulsory merger of all right-wing forces into an 'inspirational militant movement and the founding stone of the Spanish state', Article 46 defined the role:

The national head of the Falange Española Tradicionalista y de las JONS, Supreme Caudillo of the Movement, is the personification of all its values and honours. As author of the historic era when Spain took the opportunity to realize its destiny and with it the hopes of the Movement, the leader assumes full and absolute authority. The leader answers to God and history.[6]

The third time that Franco was attributed the title of 'caudillo' came in a disposition of 21 May 1941 which allocated 'the respective responsibilities of the senior leaders' of the National Movement and expressly confirmed his 'caudillaje and leadership'. Article 3 read: 'The appointments of staff and command posts [...] will be made in the name of the Caudillo by the president of the Junta Política and at the request of the secretary general, with the signature of both.' Given that both positions were, according to the statutes, appointed, designated and separated 'freely' by the national leader and caudillo, the arrangement was seen as a mere reaffirmation of his sovereign and constituent power.[7]

The fourth and decisive occasion that verifed the judicial and political status of Franco as 'caudillo' came with the proclamation of the 'Ley de Sucesión en la Jefatura del Estado' of 26 July 1947, approved by the Francoist Cortes and put to a national referendum (under the prevalent limits of freedom of expression), supposedly giving him the support of 82 per cent of the electorate. In it, Article 1 converted Spain into a 'monarchy' but gave its lifetime 'leadership' to a 'caudillo', who was also de facto regent and entitled to choose his successor 'as king or regent' – always with the potential to revoke his choice if necessary:

Article 1. Spain, as a political unit, is a Catholic, social and representative state which, according to tradition, declares itself a monarchy.
Article 2. The head of state corresponds to the caudillo of Spain and the Crusade, Generalissimo of the Armed Forces, D. Francisco Franco Bahamonde.[8]

Perhaps the last official public use of the legal-political term 'caudillo' took place on Franco's death, early in the morning of 20 November 1975. That same day, a decree rapidly approved by the government provided for three days of official mourning in the country, with the following explanatory statement:

Upon the death of the head of state, caudillo of Spain and Generalissimo of the Armed Forces, His Excellency Señor Don Francisco Franco Bahamonde, the convening of the Cortes and the Consejo del Reino for a joint session will be held on the 22nd, to receive the oath prescribed in the Ley de Sucesión en la Jefatura del Estado.[9]

Leaving aside the formal legal sphere, the evolution in the lexicon of popular language and the media of the title of 'caudillo' (soon in upper case and always in the singular) as an expression of the highest power in the state living in the person of Franco should also be recognized. It is clear it was used much earlier than its conversion into an official title in the September 1937 order instituting the 'Fiesta Nacional del Caudillo'. In fact, the word was in circulation from 1 October 1936, largely as part of a press and propaganda campaign aimed at projecting the political figure of Franco to the forefront of the insurgent side and above the rest of the rebel generals.[10]

Thus, for example, on the same day, 1 October 1936, the Galician newspaper *El Eco de Santiago* presented Franco as the 'illustrious general' named by the Junta de Defensa Nacional as 'head of the government of the state' and 'Generalissimo of the armed forces', but added the title of 'caudillo', invested upon him for his 'extraordinary courage' and for being 'one of the most glorious [names] of the African Army'. The next day, 2 October, the monarchist newspaper *Abc* (in its Seville edition) reported on the assumption of full powers by the 'head of the new Spanish state', calling him a 'caudillo that has all the powers of the state' and is the 'founder of the new fatherland'. A few weeks later all the press in the insurgent zone bore on their covers some form of the compulsory instructions: 'One Fatherland. One State. One Caudillo' (for example, *La Gaceta Regional*, Salamanca, 5 November 1936). Other forms of it were: 'Una Patria. Un Estado. Un Caudillo. Una Patria: España. Un Caudillo: Franco' (*El Heraldo de Aragón*, Zaragoza, 24 February 1937), or 'Una Patria: España; Un Estado Nacionalsindicalista; Un Caudillo: Franco' (*El Telegrama del Rif*, Melilla, 30 April 1937). It is hardly necessary to recall that this triple rally cry was a translation of the famous formula used by the German National Socialists since the beginning of the 1930s: 'Ein Volk! Ein Reich! Ein Führer!' (One People! One Empire! One Leader!)[11]

The promotion of Franco as Caudillo of Spain by the grace of God (and/or any combination of: 'of the Crusade', 'of the Victory', 'of the Empire', 'of neutrality', 'of peace', 'of the faith', 'of the fatherland', 'of the new Spain') was not only channelled by the written press.[12] The rest of the news media and propaganda of the time, albeit less widespread (radio, movie newsreels, posters, postage stamps, later television, etc.) also participated in this cult of the charismatic personality of Franco with all its vigour and respective power. In this regard, one should remember the template designed in 1937 that enabled the painted reproduction of the image of Franco in a military cap on walls throughout Spain above a laudatory text that said: 'Franco. Caudillo of God and fatherland. The first victor in the world of Bolshevism on the battlefield.' There were also poetic eulogies to raise his profile, circulated in their thousands during the war and after. Probably none was as famous and widespread as the bombastic sonnet by Manuel Machado of 1939 entitled '¡Bienvenido Capitán!' (Welcome Captain!):

> De tu soberbia campaña,
> Caudillo noble y valiente,
> ha surgido nuevamente
> una grande y libre España.

> (From your superb campaign,
> Caudillo noble and brave,
> has emerged again,
> a great and free Spain.)[13]

Formal education also contributed to the mythology of the Caudillo through several channels: the official portrait in the classrooms, mentions in textbooks, rituals and public ceremonies of respect. A good example of this propaganda in education was the reference to Franco in the *Catecismo patriótico español* (*The Spanish Patriotic Catechism*), a book declared a 'text for schools' by order of the National Education Ministry in January 1939. It was the work of the Dominican friar Albino González Menéndez-Reigada (bishop of Tenerife in 1924 and of Córdoba in 1946). In its pages, children were told that the Spanish state was 'under the supreme authority of the Caudillo, Generalissimo Franco' and that he was 'the embodiment of the country and has the power from God to govern us'.[14] Several years later, in 1953, one of the regular school encyclopedias (for those pupils between 10 and 12 years old) reiterated everything a Spanish child should know about the subject in an equally catechism-like way: 'What is the state? It is the nation organized for the fulfilment of its purposes. The Spanish state has a leader, who is Caudillo Franco.'[15] And still in 1964 ten-year-old schoolchildren were taught the meaning of the 'Day of the Caudillo' by a comprehensive political-ideological explanation in tune with the foundations of the regime:

> On 1 October 1936, Franco was elected head of state and caudillo of Spain in Burgos. Since then, he has devoted his entire life and his knowledge to the fatherland and if during the War of Liberation he won brilliant military victories, the arrival of peace has brought no less resonant political triumphs. In gratitude for his services, we promise him on this day our commitment and love.[16]

The conclusion that can be drawn from both popular and official public uses of the term 'caudillo' in reference to Franco is very evident: what started as a mere propaganda term came to accompany his official and formal status as 'head of state' and 'Generalissimo', and very soon, in less than a year, it eventually superseded those words to specify a superior and inclusive leadership which denoted the complete concentration of all state powers in one person without temporal limitations. Ramón Serrano Suñer stressed that process of personal assumption of full power in his speech of 18 July 1938, when he condemned with sarcasm the liberal premise of a separation of powers: 'Civil power! Military power! Here there is but one single power, total, indivisible and sacred of a united Spain!'[17]

The Italian jurist Giovanni Mammucari well appreciated in 1955 that the progressive transformation carried out between October 1936 and September 1937 would be sanctioned by the Ley de Sucesión of 1947 in a very precise and thorough manner:

The Caudillo, therefore, is head of state in Spain and, at the same time, head of the government, supreme commander of all the forces of land, sea and air, as well as head of the single party, the Falange Española Tradicionalista y de las JONS, also called the 'Movement'. [...] The Caudillo is not elected, nor is he confirmed and much less can he be removed, there is no other power above him.[18]

The conclusion of a much later study by another jurist should also be remembered. Juan Ferrando Badía stated in 1984, almost ten years after the end of the Francoist regime:

The figure of the Caudillo was the crucial institution of the regime because he embodied the supreme institution of the political hierarchy, not only in the order of representation, but also in the exercise of power. The features that characterized the head of the Spanish authoritarian state were the following:
1. Personal exaltation of the leader and his identification with the so-called historical destiny of his people.
2. Full power concentrated in his hands.
3. Absence of an institutional control of his leadership: as the head of state, Franco was only answerable before God and history.[19]

To sum up, in his capacity as leader, Franco expressly concentrated *plenitudo potestatis* (full state power) and exercised the highest state authority, combining executive, legislative, judicial power – in short, sovereign and constituent functions without discrimination and at the same time – for his lifetime and without the possibility of removal. As pointed out by José Zafra Valverde, a jurist in open sympathy with Franco and his regime: 'Without assuming the title of king or similar, Franco was a sovereign monarch, rather than a nominal, courtly and ceremonial monarch. His office was the *dux populi*, as in the biblical origins of the monarchy.'[20] In a speech in Valladolid in October 1960, Franco himself defined his leadership as being 'command' and 'captaincy' with a clear and rounded profile:

The captaincy calls and requires perfect synchronization with the most profound and legitimate rhythm of the time in which we live, looking clearly into the future and at the same time with a capacity to renounce easy success, an abiding love for the solidly established and far-reaching enterprise, serenity and firmness in adverse circumstances, fidelity to principles and incorruptible willingness to serve. [21]

Certainly, Franco never entertained the possibility of abandoning his position, for reasons he gave a couple of months after that statement, in his message at the end of 1960 to celebrate the twenty-fifth anniversary of his exaltation to the role of head of state:

Who receives the honour and accepts the weight of supreme leadership [*caudillaje*] at no time can legitimately accept relief or rest. It must consume his existence at the forefront of the founding enterprise that was called for by the voice and the commitment of his people, rooting and perfecting the whole system. [22]

Consequently, throughout the whole Franco era, the personal figure of the Caudillo was the object of veneration and exaltation officially consecrated and cultivated, reproduced in public spaces (with memorials, monuments, street names, official ceremonies, civil rituals, etc.) and in social activities (community festivals, commemorations, temporary milestones, etc.) with both his comprehensive effective power and his legal authority unquestioned and of providential origin. In the face of this situation, one has to wonder: how and when did the word 'caudillo' come to denote all those personal prerogatives of Franco and by what processes, channels and means?

Etymology and Uses of 'Caudillo' Before the Civil War

Even though the etymology of the word is obscure and debated, it seems clear that in the Spanish language the word *caudillo* could only derive from two possible sources. On the one hand, one might consider that it comes from the Latin word *caput* (head) via its derivatives *capdellus* or *capitellus*, as it was used in late Latin and the early Middle Ages, meaning 'ringleader' or 'war lord' (similarly, *dux* – 'leader' or 'guide' – in Italian derived into *condottiero* or *duce*). On the other hand, some authors suggest that it could derive directly from an expression of early Castilian Spanish that translated the Arabic word *cadí* (plural: *cadíes*) in the sense of 'the one who decides', a figure typical in the Muslim judiciary who assumes not only judicial powers but also legal and executive functions. In both cases, the term suggests a leader, someone who is put in charge of others and directs and leads, mainly (but not only) in warfare and military operations. That is to say: a conductor of armed forces and one who commands these and other crowds.[23]

For example, the entry for *caudillo* in the 1911 edition of *Enciclopedia Universal Ilustrada Hispano-Americana*, defines the word as a Hispano-American neologism with a mostly (but not exclusively) military meaning: 'one who as head guides and sends people to war' (also he who 'is the head and director of any guild, community or body'). In fact, the work was repeating verbatim the definition provided by the *Diccionario de Autoridades de la Real Academia de la Lengua*, which still had this entry virtually unchanged in all respects in its 1984 edition.

According to some testimonies, the word *caudillo* was already in circulation in the sixteenth century and spread particularly in colonial America to denote leaders, heads and commanders of the conquering troops who penetrated those lands and extended the frontiers of the Spanish Empire. From the beginning of the nineteenth century the word started to spread massively, during the wars of emancipation from the Spanish crown and the subsequent civil wars that engulfed the independent countries. In this context of uncertainty and widespread violence, the succession of fragmented military conflicts, both internal and external, there emerged in almost all the new American nations the formation of bands and groups of armed men who were trying to impose some kind of order and equilibrium under the direction of a 'popular leader' who held (or lost) leadership through the force of his personality in terms of bravery, charisma, the ability to command and military success. As explained almost a century ago by the Venezuelan historian Laureano Vallenilla Lanz, the leader who thus emerged was not a bandit, an outlaw or a common criminal (except to his enemies, who thus wanted to criminalize his cause and person). He was, on the contrary, 'the necessary policeman' in times of anarchy and chaos, when

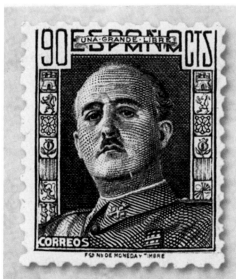

1. Stamps showing Franco in his 40s, 50s and 60s

2. Franco as a commander in the African Army, 1916

3. Franco as Caudillo after the victory of 1939

4. Franco and Hitler at Hendaye (on the Spanish–French frontier), 23 October 1940

5. Franco as Caudillo and head of state, late 1950s

6. Franco and his wife Carmen at a social event in the mid-1960s

7. Franco and Prince Juan Carlos in 1972

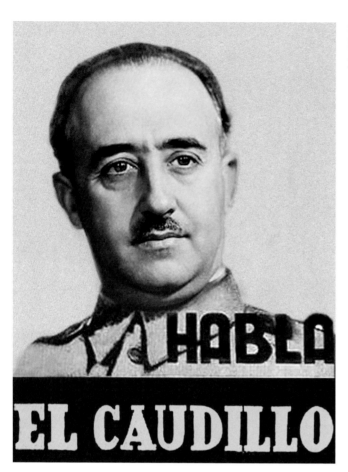

8. The front cover of a book of Franco's speeches, published in 1939

9. Postcard depicting General Franco with 'Long Live Spain, Italy, Germany and Portugal' slogans and flags – from the time of the Spanish Civil War

10. Franco on the cover of *Time* magazine, October 1943

FRANCO OF IBERIA
An advance against him is an advance against Hitler.

11. A 1953 coin featuring Franco

SEOANE

TRECE ESTAMPAS
DE LA TRAICION

BUENOS AIRES - MONTEVIDEO
JULIO DE 1937

12. The cover of a book of caricatures published in Latin America (Uruguay and Argentina) in 1937

el generalisimo

13. The Generalissimo, a poster issued by the Madrid Defence Council (Junta de Defensa de Madrid) in late 1936

POR BULERIAS

¡Bien pagáa...! ¡Bien pagáa...!

14. Caricature of Franco published in an exiled Republican magazine in 1953, the year in which Franco allowed the US to build military bases in Spain. The caption reads 'Very well paid!'

15. Caricature of Franco published in exile in France by a Republican organisation during the 1940s

the destruction of traditional social balances made for an armed force led by a
strong and feared personality, a requirement for the restoration of minimum
order, at local and regional levels, and even at state level:

> It is clear that in almost all these nations of Hispano-America, sentenced
> by complex causes to a turbulent life, the caudillo has been the only force
> of social preservation, fulfilling the phenomenon that men of science have
> noted in the early stages of the integration of societies: leaders are not chosen
> but imposed. The election and the succession, even in the irregular way in
> which it begins, constitute a further process. It is the typical character of a
> state at war that the preservation of society against incessant attack calls for
> compulsory subordination to a leader. Those unaware who read the history of
> Venezuela found that even after independence was assured, social preservation
> could in no way be entrusted to the law but to the most prestigious and feared
> caudillos, those who had imposed order in the military camps and fields.[24]

This describes how the first half of the nineteenth century in the emancipated
Latin America (and also after) was the 'era of the caudillos' and the time of the
caudillajes, a time of more or less authoritarian governments under the personal
guidance of great figures or heroes who had military successes of some kind
in the defence of their country, its cause or that of its countrymen, clients and
followers. In the more recent words of two other Venezuelan historians:

> It is understood that caudillo means a warlord, both personal and political,
> who employs an armed group that accepts him as leader, a fundamental
> cornerstone to power. Caudillismo is the dominant political activity deployed
> by the caudillos in a particular historical moment. It is a form of de facto and
> pragmatic domination.[25]

These armed leaders became caudillos with little regard to their social origins
(humble, mesocratic or powerful), their previous occupations (military, farmers,
ranchers, merchants, lawyers), their degree of cultural achievement (illiterate,
illustrious, graduates) or their declared ideology (liberal, conservative, Catholic,
anti-clerical). Subsequent caudillos dominated the political life of Latin

American nations with varying degrees of success, longevity, social support and institutional endowment: from José Tomás Rodríguez Bobes at the forefront of the monarchists and José Antonio Páez at the front of the patriots in Venezuela, to Ramón Castilla in Perú, Juan José Flores in Ecuador, Antonio López de Santa Anna in México, Rafael Carrera in Guatemala, José Gervasio Artigas in Uruguay, José María Obando in Colombia and Juan Manuel de Rosas in Argentina.[26]

In short, the concept of 'caudillo' broadcast in independent America probably returned to Spain in the nineteenth century to denote military leaders who, as *espadones* (swords) in the 'era of the *pronunciamentos*' (coups), ran the factions of the liberal monarchical regime that were harshly consolidated against Carlism or Republicanism: Baldomero Espartero as caudillo and *espadón* of the 'party' of the progressives and Ramón María Narváez as the equivalent for the moderates. The *raison d'être* of this role for the generals as military strongmen in the political life of Spanish liberalism lies in the very strength of the army as a key institution of a weak state apparatus, engaged in a succession of endless conflicts and subjected to increasing and serious social and political challenges. In the words of the Republican leader Emilio Castelar during the six years of democracy (1868–74): 'We are so weak that we cannot live without the generals.'[27] The consistent use of the word 'caudillo' to signify those capable of moving troops in support of one or another programme or party was logical and natural. The term could also apply to prominent figures in political life without any military command: Antonio Cánovas del Castillo called the financier and politician Juan Álvarez Mendizábal 'caudillo of the mob', while Alejandro Lerroux, in his radical period in Barcelona, was well known and acclaimed as 'caudillo of the masses' of the Republican and working class.[28]

In the decades before the Civil War, the term 'caudillo' returned to public prominence largely as a result of military operations to defend Spanish sovereignty in Africa and to implement peace in the Protectorate of Morocco (1908–27), a task that led to financial and demographic haemorrhages and growing socio-political conflicts in the metropolis. The right-wing Spanish press began to use the terms 'glorious caudillos', 'heroic caudillos', 'caudillos of Africa' or 'undefeated caudillos' for the military commanders and officers that led the troops of the Army of Africa (as in the cases of the generals Berenguer,

Sanjurjo and Fernández Silvestre, and Colonel José Millán Astray, the founder of the Legion in 1920).[29] For example, in January 1923, the popular Madrid weekly *Nuevo Mundo* devoted an illustrated story (signed by journalist Juan Ferragut) to then Major Francisco Franco, who had played an important role after the disaster of Annual which had put at risk the city of Melilla in the summer of 1921.[30] In it, talking about the Africanista military leaders, Ferragut did not hesitate to include among 'the best, the caudillos, those who when the panic of the shameful defeat spread were strong, heroes and Spaniards', with General Sanjurjo and Colonel Millán Astray expressly cited. Before the end of that year, on 31 October, another Madrid weekly, *Mundo Gráfico*, reported on Franco's marriage in Oviedo with a full page and a portentous headline: 'The Wedding of a Heroic Caudillo'.

The professional military journals were also regularly using the term with the same meaning, as evidenced by an article published in the Ceuta *Revista de Tropas Coloniales* in June 1924 under the title 'El Caudillo de Xexauen', a homage to General Dámaso Berenguer, 'The sweetheart of the Army of Africa'. In its issue of March 1925, the same magazine, already edited by Franco as colonel, included an article on its new editor by the conservative politician Antonio Goicoechea which did not hesitate to praise him as the Africanista military leader with this complimentary phrase: 'For his youth, for his history, for his triumphant career, the new Colonel Franco is a child of the military environment of the Legion and a unique prototype of it. [...] The bold soldier has become a caudillo.'

Exactly one year later, in March 1926, on his promotion to general, Franco was again included among the 'names of the most significant caudillos' (understood as 'illustrious warlords' and alluding to the conquerors of the sixteenth century) in a tribute paid to him by his fellow officers on his move to the Infantry Academy of Toledo. The citation delivered on that occasion included a dedication which, like the previous text from Goicoechea, is strangely premonitory:

When the step of the world of the current generation is not more than a brief comment in the book of history, the memory of the sublime epic written by the Spanish army at this stage of the development of the life of the nation will endure. And the names of the most significant caudillos will be covered in glory, and above all of them will rise triumphant that of General Don Francisco Franco Baamonde [*sic.*] for achieving the heights reached by other illustrious men of war, such as Leiva, Mondragón, Valdivia and Hernán Cortés, and to him his comrades dedicate this tribute with admiration and affection for his patriotism, intelligence and bravery.[31]

The use of the term in the singular and upper case seems to have begun during the dictatorship of General Miguel Primo de Rivera (1923–30) and as part of the process of 'charismatic construction' of his public figure as an authoritarian but effective ruler, to compensate for a lack of constitutional or traditional legitimacy. This process required the mobilization of diverse resources (print and radio media, civil and military patriotic ceremonies) and innovative formulas (the creation of an Office of Information, press campaigns orchestrated at national level, the financing of activities, related media and journalists). In the wake of that operation, he was presented as the 'Iron Surgeon' who came to cure the ills of the fatherland (in the best line of the regenerationist Joaquín Costa) or as the 'National Caudillo' (a kind of translation of the term 'Duce' applied in Italy to Mussolini, whose propaganda apparatus was admired and imitated). It should be emphasized that the experience then acquired would be present in the early stages of shaping the political propaganda of the Franco regime, a favourable circumstance because many of those responsible for this work under Primo de Rivera would assume the same role under Franco: José María Pemán, José Pemartín, Julián Cortés Cavanillas and Máximo Cuervo.[32] In any case, it is significant in the history of the word that, at the time of the removal of the dictator by King Alfonso XIII in early 1930, the bulletin from the Comité Ejecutivo (Executive Committee) de la Unión Patriótica (the attempt at a party founded years earlier to gain civilian support for the dictatorship), carried on its cover, in large capitals, the headline: 'On 28 January our Caudillo Ceased his Government'.

Perhaps, given the use of the term in a political and personal sense under the Primo de Rivera dictatorship, the word had little prestige and less usage during the five years of the Second Republic between 1931 and 1936. As studies of the political lexicon of the period tell us, its use was almost always associated with 'contexts of negative connotation', in tune with the 'special democratic sensitivity and anti-militarism of the age' (the terms 'caudillo' and 'mesnada' – his group of armed followers – did not appear in the socialist vocabulary). That negative content was still clearer in the derivative 'caudillismo' ('Our struggle against caudillismo will be relentless').[33]

However, in the right-wing sectors most hostile to the democratic Republican regime, the term was not rejected at all. José Calvo Sotelo, a former minister of the dictatorship and leader of authoritarian monarchism in open opposition to the Republic, always advocated military action against it and appealed regularly to the 'caudillos' who would be speaking in the 'charged atmosphere of Spain', just one month before the military attempt of August 1932 led by General Sanjurjo. Little more than one year later, he would reiterate: 'Nations need great leaders. They need caudillos and when they remove them – great naivety! – they sink beneath an anonymous and infamous leadership (*caudillaje*).'[34] For his part, José Antonio Primo de Rivera, son of the dictator, convert to fascism and leader of the Falange Española, in mid-1933 appealed to a caudillo who was 'a prophet' with 'a dose of faith, health, enthusiasm and anger that is not compatible with refinement'. In the ranks of the political Catholic opposition, in tune with its legalist strategy, the more civilian term *jefe* became popular (in preference to more traditional terms for leader, director and nobleman) to refer to its political 'caudillos'.[35] Thus José María Gil-Robles, the undisputed leader of Spanish political Catholicism, was hailed as 'Jefe', with a capital letter and with common threefold mantra in all gatherings of the CEDA: 'Jefe, Jefe, Jefe!' (a slogan that, in part, recalled the triple divine invocation of the religious cult: 'Holy, Holy, Holy, is the Lord, God of the Universe').

In the critical context of the eve of the Civil War, there is a remarkable and revealing case of the use of the term in the Socialist ranks that deserves mention. In his speech in Cuenca on 1 May 1936, Indalecio Prieto warned his colleagues of the risk of a military intervention against the Popular Front government and did not hesitate to name the ideal candidate to act as 'the caudillo of a military subversion':

I will not say a single word to the detriment of this illustrious military figure. I've known him well, when he was commander. I've seen him fight in Africa; and for me, General Franco [...] becomes the supreme figure of bravery, is a calm man in a fight. I have to own this truth. However, we cannot deny [...] that within the military, in considerable size and numbers, there are ferments of subversion, wishes of rising against the Republican regime, not so much because of what the Popular Front represents in its present reality, but because, predominant in the politics of the nation, it represents hope for the near future. General Franco, for his youth, his skills, his network of friends in the army, is the man that in time, can shortly lead (*acaudillar*) with the best chances – all of which arise from his personal prestige – a movement of this type.[36]

The Civil War and the Return of the Military Caudillos to the Public Sphere

The military rebellion by the Army of Africa that began on 17 July 1936 was not the prelude to the success of the simultaneous uprising in the rest of Spain, as had been anticipated by the generals, whose operational model was the well-known military coup by Primo de Rivera of September 1923. At this time the insurrection was not undertaken unanimously by all the military, and in just three days (17, 18 and 19 July), it became clear that the rebels were opposed by a significant portion of their comrades in arms, quickly reinforced by rapidly formed armed party and trade union militias. By virtue of this division of military forces and civilian resistance, the military coup sponsored by a large but not overwhelming faction of the army was only partially victorious in half of Spain, thus opening the way for a civil war of unspecified duration and an outcome, in principle, even more uncertain.[37]

In the areas where the military coup achieved its objectives, power was in the hands of the chain of command of the rebel army, in accordance with the mandatory declaration of a state of war and the previous eradication of hostile or undecided elements in their ranks. The consequent relentless militarization was followed by social and political reaction which repealed the democratic reforms adopted by the Republican governments in order to destroy working-class party organizations and trade unions, whether reformist or revolutionary. To avoid the dispersal of command generated by setbacks and the unexpected death in a plane crash in Lisbon of General Sanjurjo (supreme chief of the uprising tacitly accepted by all), General Emilio Mola constituted in Burgos on 24 July 1936 the Junta de Defensa Nacional 'that assumes all the powers of the state and legitimately represents the country before foreign powers' (according to its establishing decree).[38] Chaired by General Miguel Cabanellas in his position as the most senior officer in rank, the Burgos junta was composed of the top brass of the rebel generals: Mola, Saliquet, Ponte, Dávila, Franco, Queipo de Llano, Orgaz, Gil Yuste and Admiral Moreno, with colonels Montaner and Moreno Calderón (as secretaries). However, the military operations were under the control of the three generals who directed the troops operating at the fronts: Mola, who commanded all the centre and northern troops; Queipo de Llano, who held the area around Seville; and Franco, who led the troops from Africa, whose transfer to the peninsula would enable him to undertake the march on Madrid.

The context of civil war from 20 July 1936, with its fragmented geography of local micro strongholds and small active forces facing each other (according to Cardona, at the beginning, 'both sides fought with quite primitive columns'), was the ideal platform for the insurgent side to revive the word 'caudillo' in its usual sense of a courageous and heroic 'military leader and warrior'. And perhaps the same reason explains its radical exclusion from the vocabulary of its Republican enemies, whether democratic reformists or social revolutionaries. This reactivation was supported by the fact that many of the insurgent leaders had been trained in the Army of Africa and knew and appreciated the term; in addition, its Africanist lexicography (as part of their ideological worldview) would soon become the main and dominant element of the public and official rhetoric of the incipient insurgent institutional apparatus.[39] Furthermore, that term and its context were also known, appreciated and used by many journalists and right-wing politicians who cooperated from the outset with the military rebels in the difficult task of constructing an alternative state to the hated Republican democracy.

The return of the word 'caudillo' to the public arena can be followed in proclamations, rants, speeches and statements made by the leaders and rebel officers from the beginning of the war. It can also be tracked in the news, articles and interviews printed in the newspapers and media favourable to the insurgents and immediately subjected to their control. As a result of the declaration of the state of war by the junta of Burgos, on 28 July 1936 military court martial and summary punishment were dealt out to authors guilty of the offence of rebellion: 'Those who impart false or biased news in order to damage the prestige of the armed forces and those that cooperate in providing services to the army'.[40] The censorship of all communications and information was immediately complemented by directives and propaganda slogans for compulsory inclusion as well as the removal, deportation and elimination of all hostile personnel or media.

Just a few days after that key measure of the militarization of information policy, on 5 August the Burgos junta instituted a press office to undertake 'suitable work relating to this field'. No doubt forced by the progress of the war, on 24 August the press office was renamed the Office for Press and Propaganda and its powers increased to make it a 'body exclusively responsible for all services related to information and propaganda by means of printing, photocopying and others such as radio'.[41] From the outset, the office was led by two key figures: right-wing journalists Juan Pujol Martínez (who had been a CEDA member of parliament and director of the Madrid newspaper *Informaciones* before the war) and Joaquín Arrarás Iribarren (who had worked as a correspondent for *El Debate* in Morocco, was a member of the authoritarian monarchist group Renovación Española and would be the first official biographer of Franco). As Gustau Nerín wrote: 'the rebel generals [...] immediately turned to those journalists who had written eulogies to the colonial army in the 1920s.'[42]

While the Burgos team was taking shape, Franco also assumed the task of controlling the press and propaganda through the services of Luis Bolín Bidwell, former correspondent of *Abc* in London, who had organized his flight from Las Palmas to Tetuán at the start of the uprising, accompanying him and performing various international tasks. Bolín was soon joined by two other figures: the famous General Millán Astray and the physician and journalist Víctor Ruiz Albéniz (who had been the chronicler of colonial campaigns under the pseudonym El Tebib Arrumi – 'Christian Doctor' in Arabic). Both joined the team of assistants to Franco when he moved his headquarters from Tetuán to Seville at the beginning of August 1936 following the victorious advance of his troops towards Madrid via Extremadura and the Tagus Valley. After the election of Franco to single supreme command at the end of September, the

Office for Press and Propaganda would move to Burgos and be strengthened by new additions such as the eccentric writer and literary critic Ernesto Giménez Caballero, an early admirer of Mussolini and precursor of Spanish fascism in his book *Genio de España* (1932).[43]

Completing the initial team of insurgent propagandists were the staff of the daily royalist *Abc* of Seville: the editor Juan Carretero; his uncle and the newspaper's proprietor, Juan Ignacio Luca de Tena; Manuel Sánchez del Arco, editor-in-chief; Juan María Vázquez, Antonio Olmedo, Tomás Borrás, José María Pemán and Luis de Galinsoga as permanent or occasional columnists. This prestigious journal and group, which no doubt well remembered the monarchist loyalty of Franco (in contrast to the Republicanism of Queipo or disregard of Mola), would become an influential platform for the insurrectionists (its circulation widely exceeded 100,000 copies per day) and inclined to promote the figure of Franco: '*Abc* of Seville, the leading newspaper of Nationalist Spain' and 'the journal which assigned more space to Franco'.[44]

This national newspaper, printed daily in Seville (its counterpart in Madrid was seized by the Republicans, who radically changed its editorial line), initially gave priority to the figure of General Gonzalo Queipo de Llano for obvious reasons (he was the leader of the revolt in Andalusia), attributing to him the title of 'caudillo' on several occasions, as it had to the late General Sanjurjo.[45] However, its pages gave increased prominence to General Franco due to his crucial importance at the head of the decisive Moroccan troops and his history of military successes during the occupation of Extremadura and advance through the Tagus Valley to Madrid.

The first mention of Franco in the Seville *Abc* occurred on Wednesday 22 July 1936, when it was clear that the military coup had become a civil war. There were several quotes from the radio proclamations and telegrams of General Franco, introduced as the 'head of the Army of Morocco', all of them underlining the success of the military movement ('Greater success could not have been achieved'), assured of the next triumph ('The end is near') and indicating that the enemy would be beaten soundly ('the red anarchy that tyrannized us, transforming our glorious home into a miserable Russian colony'). The next day, 23 July, the cover of the journal printed 'the patriotic address by General Franco at the beginning of the Movement', which was nothing more than the speech of 18 July in Las Palmas on the occasion of the declaration of a state of war. Three days later, on 26 July, also on the cover and inside pages, Franco figured prominently with the publication of the speech made the day before in Tetuán to the Spanish military under the heading 'Patriotic Speech of the Caudillo' (the first time in the war the term was used to refer to him). That speech of 25 July included the words 'caudillo' and 'crusade' in its original text: 'And since I speak to the military or professionals of the army, to the armed forces, I have to recommend faith in the crusade, the firmness of the caudillo, without losing heart for a single instant.'

On 28 July 1936 Franco flew to Seville to prepare for the arrival of Moroccan troops who were going to start the march on Madrid. On the same day, the newspaper, aware of his presence in the city, pronounced him 'General Franco, distinguished head of the liberating movement'. A day later, before his return to Tetuán, the cover of the newspaper reproduced his statements with this informative preamble:

Yesterday General Franco was in Seville. It is not necessary to describe this illustrious caudillo, one of the organizers of the military movement to save Spain. General Franco, that brave captain of the Regulars, the commander of the Legion, whose heroic spirit is second to none, does not require presentations or praise. Franco's name is famous in all households in Spain.

On subsequent days, the newspaper followed the activities, statements, speeches and manifestos of Franco, always presenting him as 'His Excellency, the general', 'most Spanish caudillo', 'distinguished general' or 'illustrious caudillo' (examples from copies of 30 July, 3 August and 16 August). His progressive rise over the rest of the generals, a direct result of the success of his troops on the march to Madrid (compared with the stagnation of Queipo and Mola in their respective areas), can be seen on the cover of the paper from 23 August 1936. Under a large full-page photograph which showed Franco accompanied by Lieutenant Colonel Yagüe (who commanded the columns in the field), a caption identified him as: 'General Franco, head of the Movement to save the fatherland'. A couple of weeks later, on 10 September 1936, the daily repeated almost the same iconic and lexical formula: a huge picture of

Franco on the balcony of his headquarters in Cáceres with a caption that read: 'General Franco, chief of the forces of the national army'. That promotion of him was complemented by a call for the strongest national unity under military guidance that entailed, by pure logic, a personal single command of all military and political operations. On 9 September an editorial by Luca de Tena ('Before the New Spain') pointed out that 'military authority is right in wanting to nip in the bud any differences, wherever they originate.' Two days later the journalist Francisco Cossío reiterated this in a prominent article entitled 'National Front':

Who can sum up in these moments the common yearning for national salvation that we all desire? Only the army. It imposes a rigid discipline that binds together all Spaniards. [...] The army should be the great binding of this enterprise of national solidarity.[46]

When the powers of the Burgos junta were transferred to the new head of state and supreme commander, the paper did not hesitate in giving that act preferential attention insofar as it met its demands for a seamless and single command to overcome the enemy. The news of the appointment of Franco to both posts on 30 September was completed with a short biography (one of the first to appear in the Spanish press) which stressed his bravery as an Africanist officer, with this climax: 'The rest of the history of the Caudillo is so current, it need not enter in these composite notes. Hopefully the judgement of history will compare General Franco with the geniuses of war.'

Tributes were endlessly lavished on the new 'caudillo', 'supreme commander' and 'head of state' (so called in the accounts of 2 October, describing the ceremony of the transfer of power in Burgos). It was also appreciated (in a report of 3 October) that this concentration of powers was so total that it well deserved the label of 'dictatorship' in the most positive sense (as the term had been used by the right during the government of Primo de Rivera): 'In this way the Junta becomes an official government, under the presidency of General Franco, who is the only leader and gathers in his hands power at least the equal of any dictator.'

The Seville daily was correct in this judgement and that same accurate assessment would be reflected in the reporting of the same act published on 2 October by *La Gaceta Regional* of Salamanca, where the cover bore a large headline bringing the news of the transfer of power with these words: 'The New Dictator of Spain Addressed an Overwhelming Crowd'. And in its main report, also on the cover, it reiterated without lexical remorse and with conceptual precision the term 'dictator', which was not then an ominous word for the military rebels and their civilian supporters, even if it was edged cautiously for the benefit of others:

> The bands play, but the music fades and the sound of the instruments are muted by the applause of the crowd. Cheers and thunderous ovations that the people, the true people, offer to the new head of the Spanish state, dictator. [...] The dictator reviews the troops and militias. [...] Here we will only give an impression of the vibrant words of the heroic general, today dictator of Spain. [...] Above, overlooking the crowd, with the gesture of Caudillo [*sic.*], the man who will assume full power within a few minutes. Below, the confused people and the army, ready to respond with their lives and properties to the words of the dictator. [...] In the Plaza de Alonso Martínez is today represented healthy Spain, the Spain that stands up, and in front of it, as undisputed commander, a serene and firm leader: a dictator, General Franco. Long live Franco! Long live Franco! Long live Franco! Long Live Spain! Long Live Spain forever!

From that founding moment, the use of the word 'caudillo' gradually diminished in the official rhetoric of insurgent Spain when refering to other military chiefs, for obvious reasons. Symptomatically, a biography of Franco and other 'distinguished soldiers of the new Spain' (Mola and Varela) that came to light in January 1937 in Melilla still called the three men 'caudillos of the war'. Still, the author tended to emphasize the pre-eminence of 'Franco, the Generalissimo of our armed forces', stressing that Spain was 'under the unique and supreme direction of our Caudillo'. The plural gave way to the singular and lower case to upper case. That transformation had a reason well underlined with a unique bombastic style:

> General Franco Bahamonde has reached the highest post of the nation, haloed with lights of immortality because, apart from his morality, he is the

personification of the heroic Spanish army, to whom we owe the bliss of having saved Spain from that fixed-date of inevitable ruin. [47]

Indeed, on 1 October in Burgos, the Franco regime was born in the midst of a bloody civil war and on the back of a collegiate military dictatorship which had opted to deliver all its absolute powers to one of its members, for life. The recipient until then had no reservations about being called a 'good dictator' or considered an 'authentic dictator'.[48] He was a dictator who would soon become, simply, the 'Caudillo of Spain', giving birth to a corresponding body of ideological doctrine that would try to legitimize this new absolute, sovereign, constituent and providential ruler.

The Political Culture of the Spanish Anti-Liberal Right on the Eve of War

As recalled in a classic work by Manuel García-Pelayo, all societies in history have developed various political orders which rest on 'ideas and belief systems intended to maintain the values that supported them, to consolidate the structure in which they operated and to provide guidelines (to their members) for orientation and action'.[49] This set of ideals, values and guiding principles of all human political society, however much integrated, respected or violated, forms the basis of the different conceptual categories that attempt to describe its essence, role and functioning: 'forms of political power' (understanding 'power' as the ability of men to force the conduct of others according to his will, in the words of Hans Gerth and Charles Wright Mills); 'types of legitimate authority' ('authority' being a power considered 'legitimate' because its 'strength' becomes 'right' and 'obedience' becomes a 'duty', according to Max Weber); 'forms of social and institutional domination' (which presuppose 'relations of interaction' between rulers and ruled that demand at the very least prestige for the superior and subordination of the inferior, in the argument of Georg Simmel); or underlying patterns of 'political culture' (considered as a system of ideas that have effects on the socio-political dynamics, according to Gabriel Almond, Sidney Verba or Lucien Pye).[50]

The diverse forces and socio-political trends that in Spain organized and executed the July 1936 military uprising, fought and won the Civil War and established a victorious institutional regime that lasted almost 40 years, of course had their own 'political cultures' that sustained different types of legitimate authority and supported 'forms of political power and domination' that are well outlined and known. Further, as clearly demonstrated in several recent works (in particular the comprehensive studies of Ferran Gallego on the formation of the political culture of the Franco regime and Ismael Saz on Francoist Nationalism), the war led to a rapid convergence of interests and principles among all those political cultures of the anti-liberal Spanish right, for the simple reason that it imposed the need to remain strongly united against the enemy to overcome the challenges of war, achieve victory and survive without any subsequent risk of regression.[51]

On the eve of the Civil War, the socio-political culture of the Spanish anti-liberal right (also called 'Spanish reactionary thinking' or 'counter-revolutionary front') registered at least four operational currents that were well established but unevenly rooted amongst the Spanish population. Of course, as several analysts have stressed, each of these currents had their respective repertoire of doctrines refined by years of tradition, prestigious names, ancient or modern organizations and formulas of socio-political action of varying effectiveness, with their own groups of followers, loyal militants and activists.[52]

First, the immense weight of political Catholicism should be highlighted, heir of the veteran 'Augustinian politics' promoted by the Church hierarchy and its intellectual spokesmen in multiple forms, responding to the ancient and essential theological premise that 'all authority comes from God' – with its corollary of the subordination of the human order to the superior and prior divine order. A movement articulated during the Second Republic by the CEDA, whose political profile was clearly religious, corporate, hierarchical and conservative, despite its legalist and pragmatic political strategy during the five Republican years and up to its debacle in the general elections of February 1936. The failure of that possibilist strategy and the outbreak of war wrecked the political capital of the CEDA as a party and of its leader, José María Gil-Robles, who would only cooperate with the insurrection from the sidelines in Portugal. But the movement would not disappear, much less its doctrinal heritage, political staff or the masses of followers of Spanish political Catholicism. On the contrary, the ideology of National Catholicism and the idea of a 'crusade for God and for Spain' would arise as a powerful ideological formula for the legitimization of the uprising and the new state.[53]

Second, in terms of popular support (but not in terms of able political personnel), was Alfonsist authoritarian monarchism, which had just suffered the collapse of the Primo de Rivera military regime and maintained a symbiotic relationship with political Catholicism only broken by the different degrees of loyalty to the monarchy as an institutional formula. After the debacle of 1931, monarchism became more critical of the liberal-democratic tradition and moved in favour of targets such as the end of political parties and parliaments, the establishment of detached and strong technocratic governments, the rebirth of integral nationalism and the restoration of the identity of throne and altar in corporate and disciplined state projects. It was the alternative that would encourage with singular doctrinal coherence the journal *Acción Española* (in the wake of Charles Maurras's Action Français movement), whose illustrious spokesman was José Calvo Sotelo, a former supporter of the dictatorship who would be killed on the eve of the revolt of 1936, eliminating one of the most prestigious leaders of the authoritarian monarchic movement.[54]

Third, in some geographical areas (above all, the Basque provinces and Navarre), there remained the political culture of the old Carlist tradition, the oldest of the anti-liberal political currents and the most restrictive on religious and moral issues. Rejuvenated since the beginning of the twentieth century by figures such as Juan Vázquez de Mella and Víctor Pradera, traditionalism offered a true source of political and ideological alternatives to the exhaustion of the liberal system and the dissolution of the national idea and moved progressively closer to the new principles of Alfonsist monarchism and Catholic corporate authoritarianism. Its reduced territorial base, coupled with the secular failure and weakness of its dynastic candidates and the limited national prestige of its leaders, diminished its power and manoeuvrability. However, the crisis opened by the proclamation of the Republic in April 1931 seemed to corroborate in retrospect the correctness of its anti-liberal intransigence and its belligerent Catholicism.[55]

Finally, from 1933, was the crystallization of the fascist alternative inspired by the Italian model in the hands of the Spanish Falange, founded by José Antonio Primo de Rivera, the son of the dictator, who was shot by the Republicans four months after the war started, leaving the movement decapitated at a critical juncture. In tune with its inspiration from Mussolini, the Falangist formula projected a new concept of a totalitarian state, complete with the political militarization of society, a hierarchical citizenship and the doctrine of charismatic leadership based on a civil and secular religion of the sacred and deified fatherland. However, despite its modernity, aestheticism and youthful appeal, Falangism barely competed with other alternatives until the war offered a unique opportunity for its expansion and consolidation as a movement and mass party.[56]

In any case, aside from the weight and influence of each of these political cultures, the truth is that there had been an intense process of convergence and cooperation between them during the Republican period, particularly after the crisis of October 1934 and the electoral defeat of February 1936. That process was necessitated by the perceived seriousness of the risk faced by the right and the strength of their common enemy: the reality of the reformist liberal democracy and, behind it, the threat of social revolution as its potential and forced outcome. As the fascist leader Onésimo Redondo warned in 1931: 'Jacobinism is today Bolshevism. Or something that will lead to it.' The reply from the Alfonsist monarchist ranks, in the words of the journalist Joaquín Arrarás in 1932, left no doubt of the consensus with that judgement and its outcome: 'Adversity is the link that today gathers, concentrates and tightens the whole family.' The consequent call for unity was perfectly indicated by another illustrious monarchist of Acción Española, Pedro Sainz Rodríguez, on the eve of the crisis of October 1934, with an indirect appeal to the military role demanded by the situation: 'The imperative logic of a single command is something that is not discussed, it is a necessity which reality imposes in the tragic moments of the people.'[57]

Moreover, the relative ease of this convergence was based on the presence of several components shared in varying measures by all those cultures: the assertion of the Catholic tradition of the nation as an inalienable and defining component; the defence of a restored and integral nationalism that admitted no doubts or pacts with the 'Anti-Spain'; the promotion of an idea of reform of the state that broke radically with liberalism and democracy; the conception of social hierarchical relationships and of militarized discipline that aimed to tackle social divisions and class struggles; and, progressively, the conviction that only organized violence and preferably the force of the military could address social and national dissolution.

Indeed, from the electoral defeat in February 1936, the key role in the backlash against these deadly dangers ceased to be in the hands of the civilian party movements and passed to the control of the Spanish army, in a process of political satellization well understood by all contemporaries and demanded by many political leaders. Calvo Sotelo had already demanded, clearly and precisely, in January 1936 a return to the more traditional military praetorianism:

> There are those who will find in these words an indirect invocation for force. Good. Yes, there it is [...]. To whom? To the essentials: to the military force at the service of the state. [...] Today the army is the foundation of support for the fatherland. It has risen from the role of the enforcer, blind, deaf and dumb, to that of the spinal cord, without which life is not possible. [...] When the red hordes of communism advance, there is only one brake: the strength of the state and the transfusion of military virtues – obedience, discipline and hierarchy – to society itself, to make them leave the unhealthy ferments that Marxism has sown. That is why I call upon the army and the patriotism that drives it.[58]

The same idea was also suggested on the eve of the uprising by both José María Gil-Robles and José Antonio Primo de Rivera, despite their fear of the consequences that this military role might have for their own political plans. José Antonio made his suggestion in his 'Carta a los Militares de España' (letter to the military of Spain) sent from prison on 4 May 1936: 'without your strength, soldiers, it will be titanically difficult to succeed in the fight. [...] Spain's existence depends on you.' Gil-Robles had warned parliament a fortnight earlier: 'when the civil war breaks out in Spain, it should be known that the weapons have been loaded by the neglect of a government that has failed to fulfil its duty.'[59]

The Civil War as the Facilitator of the Francoist *Caudillaje*

When the uprising began, the whole literary, ideological and doctrinal arsenal of the militaristic and Africanist tradition of the Spanish army was launched. In fact, whatever the sympathy of the rebel military chiefs for one or other of the 'political cultures' of the Spanish right (and obviously Catholics and monarchists were to predominate over Carlists and Falangists), all were fully in agreement on the purely military character of the Movement. It is unlikely that anyone contradicted any part of what General Mola declared in this regard and as a warning to the navy in a speech broadcast on 13 September 1936 (just before the Junta de Defensa Nacional decreed 'an absolute departure from all political partisanship' and the subordination of all 'to the army, an effective symbol of national unity') declared:

> I have a blind faith in these brash boys that today demand [a barely veiled reference to partisan, Falangist and Carlist militias]; but let it be understood that in the task of national reconstruction which they are eager to carry out and they will – who doubts it? – in this formidable undertaking we, the military, have to lay its foundations; we have to launch it; it is our right, because that is the nation's wish, because we have a clear idea of our power and only we can consolidate the union of the people with the army, which has been kept distant until 19 July by the absurd propaganda of stupid intellectualism and suicidal politics.[60]

It is unnecessary to emphasize that the few challenges to that exclusivity of military power in the insurgent area were quickly nipped in the bud by the military authorities right from the beginning until the very end. It is enough to recall two quick interventions by Franco, already supreme commander of the armies. The first was the expulsion from Spain in December 1936 of the Carlist leader Manuel Fal Conde for his claim that the *requeté* – Carlist militias – should be made a virtually autonomous arm from the rest of the army. Second was the arrest, trial and condemning to death of Manuel Hedilla (interim successor to José Antonio Primo de Rivera as Falange leader) and other Falangist comrades for their opposition to the forced unification of political parties enacted in April 1937.

In this regard, as shown by recent studies on the coming together of the insurgent war effort (for example, the works of Gabriel Cardona, Jorge Martínez Reverte, Michael Seidman or James Matthews), it is evident that the contribution of volunteer militiamen from the Falange and traditionalist groups (more than from monarchist parties) was very prominent and appreciated by the rebel military commanders: by the end of 1936 there were almost 37,000 Falangist militia, 22,100 Carlist *requetés* and a little over 6,000 Alfonsists. But it is also clear that these 'national militias' (always integrated within military units and under professional control) never became more than 34 per cent of the forces mobilized until the autumn of 1936: around 65,000 men out of a total of 189,000 armed soldiers. Moreover, these volunteer troops, driven by their partisan political and ideological commitment soon ceased to be the principle source of recruitment.[61] As well as the militiamen, the rebel army used and perfected traditional compulsory military recruitment channels. The war could not be won with so few volunteers and they had to resort to the forced mobilization of others, young and not so young (between 18 and 45 years) to maintain operations and nurture the war effort. The Nationalist armies would thus mobilize 1.2 million men in 15 drafts up to the beginning of 1939. This successful, huge logistical operation of preparing human and material resources was performed by the military, under their rules and supported by a well-prepared and established military plan.

As far as the 'mobilizing myths' that were used to stimulate the fighting zeal were concerned – without neglecting the Falangist contributions in their robes of modernity and international prestige – the truth is that the fundamental, recurrent and omnipresent motivations put forward by 'the army of Franco' were more classical and traditional than anything else. Above all, Spanish, Unitarian, integralist and historical nationalism: 'Spain, evangelizer of half of the globe; Spain, hammer of heretics, light of Trent, sword of Rome, cradle of San Ignacio', as praised by Marcelino Menéndez y Pelayo and learned by heart by the cadets of the military academies since the end of the nineteenth century. And, at its side, Catholicism that had identified with the idea of the crusade 'for God and Spain' which for centuries carried the idea of 'Spain as a favoured country and destined for the realization of the Kingdom of Christ'. At this point, it seems that the speeches made to mobilize the masses on the insurgent side appealed through inertia and default to the common and substantive heritage in all the Spanish right and in the soul of the two bureaucratic corporations that articulated the making of the new state: 'the mystic cult of the nation' of the military who felt the army was 'the only patriotic institution and possessor of the truth'; and the political theology of National Catholicism of priests with their talk of the providential and purifying crusade.[62] At the same time, the Church continued to be the classic integral instrument of 'morality' in the ranks of the army through the services of military chaplains responsible for 'spiritual assistance'. In the recent words of James Matthews:

> The alliance between the Church and the military was hatched soon after the uprising and, during most of the Civil War, 'national' and 'Catholic' were synonymous words. [...] The sacred language of the spirit of crusade had the power to make death tolerable, and even positive, in official discourse. The men who fell were martyrs of the cause and therefore 'incorporated into the iconography of worship'. This can be seen in the slogans painted on the walls of the buildings of Nationalist Spain: 'Before God there will be no unsung hero'.[63]

One of the points of convergence for all the political cultures of the Spanish anti-liberal right was the doctrine of the *caudillaje* as a form of supreme authority, command and government demanded by wartime circumstances, national traditions and international imperatives. At this point, agreement was unanimous and the well-known result was the rise of Franco as a charismatic and providential caudillo for life, with full constituent powers and sovereign and unappealable judgement. For some he was above all the caudillo of the victory for his military triumph, caudillo of the crusade by divine will or caudillo of the national revolution by virtue of his Falangist political leadership. Of course, the Caudillo himself would always maintain his three sources of legitimacy, harmoniously balanced and coordinated, without prejudice to his sovereign, supreme, arbitrary and decision-making authority.[64]

The rebel military commanders began the process through their own roles in the insurrection and directing war operations, and it was they who, at the end of September 1936, proceeded to elect General Franco as 'Generalissimo of the armies' and 'head of the government of the state' without consultation or intermediation with anyone, aside from the political preferences expressed by Rome and Berlin – which were much more influential than any other Spanish domestic political opinion.[65] The imposition of a 'single command' in the person of Franco was in tune with the hierarchical and disciplined vision of military chiefs in a situation of national emergency, in response to the principle of unity of command and an evident sign of 'Caesarism' as a result of his successes ('the Caesars were generals victorious', read a slogan immediately adopted by the insurgent propaganda).[66] The use of the word 'caudillo' was equally logical in view of its previous wide circulation to denote a heroic and admirable military chief who assumed all-embracing political powers. In fact, the term allowed for the merger of two powers formally 'transferred': the military authority to fight the war (Generalissimo) and the political authority to build the alternative state apparatus (head of state). The definitive consecration of the Caudillo by his comrades in arms was the victory parade held in Madrid on 19 May 1939, when Franco oversaw the parade of over 100,000 soldiers (the triumphant 'armies of Franco') and received the highest Spanish military award for his prowess. The decision of 'the military family' to honour their senior captain and leader was explained thus in the corresponding decree:

Having won the war definitively, which Anti-Spain unleashed on our fatherland, the entire nation, led by all the Knights of the Grand Cross laureate of San Fernando, gathered together, requested the award of the Grand Cross laureate of San Fernando for the Caudillo, who knew how to win the war with his genius [...]. It is not because a general in chief dutifully fulfils the requirements of Article 35 of the regulations of the Order of San Fernando for membership, but in the present case is the great leader who saved his country, restoring independence and order and also undertaking for the whole world the best service that could be provided for peace by defeating Bolshevism in our fatherland to save a seriously threatened civilization.[67]

For the ecclesiastical hierarchy, the almost immediate conversion of the insurgent war effort into a crusade for the faith of Christ was soon completed with the elevation of Franco to the category of *homo missus a Deo*, sent by Divine

Providence to defend the Church and restore its role in the Spanish nation, in keeping with the tenets of National Catholicism. The cardinal primate and archbishop of Toledo, Isidro Gomá, reported to the Vatican from the beginning that, of the rebel commanders, Franco was the most favourable to the Church ('The one who has better credentials at this point; that is, Generalissimo Franco, a practising Catholic all his life'). He soon received confirmation of Franco's goodwill in the form of legal, economic and cultural measures that restored the rights and privileges of Catholicism that had been suppressed by the Republic.[68]

The transition to 'caudillo by the grace of God' was very quick because it connected with the old theological idea of authority as divine investiture and shadowed the formula of *Rex per Gratia Dei* common in the historical Spanish and Catholic tradition. At the end of the war, the day after the victory parade, the ceremony of Te Deum in thanksgiving for the victory was celebrated in the Church of Santa Bárbara of Madrid, with Franco entering under a canopy and received by the full episcopal hierarchy, only confirming an existing situation now sanctified by the public prayer of the Primate:

> God, to whom all are subject, to whom all things serve, make the reign of your good servant Caudillo Francisco Franco times of peace and joy, so that the man whom we put in front of our people under your guidance have days of peace and glory. We ask today, Lord of Lords, to look benignly from the throne of your Majesty to our Caudillo Francisco Franco to whom you granted a people subject to his government and to assist him in all your will.[69]

For the unified political party, the dominant Falange perfectly agreed with the *caudillaje* of Franco because of its own hierarchical and charismatic concept of political leadership. In addition, the loss of José Antonio Primo de Rivera and the difficulty of replacing him as head of the old Falange had crucially undermined the party, preventing it from resisting the decision of Franco, decreed on 19 April 1937, to take over its structures, symbols and supporters to merge with other right-wing political groups, thus founding a new unified party that served as the third pillar, along with the army and the Church, of his regime of personal power: the Falange Española Tradicionalista y de las JONS.[70] As Dionisio Ridruejo, then a young Falangist leader in charge of official propaganda, would recognize, opposition would be suicidal and acceptance was in the interests of both parties because it solved a real problem: 'a movement without a leader and a leader without a movement'. Accordingly, the conversion of Franco (a military caudillo with religious backing) into the new Falange leader was accepted as the only way to perform the 'national-syndicalist revolution' at a time of war and thanks to a *caudillaje* grounded in military power with all-encompassing and supreme powers but always advised and counselled by his faithful followers and servants:

> The Caudillo is only limited by his own will, but this limitation is the *raison d'être* of the Movement: the proclaimed dogmas, the chosen minorities and the faith of the people. Thus the Movement – an instrument of the Caudillo (of the state which is invested upon him) popularizes, on one hand, his will and serves, on the other, as a touchstone and voice of advice for the decisions of that very same will that other organs (the army for its power, the bureaucracy for its administration) will implement.[71]

The convergence of the three institutions on the need for the *caudillaje* of Franco as a virtual victorious Caesar, providential and sovereign, cemented the consistent cult of charismatic personality that would continue until his death in 1975, although with variations of mode and intensity. Sometimes his status as military caudillo of victory was underlined (during the early stages of war, when the title of Generalissimo was used profusely in propaganda and the regime was to be a new military directorate similar to that of the 1923 regime – *mutatis mutandis*). At other times, Franco was emphasized as being the Falangist Caudillo of the national revolution (as happened between 1937 and 1942, when the international context tempted the emulation of his Fascist and Nazi backers and the regime presented itself as Spanish totalitarianism). Sometimes his profile as the religious caudillo of the crusade was emphasized (from 1943 until 1959, when his National Catholic legitimacy became the form of introduction before the victorious powers of the world war and during the first postwar era). Finally, at other times, his role as caudillo of Spain and head of state without more contentious adjectives would be stressed (as would occur from 1959, when technocratic efficiency and modernizing successes served to find new respectable civil and 'functional' legitimacy in the outside world).

Through this same versatility of functions and situations, the Caudillo became, before the law, the 'supreme and unique institution' of the Franco regime. This was accurately highlighted by Giménez Caballero in one of the most widespread propaganda addresses to 'the combatants' during the Civil War, which was also a call for all to close ranks around his person for reasons of mere survival:

> We the fighters – this new and traditional army of Spain – we know Franco and worship him fanatically. [...] And everyone knows – especially the reds, the enemy – that without FRANCO all our dreams, all our sacrifices, 'everything' and 'all', would collapse and be lost. [...] And before this grandeur and this glory SPAIN! – SPAIN OF FRANCO AND THE FALANGE, FALANGE OF GOD AND THE ARMED FORCES.[72]

Of course, the unconditional military victory achieved in April 1939 would always be the foundation and original source of legitimacy for Franco to govern as caudillo of Spain. That same military force guaranteeing the irreversibility of that victory remained the ultimate *ratio* of the existence of the regime. Franco himself made clear both aspects at various times throughout his public life. That was the case in his inaugural speech, delivered on 17 March 1943 before the newly constituted Cortes. He affirmed: 'With the rights arising from the legitimacy of power of a man that saved a society, we institute a system of enlightened and paternal government.' Three months later, on 17 July 1943, he reaffirmed this idea in his speech commemorating the start of the war: 'Our policy is based on the right of our victory, backed by the force of reason, strengthened by the will of the people and faithfully kept by the loyalty of our armies.'[73]

The subsequent appeal of the Caudillo to his comrades in arms to preserve the fruits of the victory was constant and recurrent throughout the existence of the dictatorship, particularly in its most difficult times. In October 1945, with international condemnation raging, Franco turned to the senior commanders in the Escuela Superior del Ejército with these words:

While those times of true peace, solidarity and improvements that we all crave do not arrive, I exhort you, in the middle of your work, to remain jealous and vigilant in defence of the sacred unity of our fatherland, attained at so high a price, standing firm against any cracks that are attempting to open in our ranks, because it is demanded by the mandate of our dead, the existence of our nation and all those who have worked these nine years for our resurgence.[74]

A little less than a decade later, in November 1957, in new and critical circumstances, the Caudillo again addressed his army comrades to remind them of the vital role assigned to the military in his regime along the old praetorian tradition of Spanish history. The speech took place in the courtyard of the Alcázar of Toledo, the iconic place that had witnessed one of the most revered wartime events for the Francoist army, a symbol of its bravery and perseverance:

If whatever we do in order to forge unity amongst the peoples and lands of Spain is transcendental, it is equally or more transcendental when we apply it to the army. The army is the backbone of the nation. What unifies, sustains and maintains the rigidity of the whole. Through the bone marrow runs the vital essences of the sacred values of the fatherland. It is not the head that directs and reflects, or the other parts that organically make it up, but the spine that binds and holds it. With this broken, the body would be in tatters.[75]

Near the end of his life, in September 1975, Franco again returned to the theme before a committee of generals, leaders, officers and non-commissioned officers of the armed forces who came to show their commitment in the face of the difficulties they then confronted:

For me it is always a great satisfaction to find myself with my colleagues of the military family and even more in these times which require greater unity and effective service, not to lower our guard, but to stand firm in our purpose to defend Spain in this tormented world. We are not indifferent to outside problems that require us to maintain our serene and watchful position of constant vigilance.[76]

Charisma and Political Legitimacy:
The Doctrine Underlining the *Caudillaje*

Of course, the construction of the Caudillo's regime of personal and sovereign power was not exceptional in twentieth-century history. It was, rather, one of the most definitive cases of the new type of dictatorial regimes that emerged in Europe during the 'age of dictators' of the years of both world wars and the period between them (1914–45). These were regimes that, unlike the earlier nineteenth-century dictatorships (either monarchist or military), were constructed through a process of 'charismatization' of personal authority and 'around a cult of the exemplary, missionary leader, destined to re-forge national unity and lead the people into a new era'.[77] While the roots of dictatorship should be sought in the idea of a strong and powerful leader that has existed in Western political thought since the times of Alexander the Great and Caesar, its new modulation at the dawn of the twentieth century was indebted to the contributions of Thomas Carlyle (with his romantic praise of the heroic leader), Friedrich Nietszche (with his theory of the dominant superman), Gustave Le Bon (with his premise of a mass era that demanded great leaders) and the school of political scientists that had called into question the purely rational basis of Western liberal political systems (from Roberto Michels to Gaetano Mosca, including Vilfredo Pareto and other 'heirs of Machiavelli' of the time).[78]

The triumph of the democracies in the Great War of 1914–18 did not mitigate this trend of the personalization of supreme authority in a charismatic and single leader. Essentially, the effects of the war on borders, mentalities and societies provided the context for the emergence of a plethora of new dictators, sovereign bearers of 'creeds of national redemption' and 'gospels of purifying violence' across the continent: from Lenin in Bolshevik Russia in 1917 to Mussolini in Fascist Italy in 1922, also including Marshal Pilsudski in Poland in 1919, the regent Horthy in Hungary in 1920 and Kemal Atatürk in Turkey in 1921.

The phenomenon of such new dictatorships and political movements was so evident that it led Max Weber in 1921 to formulate his concept of 'charismatic authority' as one of the three existing types of 'legitimate justification for political authority'. Weber used the term 'charisma' (from the Greek *charis*, translated into Latin as *gratia*) in its original sense of a special and outstanding quality of a person who seems to be vested with an original gift, a particular and luminous grace which arouses devotion in others and reverence to their pronouncements and decisions. The use of the term changed from its first religious and sacred beginnings (the magician, the prophet, the apostle) with the new political times to denote the aura of holiness and infallibility of the new autocratic leaders that awakened 'popular idolatry' and partly resurrected 'the ancient cult of the deified ruler'.[79]

The new type of Weberian charismatic authority was in opposition to and co-determined by the other two basic ideals registered in history: 'traditional' authority (which lay in the usual and customary law, either dynastic or theocratic) and 'rational' authority (legally defined by rules and institutions above the individual, whether partially representative, plebiscitary or liberal-democratic). According to Weber, this 'charismatic domination' was based on the 'extraordinary rendition to the sanctity, heroism or example of a person and of the order created or revealed by him'. Its contrast with other forms of legitimacy derived from that extreme personalization of the duty of obedience to a unique, outstanding and exceptional command:

> In the case of legal domination, obedience lends itself to an impersonal and objective legal system and persons established by that regulation under the formal legality of his commands and within the scope of those people. In the case of traditional domination, obedience lends itself to a competent person by virtue of the tradition and linked to the tradition by virtue of personal loyalty. In the case of charismatic domination, the leader with charismatic qualities is obeyed by virtue of the personal confidence in his heroism, relevance, or exemplary character in which the belief in that charisma was enshrined.[80]

Following that fruitful Weberian category, writers of the age and after would underline the novelty of the new charismatic regimes that concentrated all state power in a singular person (the 'personal power' of Georges Burdeau) who was a depositary of *plenitudo potestatis*, for a lifetime, without time restrictions and in an uncontested manner. This was the modern dictator who, as highlighted in 1921 by the jurist Carl Schmitt, was not only the classic dictator (limited to the performance of a mission) and necessarily temporary, but a true sovereign and constituent dictator destined to stay (because he was the source of law and founder of a new regime).[81]

In short, the new charismatic dictator defined a magistracy of absolute, unique and unrepeatable power precisely by that 'charisma' that must be understood as the quality of the ruling sovereign to which the governed are subject de facto and *de iure*, recognizing his legitimacy, his prestige and his authority according to his uniqueness and significance for the country, nation or group. It was a kind of 'immense Caesar' of flesh and bone, bearer of an extraordinary mission to be the saviour of a nation, people or class and the guarantee of its renaissance: the author and recipient of new forms of civil 'political religion' or of a religious sanctification of politics.[82] That was the novel doctrine of legitimation of the absolute power of Italian Fascism in the person of Mussolini, of National-Socialism in the figure of Hitler and even of Soviet Communism around Stalin, all models well known and disseminated long before the Spanish war created the context for the implementation of the principles in the case of Franco.[83]

As an illustrative example of that new charismatic legitimacy as a source of sovereign authority, one should remember the degree of the mythologized personal cult of the Duce in Italy, which spawned Fascism as a central part of its civil and secular 'political religion' (according to Emilio Gentile). In March 1934 the organ of the Fascist Youth proclaimed the mythical and supernatural virtues of the 'new God of Italy' with these rhetorical clichés common until almost the end of the regime:

> His figure stands out, already monolithic, now, in history, in projections for the future, dominating men and things, as a prince of the state, as a genius of the race, as redeemer of Italy, as a Roman, in reality and in myth, of imperial Rome, as the personification and synthesis of the popular ideal, as the great initiated [...]. He followed from the beginning the practice of the hero [who] sets off alone to conquer the world, who exists before and only in his creation of the spirit [...] Mussolini has been the shining light, he is the inspiring and creative genius: he is the animator who drags and conquers; it is he: the solid entirety of myth and reality.[84]

In the subsequent case of National Socialism, it is appropriate to recall the features and contexts which, according to the canonical analysis of Franz Neumann (in 1942), were essential characteristics of that 'Germanic religion' that responded to a concept of political leadership defined under the formula of the Führer Prinzip:

Adolf Hitler is the supreme leader. He combines the functions of supreme legislator, supreme administrator and supreme judge. He is the leader of the party, army and people. In his person the power of the state, the people and the movement are unified. [...] That person is the lifelong Führer. [...] He is independent of the other institutions. [...] Right is what the Führer wants and legislation emanates from his power. Similarly, the Führer embodies the administrative power, which is exercised in his name. He is the supreme chief of the armed forces and supreme and final judge. His power is legally and constitutionally unlimited. [...] The supreme leadership is not an institution governed by rules and precedents nor a position of delegated authority, but the investiture of power in one person, Adolf Hitler. The justification of this principle is charismatic: it is based on the claim that the Führer is endowed with qualities that ordinary mortals do not have. From him emanates superhuman qualities that penetrate into the state, party and people. [...] In periods of civil war, religious disturbance and deep social and economic upheavals that produce misery and pain, men are sometimes unable – or are deliberately unable – to perceive the laws of the process that has led them to this situation. The less rational strata of society are looking for leaders. Like primitive men, they look for a saviour who removes their misery and frees them from poverty. There is always a factor of calculation, frequently on both sides. The leader uses and enhances the sense of reverent fear; henchmen flock round him to achieve their aims.

Obedience is a necessary element of charismatic leadership, both subjective obedience – as an onerous burden – as well as objective – as a means of forcing the fulfilment of duty.[85]

The doctrines of legitimation of the power of Franco in Spain used these theories of charismatic power abundantly and profusely to justify the Spanish *caudillaje* of a 'divine Caesar of a fulminant victory' (in the words of the hyperbolic Giménez Caballero). But, as has been pointed out, unlike the cases mentioned above, the creation of a new type of charismatic authority around the figure of a military leader who had waged and won a civil war combined several unique components: (1) military support that always underpinned Franco's role of Generalissimo with 'all the powers of the state' by express delegation of his comrades in arms; (2) religious support that converted him into a 'crusader of the faith of Christ' and a 'providential man' anointed by God to govern the nation; and (3) political support that placed him as national leader of the only official party of the regime, 'only responsible before God and history'.

The result of the merging in a personal 'single command' of those diverse yet complementary powers of legitimation (military, religious and political) was the attribution to Franco of the title of caudillo of Spain, by the joint willingness of the army, by the grace of God administered by the Catholic hierarchy and by the leadership of the single-party state which consolidated and organized his civilian supporters. A good example of this symbiosis in propaganda terms can be seen on the cover of the newspaper *Abc* (the 'largest in circulation of National Spain') on the second anniversary of the 'glorious uprising of the army', on 18 July 1938. The text (which could be the archetype of the tributes of the Francoist press at that time) was a declaration of faith of combined National Catholicism, national militarism and national syndicalism whose apex and keystone was the charismatic figure of the Caudillo:

> We believe in God. We believe in Spain. We believe in Franco. We trust in God. We trust in Spain. We trust in Franco. We love God. We love Spain. We love Franco. [...]
>
> Our rapport with the ideal of a united and traditional fatherland, faithful to the spirit of the glorious dead of the crusade, its martyrs and heroes, today has a strict, unambiguous, sign that is designated to us by the hand of God and for the destiny of Spain. This sign is Franco. With Franco, with the national Movement, that he not only leads, but of which he is the architect, inspiration and creator, with whatever Franco thinks, feels and wants, we solemnly reiterate our identification with this day of 18 July, in

order to commemorate the date in which the faith and patriotic love of the providential man redeemed Spain.[86]

Of course, the passage of time would not change the tone of the celebration, despite the changes in context. The newspaper *Extremadura* (Cáceres) demonstrated this on 18 July 1946, featuring a portrait of Franco with the caption 'CAUDILLO AND LORD', reiterating his exceptional qualities: 'Franco, captain of the victory, national caudillo of the Falange, supreme commander of the armies, head of state, a synthesis of the highest Spanish virtue saved in July 1936'. And 20 years later, as part of the festivities of 1 October 1966, the same newspaper renewed its vows of loyalty to the 'Caudillo of Spain' in appreciation of the 30 years of peace and prosperity achieved under his mandate, 'asking God to continue to bless him in the highest task, preserving for many years his precious life for the good of the fatherland, which is protected by his trusted hand'. Just two years earlier, on the occasion of a visit by the papal legate to the basilica of the Valle de los Caídos, the nerve centre of the cult of the Caudillo in the Franco regime, Admiral Carrero Blanco had revived that charismatic authority of Franco with a resonant speech widely reported by the Spanish press:

The divine goodness, moved no doubt, by the sacrifice of so many martyrs [in the Civil War], gave us an exemplary caudillo who not only led us to victory on 1 April 1939, but also knew how to cut sharply at the origin of the evil to fix it at its root, settling the political future of the fatherland on the redemptive formula to join the social with the national under the rule of the spiritual. To him we the Spaniards owe our freedom, our inner peace and that our children and our grandchildren are educated in the Catholic faith. The free world is indebted to him for not permitting a communist state in the Iberian Peninsula, where, as has happened in Central Europe, the Church would be silenced. The same day that our war was ended, the Caudillo promulgated a decree ordering the erection of a monument to perpetuate the memory of the fallen, to honour those who gave their lives for God and country, and to serve as an example to future generations.[87]

Obviously, the careful presentation of Franco in the Spanish press was a response to the iron-fisted government control of the media that had already been imposed during the Civil War, and the subsequent promotion of him, both personally and politically, was carefully monitored by the bodies responsible for official propaganda. For example, one should remember the tenor of the binding instructions to all the newspapers sent in November 1941 and December 1942 by the Delegación Nacional de Prensa (National Delegation of the Press), the branch of the Home Ministry in charge of censorship and media control:

> All newspapers should publish, at least, one photograph of the Caudillo in the foreground [...]. Newspapers will devote very special attention within the important events celebrated today to the speech delivered by the Caudillo that will be published in full on the front page. The composition should be full-page in bold and with a space of more than a column.[88]

The Charismatic Cult of the Spanish Caudillo and its Legal-Political Formulation

The resulting personality cult of Franco as mythologized caudillo of Spain thus became one of the central elements of the propaganda apparatus of the regime and its socio-political foundation. Clear proof of the attention given to this task from the beginning were the official instructions given in May 1937 to the newsreel films. At the end of their transmissions there should be an official portrait of Franco accompanied by the national anthem. A year later, instructions in this regard were exhaustive and revealing of the willingness to mythologize the Caudillo as a nearly divine personage: 'All news dedicated to the Caudillo or on which he noticeably appears, must be included at the end of the newsreel and always, if possible, with a glorifying finish of apotheosis.'[89]

Aside from the political propaganda of variable quality and of the workings of the political leadership and official journalists, the development of the legitimizing doctrinal body was under the control of a remarkable group of jurists, most of whom occupied influential chairs of political law and philosophy of law in Spanish universities (conveniently cleansed of enemies) and directed and monopolized the new Institute of Political Studies, established in 1939 to serve those same aims and purposes.[90]

One of the first authors in this task was the young and prolific traditionalist jurist Francisco Elías de Tejada Spínola (1917–78), who soon became a professor at Salamanca and then at Seville and Madrid. Not long after the victory in 1939, the brochure *La figura del Caudillo* stated that the Caudillo was 'essentially a military leader triumphant', a new 'Alexander' who 'has no Achilles heel' and was a 'source of sovereignty' because 'he is predestined by God to govern a political society in the moments in which the normal organization cannot fulfil its mission'. In tune with his affiliation, Tejada Spínola claimed intellectual support from both Catholic political theologists (Jaime Balmes and Donoso Cortés) and modern scholars (Carl Schmitt and the Italian Fascists Cesarini Sforza and Carlo Costamagna).[91]

Parallel and simultaneous to this, another jurist with Falangist affiliations formed in Bologna, Juan Beneyto Pérez (1907–94), also undertook in 1939 the task of justifying the doctrine, backed by Arrigo Solmi, Mussolini's justice minister. His famous book entitled *El Nuevo Estado Español* underlined the military origins of the Caudillo as a requisite 'of the principle of single command', and that he became 'leader in the war' and 'leader in the peace' because he was 'the supreme and total leader' with a main function: 'Governing is not only to execute, but to be in charge, to legislate most precisely.' The book ended by recalling with approval the words of the secretary general of FET y de las JONS, Raimundo Fernández Cuesta, in celebration of the second anniversary of the national uprising in Valladolid on 18 July 1938:

The Caudillo is not a head of government or a vulgar dictator. He is the charismatic chief, the man appointed by the finger of Providence to save his people. A figure that is more than judicial, historical, philosophical, that falls outside the limits of political science to enter the role of hero of Carlyle or Nietzsche's Superman.[92]

In 1939, the same year as the victory, a work signed by Beneyto and José María Costa Serrano reiterated the singular providential uniqueness of the power of Franco with these words: 'The Caudillo is the total conception and an accumulator of historical functions, legislator, judge, supreme executor and party chief. He penetrates all social and political life.'[93]

In 1941, during the culminating moment of the regime's identification with the powers of the German–Italian Axis in World War II, another jurist of renown with a chair in Madrid, Luis Jordana de Pozas (1890–1983), published in the journal of the Institute of Political Studies a dense article on 'The Principle of Unity' based on a clear-cut premise: 'If power is unitary, it has to be incarnated in one single man who exercises it in an effective and personal way.' For this reason the Burgos junta in 1936 had decided to eliminate a 'division of powers' and to transfer 'all the powers of the state' to Franco, including in its wisdom not only legislative and executive power, but also 'the judicial function' ('even if that power continued to be exercised by judges and courts'). The resulting institution of the *caudillaje*, in the person of Franco, was part of the process that 'the states arising from national revolutions' were experiencing (Italy, Portugal and Germany were expressly mentioned in similar terms). And, in keeping with the National Catholic affiliation of the author, one of the advantages of the Spanish case was precisely the religious quality of the Caudillo, evoked in a quotation from a speech delivered at the second National Council of FET: 'One single legitimate authority in its origins and in the vocation of its will [...] governs, with God's help, the destiny of Spain towards the realization of its historical enterprise leading the national revolution.'[94]

Just a year later, in 1942, when the course of the war began to take an adverse turn for the Axis powers, another Spanish Falangist jurist assumed the task of formulating a 'doctrine of the *caudillaje*' to substantiate the legitimacy of Franco's powers in a way that was to become the canonical doctrinal piece on the subject. Francisco Javier Conde García (1908–74), shaped in Germany under the guidance of Carl Schmitt (whose work he translated into Spanish), would be professor of political law at the University of Santiago de Compostela and later at Madrid until entering the diplomatic service in 1946 and enjoying a long and distinguished career. Conde was going to be, par excellence, 'the *caudillaje* theorist' (according to Alberto Reig Tapia) and 'one of the most brilliant interpreters of the new state' (in the words of Ferran Gallego).[95]

First in the pages of the official journal of the Falange, *Arriba,* and then in a book with the resonant title *Contribución a la doctrina del caudillaje,*

Conde stressed that the *caudillaje* was an institution that was supposed to fuse the highest will of unity of command and the faith in a providential man, charismatically legitimized (even though this legitimacy did not exclude Spanish tradition but rather assumed it). He also remarked that military victory, as a barely sublimated right of conquest, was the most legitimate power base for charismatic authority: 'The form of military command is the most precise and practical way to ensure the organization of power, because it reaches the highest degree of rigour in command and security in obedience.' In his argument, '*acaudillar* [i.e. to lead] is, above all, to command legitimately' (not a mere provisional dictatorship, according to the terminology of Schmitt), '*acaudillar* is to command charismatically' (because the exceptional nature of the Caudillo generates unlimited devotion) and '*acaudillar* is to command personally' (because in emergencies power has to be undivided to be effective and cannot limit its decisions for any formal reason). In a fair appreciation of the need for integration of other related political cultures (and the uncertainty of the coming times), Conde also added that charismatic legitimacy could assume or become traditional legitimacy thanks to the constitutional process (summoning of the Cortes, the subsequent definition of the state as a 'kingdom', etc.): 'The prevalence of the charismatic element in the *caudillaje* does not exclude the principle of traditional legitimacy.'[96]

With less critical but equal political conviction, the same year, at the height of Nazi–Fascist influence on the Spanish regime, a Falangist comrade explained in a simple manual the Caudillo's nature as saviour and father of Spain through his status as undefeated and victorious warrior, which empowered him to undertake the path of total regeneration of a Spain redeemed by the blood and the sword of its sins against God and history:

When a nation reaches the state of decomposition that ours had reached, there can be no salvation if there is not a profound and social change, with a new conception of the state; that is, a national revolution, and this national revolution demands at the forefront a figure, not the 'leader' of a democratic party, nor a head of government not even that of a vulgar and well-known dictator, but the figure of a Caudillo, a charismatic leader (a free gift that God grants to this creature), a man appointed by the finger of Providence, who escapes the limits of political science to become the 'supernatural hero' or the Superman. [...] The *caudillaje* is reverent before the superior and arises by God's mandate reflected in historical evolution, therefore the Caudillo is born alone, elected on his own merits and when this moment arrives undisputed and indisputable. He is accepted as caudillo by virtue of his triumphant sword, the clarity of his decisions, the sharpness of his vision to command and show the way forward. Destiny gave Spain this exceptional man in the most painful of all her challenges.[97]

The year 1942 also witnessed the emergence of the second revised edition of a doctrinal text that defined, from fundamentalist Catholic tenets, the specifics of the Spanish regime in an international context and as a result of 'the deep crisis of historical democracy'. Its author was Luis del Valle Pascual, professor of political law at Zaragoza, and the title of the work was *Democracia y Jerarquía*. It was an attempt to explain the origin and structure of the regime from the idea of overcoming the 'purely formal, inorganic and completely empirical democracy of the forgers of constitutionalism', regimes corrupted for being 'democracies, of numerical majorities, levelling and egalitarian, democracies of individuals'. To accomplish that, he formulated and collected concepts and ideas that would have a wide circulation in later years, when the Axis had been defeated and the victory of the Western democracies forced the reformulation of the defining categories of the 'new Spanish state'. Del Valle Pascual postulated the greater effectiveness of models of 'organic democracy', based on the basic social forms (corporations, families, classical municipalities) and formulated by a 'command hierarchy' according to 'a fair principle of selection'. At the front would be a 'head of state' who would be 'the pinnacle of this selection of citizens', chosen 'by the will expressed by the people by enthusiastic acclamation or plebiscite', who was the recipient of 'their full and entire confidence' and became 'supreme leader and director, commander and guide of the people'. Of course, the best model of such a system was that of 'the current Spain, around the great figure of the Caudillo', a providential and charismatic leader who guaranteed 'a more perfect unit of direction and sovereign decision'. A caudillo, moreover, whose history and career 'will serve the divine plan and will be close to the designs of God'.[98]

A comprehensive review of that legal-political propaganda generated by the regime during the crucial years of the Civil War and the world war requires at least a mention of the works of other jurists or equally prestigious political scientists: Luis Legaz Lacambra, Luis Sánchez Agesta, José Antonio Maravall, José Pemartín, Ignacio María de Lojendio, Juan Candela-Martínez, etc.[99] However, expanding the overview in that way would hardly change the process of creating the charismatic leadership of Franco. Neither would it alter the crucial role played in that process by the triad of institutional pillars holding up his regime of personal authority: the triple status of Generalissimo, providential man and supreme *Pater Patriae*.

The passage of time and the changes in international context did not substantially modify the official doctrine of charismatic legitimacy of the Spanish regime, even when the defeat of fascism and the brief international ostracism suffered by the dictatorship damaged its legal and political credentials within and outside Spain. It did alter the nature of the regime, though: the transition without trauma from the national-syndicalist state that shaped the Fuero del Trabajo (1938), the Catholic and organic democracy prescribed by the Fuero de los Españoles (1945), to the Catholic, social and representative monarchy of the Ley de Sucesión (1947) and the state of rational administration of works and services which the Ley Orgánica del Estado (1967) postulated.[100]

The reading of the official legal formulations after 1945 proves the persistence of the *caudillaje* under the new institutional moulds and conceptual frameworks. In 1951, with Franco's Spain in the process of slow rehabilitation in the context of the Cold War, a young jurist named Manuel Fraga Iribarne (1922–2012), who was then professor of political law at Valencia (later at Madrid), renewed the traditional charismatic foundation with a dose of technocratic and functionalist validation more in keeping with the times (and consciously stressing its exceptionalism and consequent uniqueness). His book was titled *Así se gobierna España* and was intended, primarily, for Western international circles within which the regime tried tentatively to reinstate itself, with growing success:

The Spanish people, in full crisis of coexistence, had accepted the supreme leadership of Franco to defeat communism militarily; but, at the same time, it asked him to reconstitute the country politically under the form of the most authentic *caudillaje*, in the better sense of the word. Seeing the failure of governments to organize the country since the crisis of 1931, it was hoped that this time there would be a single and true caudillo who would give new laws, a new constitution to the community. Like Solon, like Cromwell, like so many other national heroes, General Franco was to be father of the country, and return it to normality and order. [...] Currently, the head of state assumes the presidency of the government and occupies a position more like that of a president of a republic than that of a regent. Let's not forget that the situation is properly one of a power in emergency. That is to say that the command of Franco represents an extraordinary concentration of powers to deal with difficult circumstances; but not a tyrannical power imposed on the nation, which recognized him on all occasions as its caudillo.[101]

A decade later, in 1961, another professor of the same discipline (at the University of Oviedo) and later an equally important political protagonist, Torcuato Fernández-Miranda (1915–80), wrote a widely used textbook (*El hombre y la sociedad*) that would be one of the latest doctrinal formulations of the *caudillaje* adapted to the new times of technocratic development. Fernández-Miranda rescued the magisterium of Weber and its three types of political legitimacy (rational, traditional and charismatic) but connected it with Spanish Catholic traditional thought and its three types of legal authority (by succession, election and acquisition or conquest). In addition, he explained and justified the *caudillaje* with very explicit historical and functionalist reasons (again, exceptional and unique):

If in a situation of grave danger, a ship is without a captain and anyone who *normally* replaces him, the person that in the midst of anarchy was able to impose his voice and his command would be automatically, with total legitimacy, the ship's captain. Similarly, with the exercise of power in situations of social shipwreck and institutional power-vacuum, the person who is capable of prompting the *consent of the people* and being a director or conductor of the same, is, exceptionally, but with undoubted legitimate title, caudillo. The exposed doctrine is, ultimately, the doctrine of the *conquest*, as the legitimate source of power, of Saint Thomas Aquinas and of our Spanish theological lawyers of our golden age, Vitoria, Suárez, etc. Indeed, it responds to these concepts [...] the *caudillaje*, established as an exception. The process of permanent civil war, latent or expressed, in Spanish life since Fernando VII, reached its peak in the anarchy of the Second Republic, making civil war inevitable. From that war arose the conductor or caudillo of the crusade, in the person of Francisco Franco, *inspired* by a National Movement and proclaimed by the adhesion of national Spain.[102]

Finally, in 1973, in the critical phase of late-Francoism, an influential work by José Zafra Valverde, a member of Opus Dei and professor of political law at the University of Navarra saw the light in *Régimen político de España*. The book's author recognized unequivocally the uniqueness of a regime of 'national leadership' (*caudillaje*) that conferred on Franco 'a political office in which sovereignty is concentrated in the strictest way' and in 'the double meaning of the maximum capacity and the maximum authority' and its derivations: 'functions of authority or persuasive control, constituent, legislative and supreme administration, executive and judicial'. Such a concentration of sovereign authority had its foundation in the 'legitimacy of origin' (the victorious defence against the Communist revolution begun by the army in July 1936) combined with a 'legitimacy of exercise' ('Peace, economic progress and social justice are the three concepts that summarize the positive balance of governmental work'). This dual genetic legitimacy, effectively endorsed by what the author called '*ductoria* and *soterica*' legitimacies, is key to understanding the sovereign and absolute personal power of Franco:

> But then there is the fact of the marked personalization of political sovereignty, which from the beginning has been the fulcrum of the regime. [...] As well, in this respect we noted two forms or cases of political legitimacy that have projected their stimulating light on an ongoing will to command and a collective intent to consent. First was what we might well call a *ductoria* legitimacy (from the Latin *ductor*: guide or leader); then, and with greater fortune, a legitimacy for which we propose the title of *soterica* (from the Greek *soter*: saviour).[103]

But the doctrinal formulations generated by those circles, with all their variations and modulations, could not hide (nor wanted to) the profoundly anti-liberal and anti-democratic nature of the regime's caudillo.[104] Nor could it avoid the greater problem of any regime of charismatic and exceptional personal power: the problem of the successor to the unique leader. As Georges Burdeau also noted, it is all about regimes in which 'it is known who commands, but ignored who has the right to command' because 'the succession of personalities who embody all power' cannot be codified charismatically.[105] This serious defect of charismatic legitimation led to a process of 'institutionalization', which, as already observed by Max Weber, necessarily resulted in its transformation into other forms of legitimacy, either traditional (with the monarchy or similar historical institutions), or rational (resorting to representative election in any of its variations).

Despite the fact that the Francoist jurists had perceived the problem very early (and the succession law of 1947 was an attempt to square the doctrinal circle), in the 1960s it became increasingly more acute as Franco got older.[106] By then, the divergence of the jurists' criteria would reproduce the divergence of opinion among the political and social leaders of the Franco regime. The *continuistas* (later called *inmovilistas*) gambled on keeping the essence of the regime without Franco through the institutions of the regime and with a monarch established but limited in his powers by those institutions: 'After Franco, the institutions,' according to the political formula coined in 1966 by Jesús Fueyo Álvarez, a young professor of political law and director of the Institute of Political Studies. That was the option that Franco himself, encouraged by his alter ego, Admiral Luis Carrero Blanco, had contemplated from the outset: 'The succession of the National Movement is the National Movement, without mystifications.'[107]

The *aperturistas* (later *reformistas*) felt that there would be no possibility of Francoism without Franco and the successor to the title of king (chosen in 1969) should lead the transition to another liberal-democratic formula by will or by force. Such was the open alternative of Fraga Iribarne before the death of the Caudillo: 'democratic legitimacy is to be recognized in the election by universal suffrage of a representative Chamber.' It would also be a more veiled initiative by Fernández-Miranda, former tutor of the King and one of the great architects of a transitional process 'without the formal breakdown of legality', but with a resolute end: 'the monarchy of 18 July is meaningless. The monarchy cannot be blue, nor Falangist, nor even Francoist. [...] The monarchy has to be democratic.'[108]

In any case, alternatives to the succession problem, painful in the years 1973–5 with Franco an octogenarian and progressively less capable of regularly fulfilling his duties, would not alter the foundations of political legitimacy of his personal and unique *caudillaje*: 'While the protagonist of an era in the history of Spain lived, it was impossible to consider substantial changes.'[109] For this reason, in the eyes of international observers disinclined to support the doctrines of the charismatic *caudillaje*, the political judgement on Franco was much clearer and more negative. In 1959, shortly after Fraga Iribarne's explanation of the exceptional nature of the Francoist powers and almost at the same time as the rationalization of Fernández-Miranda over their legitimacy of conquest, the French ambassador to Spain summed up the political role of the Caudillo for his superiors in Paris with a laconic formula closer to the reality of the phenomenon: Franco was the closest thing to 'an absolute and solitary monarch'.[110] Also in that year, from his exile, Salvador de Madariaga, a liberal and tempered observer, restated it in a more exhaustive and denunciatory way: Franco was an autocratic dictator on a par with 'a military and clerical reactionary'.[111] It was a way to point out the persistent 'original sin' of Francoism as a personal dictatorship that no legal doctrine could hide or disguise, despite all their verbal rhetorical artifices:

The Francoist historiography (one could also say the legal doctrine) did not want ever to consider what the major problem of the Franco regime was: that it always lacked true moral legitimacy before the liberal and democratic consciousness of the contemporary world, given its origin (military revolt, civil war) and its authoritarian and repressive nature.[112]

3

THE REGIME
A Complex Dictatorship

It was not a civil war between Spaniards, although many times it has been designated that, even though our blood and that of our brothers has run in that fight: no. It was a fight between Spain and Anti-Spain. That of good against evil. We had to mutilate the body, prune the rotten and worm-eaten branches of the old Spanish trunk, eradicate the cancer that corroded us; to leave in Spain what was Spanish, what was ours, not what had come from beyond our borders to be the physical and moral ruin of the nation. [...] Therefore our movement could not be an empty movement that confined itself to the military and patriotic. We had to fill it with content, justify its *raison d'être*, it had to be for the perpetual good of the Spanish fatherland [...] Therefore it was necessary that we pruned our tree, including mutilating our body.

Speech by Franco in Madrid, 18 July 1953

What is Franquismo?

'Franquismo' (Francoism) is a recent word in Spanish contemporary history that denotes a type of political regime or system of institutional domination which governed the society, economy and culture of Spain for almost 40 years of the twentieth century, beginning in 1936 and ending in 1975.

It is not so easy to characterize the system represented by the Franco regime within the typology of political regimes in contemporary European and world history (or even only amongst those of the twentieth century). This is because the work of collation and comparison necessary to determine the place of Francoism among these systems needs to address patterns of identity, similarity and difference, depending on the criteria applied and the frames of reference used. In this respect, the parameters of collation and comparison are varied and not always consistent. There are several categorizations: (1) the classical Aristotelian trilogy of monarchy, aristocracy and democracy (and its degenerations: tyranny, oligarchy and demagoguery); (2) the triad of monarchy, republic and regency; (3) the categories of despotism, absolutism and liberalism; (4) variants of dictatorship (praetorian, military, civil-military), autocracy (traditional, elective, charismatic) and democracy (representative, parliamentary, presidential); (5) the binomial of Caesarism and Bonapartism; (6) the alternative of authoritarianism and totalitarianism, etc.

In any case, be it one or another of those systems (or a combination of several), what is not in any doubt is that the noun 'Franquismo' has an indubitable primary significance: it refers to a political regime with all the connotations that, from Aristotle onwards, have fashioned the public sphere of politics as a social activity organized to exercise power and shape authority within a human collective. It takes into account, of course, that power is the strength or ability of some individuals to influence others so that they will act according to the will of the former, and that authority is the legalized, legitimate and effective power of rulers which relies on voluntary, enthusiastic or resigned obedience ('to lead is not to force', in the famous phrase of the philosopher José Ortega y Gasset).

Thus, Franquismo is a particular form of organization of state power to attend to the political functions that define an organized and civilized human community. That is, a community where power is no longer only coercive brute force but has become the authority to impose duties and demand obedience to exercise a wide range of responsibilities: the legislative functions concerning the formulation of rules and regulations of communal life; the executive functions that involve decisions and actions exercised by public authorities and rulers; and the judicial functions insofar as they affect the administration of justice which maintains the *eutaxia* (balancing order amid the inevitable conflicts) of the state.

'Franquismo' also implies a second historical and political feature that significantly distinguishes it. The term has been coined to denote a system linked to a given historical figure, a unique character: General Francisco Franco

Bahamonde, who was born in El Ferrol on 4 December 1892 and died in Madrid on 20 November 1975. That is, the eponymous regime is defined by the person who exerted the maximum political power and supreme public authority in an almost absolute way during his long time in office. Of course, this does not mean that Franquismo was only the work of Franco since the system was not built, directed and maintained by a single man, even if his powers were theoretically unlimited. It means, simply, that Franco was the bulwark at the centre of public authority and the exercise of political power, without any superiors to query, limit or review his decisions and mandates.

This personification of the political regime in a singular individual is a key and crucial element in the conceptualization of Franquismo for obvious reasons. So much so that one of the great historians of the Franco regime, Javier Tusell, expressed this factor in one of the first works dedicated to examining the matter historiographically: 'Any attempt to arrive at a full description of Francoism and its fundamental characteristics would fail if it intended to circumvent the role played by the personality of Franco in the dictatorship which ruled Spain from 1939 to 1975.'[1]

Almost all historians and social analysts (jurists, political scientists, sociologists, economists) who studied Francoism share this judgement of the indissoluble marriage between the man and the regime that gives rise to the term 'Franquismo'. By way of illustration, the explanation in one of the first books dedicated to examining the history of the era, published shortly after the death of Franco by two prestigious historians, the British Hispanist Raymond Carr and his Spanish pupil Juan Pablo Fusi, should be recalled: 'Franco has been for nearly 40 years Caudillo of Spain, thus embodying the one-man government of the longest duration in the modern history of Europe.'[2] Taking the same explanatory line is one of the last major works dedicated to the global study of Francoism, the work of the historian Borja de Riquer i Permanyer:

If this work is titled *La dictadura de Franco* [*The Francoist Dictatorship*] it is because I wanted to emphasize the markedly personal nature of the political regime established in Spain by the victors of the war. It was a historical stage in which the dictator was always the key and fundamental part of political life. Without him, this dictatorial regime would have been unthinkable. Francisco

Franco did not, in fact, have an immediate political substitute nor one in the medium term. He was a decisive, fundamental and irreplaceable character of the political system. In few epochs of history – none in the contemporary period – has the fate of Spaniards depended on a regime as personal and arbitrary as that of the dictatorship of General Franco. [...] Therefore the Spanish dictatorship will commonly receive the nickname of 'franquista', a denomination that does not apply in the same way to its counterpart totalitarian systems, which will be more known by the name of the single party – Fascist or National Socialist – than by the surname of the dictator.[3]

The declaration of principles by Carr and Fusi underlines, in addition, a third decisive feature for the conceptualization of the Franco regime that should be emphasized and stressed: its extremely long duration. In other words, the model of socio-political domination that is called Franquismo had an exceptional longevity in Spanish contemporary history (and also in European history of the twentieth century). That the regime, its evolution and development, existed for almost 40 years (from 1936 to 1975) stands out in comparison with other similar movements.

Regarding the historical evolution of Spain in the nineteenth and twentieth centuries, the Francoist era constitutes the longest, after the liberal-oligarchic regime of the Bourbon Restoration (1874–1923). The comparison is not entirely apposite because the restored monarchy, during its almost 50 years of existence, recorded the reign of two kings (Alfonso XII and Alfonso XIII) and a long regency (that of Queen María Cristina de Habsburgo-Lorena), while the Franco regime had only one head of state during its four decades: General Franco himself, who took office aged only 43 in 1936 until his death at the age of almost 83 in 1975. In addition, this extraordinary tenure took place in an international context of rapid historical change and enormous and crucial transformations of all kinds: the global crisis of the 1930s, which in Spain ended in civil war; the six years of World War II between 1939 and 1945; a stage of postwar reconstruction and the Cold War during the second half of the 1940s and the early 1950s; a phase of economic expansion and international détente in the 1960s; and a period of recession and economic crisis during the first half of the 1970s.

The lengthy existence of the Francoist regime, along with its obvious correlative evolution, mean it is essential that any study aiming for rigorous historical understanding pays particular attention to this aspect. As Javier Tusell, in the aforementioned work, emphasized aptly: 'In a large part, the peculiarity of the Franco regime lies in its duration.'[4] Something very similar was highlighted by the American Hispanist Stanley G. Payne, author of an earlier study on Franquismo published in 1987; it is considered one of the best historical introductions to the era:

> The definition and classification of the regime became, obviously, increasingly complex as it extended in time. This is due in part to the same phenomenon of persistence, as it coexisted with the fascist and post-fascist social democratic eras, but even to a greater extent to the successive metamorphoses of the politics and priorities of the regime. Nietzsche once said that 'that with history cannot be defined', and certainly the Franco system had a longer history and suffered more historical changes than the majority of non-Marxist dictatorships.[5]

A similar premise has more recently been pointed out by another scholar of fascist and authoritarian phenomena in twentieth-century Europe. In the words of Robert O. Paxton, attention is drawn to the diachrony by the clear evolution of the Franco dictatorship over its 40 years of existence:

> In conclusion, a single isolated photograph from the Franco regime cannot be taken to determine what degree of importance and power the Falange (and fascism) had. The role of the movement changed over time and its power was different in several institutions. [...] At the end, in the last decade preceding the death of Franco, the regime was no longer the one that had gone a long way on the path of fascism. It had come close to Juan Linz's model of 'authoritarianism', although it had not lost all its fascist traits. The change had been both gradual and incomplete.[6]

The Debate on the Nature of Franquismo

The features of Franquismo (its status as a political regime linked to the figure of Franco and to exceptional longevity) constitute the three key assumptions for approaching what is conventionally named 'the debate on the nature of Franquismo'. That debate is a discussion (not only academic) of the appropriate conceptual definition for understanding and comprehending the type of political regime and model of social domination seen in Spain from 1936 and in force until 1975. It is an intense and long-lasting, perhaps even insoluble and unending, controversy that has involved many protagonists – policy analysts, jurists, economists, sociologists and historians. In essence, such a debate aims to define the characteristics of the Francoist political system by framing it comparatively in the different types of political systems existing in Europe and the world during the twentieth century.[7]

This definition in comparative perspective, far from being a trivial or contrived practice, constitutes a basic intellectual exercise to understand the historical causes of the origin, structure and evolution of the Spanish regime and thus clarify its links, similarities and differences with contemporary or modern political systems. It should be remembered that the first act of human knowledge is to give a distinct name to things to identify, collate and distinguish one from another in the intersubjective communication process. Accordingly, the first requirement of scientific-social knowledge is the logic of the rigorous and unambiguous conceptual definition of the analysed phenomenon to avoid misunderstandings, ambiguities, contradictions or the simply absurd: exercising the art of distinction against the vice of confusion. In the understanding of historical phenomena such as Franquismo, the comparative lens is compulsory, as pointed out by Max Weber in 1914 in response to the objections of a historian reluctant to apply comparative methods in research:

> I see it thus: that which is specific to the medieval city – something that History ought to reveal (on this we are in total agreement!) – can only be discerned by establishing what is missing in other cities (ancient, Chinese, Islamic), and so it is with everything. After that, it is the task of History to causally explain to us this specificity.[8]

The discussion on the definition of Franquismo as a particular case of political regime began during the Spanish Civil War of 1936–9. From the first moment, there were two large nuclei of alternative interpretation which, to a large extent, still survive today as the logical ends of a broader spectrum. Generalizing greatly, one could say that both interpretative schools basically agreed to conceive the July 1936 military insurrection, along with its civilian support in society, as a reactionary, counter-revolutionary and counter-reformist movement whose main purpose was to defend the class interests and traditionally dominant institutions from the realities of the socio-political reforms of the Republican government and the revolutionary threat of an organized, mobilized and very demanding working class. Apart from this basic agreement on the *social functions* of the insurgent side, the crucial difference between the two interpretations was the consideration of the *political nature* of that anti-reformist and counter-revolutionary reaction led by the insurgent army and headed by General Franco. In essence, the questions are:

1 Was it an extreme case of a traditionally conservative military dictatorship, such as those that existed then in other parts of Europe following the end of the Great War of 1914–18 and during the interwar period (like that of Marshal Pilsudski in Poland or Admiral Horthy in Hungary) and as Spain had already known in the same period (with the dictatorship of General Miguel Primo de Rivera between 1923 and 1930, for example)?

2 Or did it rather represent a Spanish version of the new fascist and totalitarian European regimes in that interwar era arising from the mobilization of sectors of civil society against democratic reform, social revolution and traditional reaction, as had first taken life and shape in the Italy of Benito Mussolini from 1922 and then with greater radicalism in Adolf Hitler's Germany in 1933?

The first interpretation used the new concept of 'dictatorship' that emerged in the contemporary period based on its original Latin meaning: a regime of force and exception created provisionally to overcome a grave crisis or emergency of state. That was the classical meaning of the 'commissarial dictatorship', because it was intended to commit a service and end after completing its mission. The new concept of 'dictatorship', as stated by the German pro-Nazi jurist Carl Schmitt in 1921, was not an exceptional temporary institution but a 'sovereign' regime with the intention of permanence (sovereignty, according to Jean Bodin, being the 'absolute and perpetual power that the Latinos call Majesty'). Its first most finished form was the domination of a group (such as the Committee of Public Health in Revolutionary France in 1793) or an individual (such as Napoleon after his coup of 1799) who assumes *plenitudo potestatis* (full state power) and pursues it without limitation because *dictator est qui dictat* (a dictator is one who dictates: 'dictate' in Latin being synonymous with 'order' or 'command').[9]

The consideration of Franquismo as a 'dictatorship' in the modern sense (which replaced the classic words of 'tyranny', 'despotism', 'autocracy' and 'absolutism') had large and prominent backing in Republican and Nationalist ranks and, later, would have substantial support among historians and social scientists. The president of the Republic and a remarkable representative of the reformist bourgeoisie, Manuel Azaña, did not hesitate to note in his diary of October 1937 the scarce modernizing features that, in his view, the Spanish right could entertain even in a war situation:

> There are or might be in Spain all the fascists you want. But there will not be a fascist regime. If force triumphs against the Republic, we would fall back under the power of a traditional ecclesiastical and military dictatorship. No matter how many slogans are translated and how many mottos are used. Swords, cassocks, military parades and homages to the Virgin of Pilar. The country can offer nothing else, as can already be seen. [...] I have explained to them thoroughly the origin, the purposes and means of the rebellion and the war; [...] the typically Spanish characteristics of the military and ecclesiastical dictatorship that the rebels implanted, whatever slogans are raised and the colour of their shirts.[10]

Paradoxically, the same opinion of the non-viability of full fascism in Spain had been put forward three years previously, in 1934, by the journalist Luis Araquistáin, the éminence grise of the radical socialist left and furious critic of Azaña's style of republicanism:

In Spain, an Italian or German type of fascism cannot be produced. There is no demobilized army, as in Italy; there are not hundreds of thousands of students without a future, nor millions of unemployed, as in Germany. There is no Mussolini, not even a Hitler; there are no imperialist ambitions, or feelings of revenge, or problems of expansion, not even the Jewish question. From what ingredients could Spanish fascism be made? I can't imagine the recipe.[11]

It is not surprising that, a month after the Civil War began, these judgements by prominent Republican leaders were also shared, with regret, by José Antonio Primo de Rivera, founder and leader of the then tiny Spanish fascist party, the Falange Española, from his jail in Alicante. Before being executed in November 1936, José Antonio recorded his concerns:

What will happen if the rebels win? A group of generals with honourable intention but of bleak political mediocrity. Basic elemental values (order, pacification ...) Behind: (1) old Carlism, intransigent, closed-minded, unfriendly; (2) conservative class interests, short-term, lazy; (3) agricultural and financial capitalism: the ending in many years of any possibility of constructing a modern Spain. The lack of any long-term national sense.[12]

It is revealing that this same opinion was harboured by prominent Nationalist leaders both then and later. For example, General Francisco Franco Salgado-Araujo, cousin and military secretary of Franco, would write in his diary on 28 October 1955 what was, in his opinion, the essence of the political model of Franquismo:

There is too much talk about the Movement, unions, etc., but the reality is that the whole shebang is held up only by Franco and the army. [...] The rest [...] the Movement, unions, the Falange and other political apparatus, have not taken root in the country after 19 years of the uprising; it is sad to record it, but it is the truth.[13]

Franco himself, in the privacy of his family, did not mind the use of 'dictatorship' to describe his regime. According to the testimony of his only daughter, he was not reluctant to be named a dictator:

> It didn't bother him at all, because in the end it was a dictatorship and to him, in his lifetime, the dictatorship of Primo de Rivera seemed good, it was not so demonized as now, that anyone could say, 'Uff, a dictatorship!', 'Call me a dictator!', and that didn't bother him because he felt that was what it was.[14]

However, against these judgements that in general tended to discard the possibility of the existence of a fascist regime in Spain for reasons of economic and social backwardness (in comparison to Germany and Italy) and sufficient traditional forces to maintain the desired order (the military and religious bureaucracy), there also circulated during the war a profusion of contrary opinions. For example, Luis Araquistáin, on the eve of the outbreak of the war, noted the presence of a peculiar Spanish fascism, 'cunning and overlooked', already defined not by the existence of a fascist leader supported by a mass civil party brazen in their violent conquest of the state, but by the assumption by the conservative right of a political programme focused on the violent repression of the workers' mobilization and the destruction of representative democratic and parliamentary institutions. In his words, the performance of the Catholic and monarchist right in Spain was:

> To end the social and secular content of the Republic and, eventually, the same Republic, the autonomy of Catalonia and the workers' organizations of Marxist inspiration. But this is fascism without disguise, adapted to Spanish realities. [...] A fascism supported especially by the landed classes, the Catholic Church and the army; more like that of Austria and Portugal than Italy and Germany.[15]

This consideration of fascism as a social project for the defence of a violently repressive and anti-liberal bourgeois order, irrespective of its strict political format, would receive full acceptance by almost all the Spanish and European left during the years of the Civil War and afterwards. Largely, this interpretation centred on the social roots and aims of fascism (downgrading its precise political mode), reflected the analysis carried out by European Marxist circles on the birth of the Italian and German dictatorships. In 1933, the Communist International had defined fascism as 'the open and terrorist dictatorship of the most reactionary, most chauvinistic and most imperialistic elements of finance capital'. In a similar vein, the respected Austrian Socialist leader Otto Bauer had analysed the roots and social functions of the new movements of the radical right:

> The capitalists and big agricultural landowners do not deliver the power of the state to the fascist hordes to protect themselves against the threat of the proletarian revolution, they deliver it to reduce wages, eliminate social benefits achieved by the working class, destroy unions and end positions of political power by the workers. Their aim, in other words, was not so much to suppress revolutionary socialism as to smash the achievements of reformist socialism.[16]

On this basis, once the Civil War started in Spain, for the left the term 'fascist' came to define (with obviously demonological and denunciatory shades) the enemy led by Franco as a whole, while the 'anti-fascist' epithet would become the common identity of the heterogeneous political spectrum who remained loyal to the Republic. It is significant that on the Francoist side, for the same demonological and generic reasons, the heterogeneous enemies were qualified imprecisely as 'reds' and 'Communists' without any major differentiations and nuances. The consequent use of the concept of fascism, emphasizing almost exclusively its social dimension and reducing or annulling its political form, is apparent, for example, in the first manifesto on the Civil War issued by the Communist Party of Spain in August 1936. In it, 'fascism' was defined simply as the movement, reactionary and undemocratic, unleashed against the reformist Republic by a coalition of 'priests, aristocrats, cowardly generals and young upper-class fascists':

> For many days now the soil of our country trembles under the thunder of cannons and stains of blood shed by the felony of a group of reactionary generals who, villainously betraying promises and repeated oaths of loyalty

to the Republican regime, have risen in arms after seizing the means with which the state could defend the integrity of its national territory. Traitors and thieves have allied themselves to the representative forces of the past linked in a degenerate and obscene 'senoritismo' [classism], incarnated in the fascist rabble, which in the hands of a gun-toting and criminal clergy, representative of the bloody tradition of the Inquisition, are destroying villages where they pass, committing horrific crimes, only possible to conceive in perverse imaginations or in those lacking any humanity.[17]

As the Civil War progressed, Nationalist Spain incorporated formal political elements present in Germany and Italy (a single party, fascist salute, corporate and imperial rhetoric, charismatic exaltation of the Caudillo, etc.). That identification of Franquismo with fascism was not only accentuated but also became more true. At the end of 1937, even the British diplomatic representatives in Spain – early and tacit supporters of the military revolt and privileged and unbiased witnesses to its evolution – warned their superiors in London of the fascist drift. One of them reported that Francoist Spain showed 'a strong absorption of the methods and ideas of Italian Fascism'. The British ambassador noted with concern this phenomenon:

What is emerging in the territory of Franco today is a form of national-socialism inspired by both Germany and Italy, although more the latter than the former. I think that the French have every reason to be concerned and we also. [...] In short, the Spain that emerges from a Franco victory will not be the Spain of Alfonso XIII nor the Spain of the Republic.[18]

Indeed, judging by the actions and public statements of Franco, Nationalist Spain had undergone a conscious and considered political conversion to fascism. From April 1937, the new unified party had assumed the previous Falangist programme almost entirely, affirming its inalienable 'will of empire' and the need to build a 'national syndicalist state' that would be 'a totalitarian instrument in service to the integrity of the fatherland'. And, as has already been seen, Franco himself from then and almost until 1945 lent credibility to this evolution with a new fascist rhetoric that affirmed his status as 'leader responsible before God and history' and stressed the 'missionary and totalitarian' nature of the new state that was under construction 'as in other countries of totalitarian regime'. This fascist inspiration was behind the attitude of the regime during World War II and explained its more or less open or underground logistical support of the German–Italian cause and furious anti-democratic phobia of the censored Spanish press. At the end of 1942, the Spanish Caudillo eloquently shared the intimate and secret judgement put forward by his chief political adviser and virtual alter ego, the future Admiral Carrero Blanco:

> It is clear that Spain has a decided wish to intervene on the side of the Axis, inasmuch as it fights our natural enemies that are this complex of democracies, Freemasonry, liberalism, plutocracy and communism, weapons with which the Jewish power tries to annihilate Christian civilization, whose defence is our historical mission in the universe, but our effective intervention is conditional on two circumstances: that the Iberian peninsula will become part of the strategic game of the great global contest, and that we have the physical possibility of carrying out an effective action.[19]

For this reason, according to those statements and actions, the consideration of Franquismo as the Spanish version of a fascist state was a popular opinion, both in academic circles and with the public in general. Salvador de Madariaga, a noble representative of democratic liberalism, who from the beginning of the war had declared himself incompatible with both sides, argued with particular vehemence at the end of 1944 for the identity of Franquismo with fascism:

> In vain you [Franco] attempt to present Spain abroad as a democracy. There is no worthwhile democracy. There is no trickery that can conceal taupe-coloured shirts, like Hitler, white jackets, like Hitler, dark trousers, like Hitler, the Roman salute, like Hitler, the title of Caudillo, a bad translation of *Führer*, like Hitler, the single party eating up the country in a full spree of corruption, like Hitler, the press tamed, like Hitler, beating dissidents, like Hitler, the Gestapo, like Hitler, the concentration camps, like Hitler, the shootings, like Hitler. General, go.[20]

Perhaps the peak and popular sanction of that identification took place in the immediate postwar world, with the fascist powers defeated, on the occasion of the formal condemnation of the Spanish regime issued by the three great Allied leaders at the Potsdam Conference in August 1945. The ban on the entry of Franco's Spain into the new United Nations Organization was reiterated with harsh judgements and words:

> The three governments (British, Soviet and American) feel bound, however, to make it clear that they for their part would not favour any application for membership put forward by the present Spanish government, which, having been founded with the support of the Axis Powers, does not, in view of its origin, its nature, its record and its close association with the aggressor states, possess the qualifications necessary to justify such membership.[21]

Thus, already during the Civil War and the immediate postwar period, the Franco regime was the subject of passionate discussion by contemporaries, with positions polarized: either to understand it as a simple but traditional bloody military dictatorship or to think of it as the Spanish version of European fascism with all its unique nuances. It must be said that almost the same terms marked the debate between scientific analysts (historians, jurists, political scientists, sociologists and economists), as has been seen.

Certainly, one should begin by pointing out that the conceptualization of Franquismo as a 'military dictatorship' has solid foundations and thus is supported today by a large part of the historiography and current social sciences. For example, Giuliana Di Febo and Santos Juliá, authors of a recent study on the subject, stress that the 'fundamental peculiarity of Franquismo' lies in the fact that it was configured as a military uprising during a brutal civil war and these origins 'marked for a long time the institutions, political orientations and the very conception and management of power'.[22]

Indeed, where it triumphed, the anti-Republican revolt of a large faction of the Spanish army in July 1936 established a regime of force to deal with a socio-political emergency (the war) and to replace existing democratic institutions (which were turned into the enemy). In this way, the rebel army (which was a substantial part of that institution), as the bureaucratic corporation responsible for the monopoly of weapons and the legitimate use of violence, tried to assume the leadership of the state at what was understood to be a critical juncture (confronting a weak civilian government that was betraying national interests), following the praetorian and militaristic tradition active in Spain since the time of the War of Independence in 1808. This deep-rooted tradition, which had the army as the backbone of the fatherland responsible for its integrity and security, was considered to be legitimate military intervention in the event of the apparent inability of civil authorities to maintain social order or to preserve the unitary central state institutions. This had been referenced by the constituent Law of the Army of 1878: 'The first and most important mission of the army is to sustain the independence of the fatherland and defend it from external and internal enemies.'[23] Thus, it had proceeded to act in September 1923 under the direction of General Miguel Primo de Rivera, the recent political model known by all the rebels in July 1936.

The consequent militarization of state and society implied by this praetorian militaristic tradition was patent in the first decisions of the rebels after a military coup was transformed into civil war. On 24 July 1936, a Junta de Defensa Nacional (National Defence Committee) was formed in Burgos which 'assumed all the powers of the state' (according to its constituent decree) and implemented a state of war and the banning of all political and trade union actions. It was a collegiate military agency involving all rebel military chiefs, with strict respect for their rank and seniority (which was why the elderly General Miguel Cabanellas presided). One of its most influential members, General Emilio Mola, would define with precision its functions and powers in a declaration of intent clearly inherited from the praetorian military tradition:

In this work of national reconstruction [...], we, the military, have to lay its foundations; we have to launch it; it is our right, because that is the nation's wish, because we have a clear idea of our power and only we can consolidate the union of the people with the army, detached until 19 July by the absurd propaganda of stupid intellectualism and political suicide.[24]

The configuration of corporate and exclusive military power in insurgent Spain was paralleled by an intense process of social and political involution which revealed the authoritarian, anti-reformist and counter-revolutionary drift of armed reaction on the march. The uncontested domain of hierarchically ordered military authorities was completed by the total subordination of right-wing parties and related organizations, which ended up abiding by the hegemony of the generals without serious discussion, both in the strategic conduct of the war and at a political level in the reconstruction of an alternative state. Franco himself, prior to his election as supreme commander, had already warned the right-wing civil leaders of the dire need to impose a fierce unity in the rearguard under military tutelage if they wanted to win the war: 'Everyone will have to sacrifice things in the interests of a rigid discipline which should not lend itself to divisions or splinter groups.' That iron unity was to be preserved by a 'military dictatorship' whose model would have to be the 'military directorate' of Primo de Rivera's times, as Franco himself acknowledged to the press.[25] The logic generated by the war spread as a hegemonic political culture, a kind of 'social militarism' that was presented as a solution for the regeneration of the country. It was defined and defended by the military medical commander Antonio Vallejo-Nágera in 1938:

> Militarism means order, discipline, personal sacrifice, precision in service. Enclosed in the military vial are essences of social virtues, as well as physical and spiritual strength. We advocate social militarization, the prevalence of militarism in society, militarism which did not, exclusively, involve standardizing all of the citizens. [...] Militarization of the school, university, office, workshop, theatre, salon, café, all the social fields, so that the scholar, the student, the white-collar worker, the blue-collar worker, the artist, the debater, will be perpetual soldiers of the empire.[26]

However, it is now clear that the Franco regime was never a simple collegiate and praetorian military dictatorship, even though it had its origins in the army and even if the army was always, even at the end, the key and crucial pillar of that institutional political system. On the contrary, the unexpected extension of the Civil War and the turbulent international framework that served as a critical context to its course and development were the main reasons for the rapid transition from the phase of domination by a collegiate military junta to a full military dictatorship of personal and individual power. In fact, after the conversion of the coup into a long war, it became imperative to concentrate command in one person to make the war effort more effective and to ensure that external support was obtained (the military, financial and diplomatic support of Nazi Germany and Fascist Italy). Recognizing this situation, the Burgos junta named, at the end of September 1936, General Franco the 'Generalissimo of the army, sea and air forces' and 'head of the government of the Spanish state', and formally transferred to him 'all the powers of the new state' (realized by the decree of 29 September 1936).

In other words, the collegiate military dictatorship became a military dictatorship of personal authority whose sole, exclusive and absolute holder was Franco, the most prestigious of the insurgent military commanders and the one who had reaped major successes on the battlefield (the unstoppable advance of his African troops on Madrid) and on the diplomatic front (making direct contact to win the support of Hitler and Mussolini). From then on, the political regime would begin to be properly reconfigured and named 'Franquismo', in honour of the crucial and decisive importance of its head in the formation and subsequent evolution of the regime.

A key factor needs to be taken into account in this regard. Franco was not satisfied with staying as a mere *primus inter pares* in relation to the comrades in arms who had elected him to the post. From the very beginning, he demonstrated a willingness to exceed his position as temporary commissarial dictator, appointed by his peers, to try to become a sovereign dictator who made use of this plenitude of powers for an unlimited time and without higher authority. On 1 October 1936, while the self-styled 'head of state' maintained the leadership of government that had been transferred to him by the junta, a Junta Técnica del Estado (State Technical Board) was created to advise and manage the civilian administrative tasks. Thus began the conversion of Franco into the absolute ruler and personification of sovereign authority and military power that had governed the destinies of insurgent Spain without constraint.

However, Franco did not limit his political activities to stressing his status as individual and personal representative of the power wielded by the army as a state bureaucratic corporation. He immediately demonstrated his intention to overcome this category of mere military dictator, albeit permanent and sovereign, to assume other sources of legitimacy and sustain his power for his own benefit and further underpin his emergent regime of personal, absolute and unchallengeable authority. Also on 1 October 1936, Franco announced his intention to organize Spain 'within a broad totalitarian concept of unity and continuity'. Indeed, from that point, he would demonstrate his willingness to emulate his German and Italian champions through the promotion of a process of political and institutional fascistization that would transform him into 'caudillo' (his official title of highest authority, equivalent to *duce* or *führer*) of Spain, alien to the centuries of decline and on a mission to recover its strength to undertake a new 'march towards empire'.

Likewise, Franco's efforts to restore to the Catholic Church all its rights and privileges lost during the Second Republic earned him the gratitude of the episcopate, which contributed to his individual political rise and provided a religious sanction of huge national and international propaganda value. The conversion of the Nationalist war effort into a 'crusade for God and for Spain' since the start of the war was thus completed with the subsequent conversion of Franco into *homo missus a Deo*, an emissary of Divine Providence and soldier of God, to lead the defence of the Catholic nation threatened by communist atheism.

Within the conscious fascistization of his regime, Franco was able to undertake one of perhaps the most crucial tasks in defining his regime: the forced unification into a single party of all the political forces that supported the war against the reformism of the Republic and the spectre of social revolution unleashed in the Republican rearguard. These forces were the new fascist radical right represented by the Falange Española, the old reactionary right embodied by Carlist traditionalism and the hitherto majority conservative right articulated mostly by political Catholicism and, to a lesser extent, by authoritarian monarchism. On 19 April 1937, in a decree issued from his headquarters, the Caudillo proceeded to dissolve all those parties and to integrate them, 'under my leadership, into a single political entity of national character': the Falange Española Tradicionalista y de las JONS. Thus, was created a 'state party' (with the old Falangist component predominant) that, after the army and the Church, would constitute the third supporting pillar of the institutional framework already perfectly characterized as 'Franquismo'.

As the writer Ernesto Giménez Caballero would point out in 1938, the need to win the war not only ruled out any opposition to Franco but sealed with a pact of blood (spilled at the front and in the repression of the rearguard) loyalty to the Caudillo of the victory: 'the Francoist Party will be that of the combatants in this war.'[27]

Thus, in April 1937, the gradual transformation of Franco into supreme commander of the armies, head of government, head of state, crusader of the faith of Christ and national chief of the single party had converted Franquismo into something more than a mere military dictatorship of sovereign personal power. The Francoist political-institutional system was no longer just a military junta with a leading and prominent head; it far exceeded the previous model of military directorate of General Primo de Rivera. This was made clear by Article 17 of the new Law of Central Government approved by Franco on 30 January 1938, at the same time as he formed his first regular government with ministers 'subordinated to the presidency', appointed and removed freely by the Caudillo by use of his absolute powers:

> The head of state, who assumed all powers under the decree of the Junta of National Defence on 29 September 1936, has the supreme authority to enact legal rules of a general nature. Provisions and resolutions of the head of state, previous deliberation of government, and on the proposal of the minister of the sector, will take the form of laws when they affect the organizational structure of the state or constitute the main rules of the legal system of the country, and decrees in the remaining cases.[28]

This transformation was the origin of a new political situation that generated the need to identify and conceptualize the resulting system using new categories. Almost all of the researchers who have dealt with the matter (historians such as those already mentioned and others such as Antonio Elorza or Julio Aróstegui; jurists like Juan Ferrando Badía or Manuel Ramírez; sociologists such as Amando de Miguel and Salvador Giner) have pointed out the relevance of understanding that conversion using concepts such as 'Caesarism with a military base', 'Bonapartist dictatorial regime', 'authoritarian *caudillista* regime' or '*caudillista* dictatorship', amongst others.

In general, these descriptive categories suggest that the new Spanish Caudillo at the heart of the regime fulfilled the same role of arbitration and charismatic dictator as Napoleon Bonaparte or his nephew Louis Napoleon Bonaparte, in the nineteenth-century First and Second French empires, respectively. According to the interpretative thesis of the Bonapartist model, Franco had become, like them, the central element of the political system and held his comprehensive authority by virtue of being the balancing figure and final arbiter between all the components and supporting factions. The ultimate nature of his undisputed power and decision-making as supreme judicial arbitrator was a response to the lowest common denominator of all interests and forces that supported the political regime that he presided over during the war and lent him their support and backing, with greater or less enthusiasm, in order to achieve victory and preserve it.

To those Bonapartist features, the typology of the caudillo model (or Caesarist – meaning a soldier who becomes a caudillo) added the role of charismatic leader whose full powers were based on his supposed exceptional skills as a soldier and as a victorious ruler against the enemy, engendering the loyalty of those under his command through his prestige and the exaltation of his person as a singular authority. The charismatic leadership, as the principle of founding authority defined by Max Weber in 1921, would owe its source of political legitimacy not to a rational election or a revered tradition, but to the exceptional charisma (personal gift) of an exemplary leader for his demonstrated abilities in a grave and specific historical situation.[29]

The Bonapartist character and *caudillista* profile of the Francoist political system are evident and indisputable, even if one focuses only on the propaganda disseminated with the consent and approval of Franco himself. As has already been pointed out, at the end of 1936 the following compulsory slogans and watchwords in the insurgent rearguard were already in circulation: 'One Fatherland, One State, One Caudillo', or 'The Caesars were the unbeaten generals'. Two years later, the writer and Falangist leader Dionisio Ridruejo bluntly affirmed: 'The Caudillo is limited only by his own free will.' Indeed, until the end of his life, Franco was primarily 'El Caudillo', the capital institution of the political regime, not only in the judicial-institutional realm but also in the daily exercise of executive and legislative power. For almost

40 years, Franco was always the beneficiary of the three basic characteristics of the caudillo political model: personal exaltation and identification with the supposed destiny of his people; the fullness of power concentrated in his hands; and the lack of institutional control of his exercise of authority since he was only responsible 'before God and history'. A caudillo, in addition, not only in military (Generalissimo) and political (supreme national chief) terms, but also providential and anointed for his lifetime by the grace of God, which added an element of sacred religious sanction to the theory of the crucial and decisive *caudillaje*.

It has already been shown how the legal literature of the regime never failed to underline that Franco founded his authority upon a charismatic legitimacy (not traditional, by succession, nor rational, by election). Torcuato Fernández-Miranda would explain it in an official political doctrine textbook, with a unique reasoning clearly indebted to the political science of Max Weber:

> The head of the Spanish state, born of the national uprising (of 18 July 1936), is constituted in the person of Generalissimo Franco, by virtue of the institution of *caudillaje*. The Generalissimo is head of state as the caudillo of the crusade. [...] The *caudillaje* is an outstanding title of authority, *individual*, and in this sense *unrepeatable* that rests on a right of *foundation* consecrated by a *proclamation* and also exceptional *adhesion*. [...] The process of permanent civil war, latent or expressed, in Spanish life since Fernando VII, reached its peak in the anarchy of the Second Republic, making civil war inevitable. From that war arose the conductor or caudillo of the crusade, in the person of Francisco Franco, *inspired* by a National Movement and proclaimed by the adhesion of national Spain. In him resides the authority of the new state.[30]

However, the historiographic, sociological and political consensus on this *caudillista* (Caesarist or Bonapartist) characteristic of Franquismo breaks down when it comes to qualifying more properly and accurately the corresponding regime type, taking as extreme parameters the already-mentioned basic alternative: is it a *caudillista* regime by nature of its totalitarianism in the mode of the Italian Fascist dictatorship presided over by the Duce, Mussolini, or the

National Socialist Third Reich and its doctrine of the Führer Prinzip applied
to Hitler? Or rather is it a merely authoritarian *caudillista* system, similar to
the Portuguese 'Estado Novo' of the jurist and economist Antonio Oliveira
Salazar or the Polish dictatorship presided over by a hero of independence like
Marshal Pilsudski, with no essential connection to contemporary European
fascist totalitarianism?

The concept of the totalitarian regime was developed during the interwar
years and later by several different political scientists and sociologists, mostly
from a liberal and social-democratic tradition (Franz Neumann, Hannah
Arendt, among others). They essentially took as a model the political structure
of Fascist Italy, Nazi Germany and Stalin's Soviet Union.[31] As a political
category, the notion of 'totalitarianism' was initially based on the theory and
reality of the concept of the state articulated by Mussolini in 1922: 'Everything
in the state, nothing outside the state and nothing against the state' – probably
his greatest and most radical doctrinal innovation, according to the analysis of
Emilio Gentile.[32] After that, the term spread in the political vocabulary of the
radical and fascist right to achieve a new crucial political triumph in Germany in
1933, when Goebbels, Hitler's minister of propaganda, announced the political
goal: 'Our party has always aspired to the totalitarian state. [...] the goal of the
revolution [National Socialist] has to be a totalitarian state that penetrates into
all spheres of public life.'[33]

On the basis of such initial political uses of the term, during the 1950s – in the
context of Cold War between the Soviet Bloc and the West – political scientists
such as Carl Joachim Friedrich and Zbigniew K. Brzezinski were reformulating
the concept of 'totalitarianism' to define all dictatorships that presented a series
of common characteristics from a formal, exclusively political perspective and
without attention to their specific social or class foundations. This definition
used as a fundamental criterion the degree of difference of those political systems
with respect to the parameters set by liberal democracy (based, in essence, on
the division of powers of the state, respect for civil liberties, the universality of
the rule of law and the open competition between groups for access to political
power through free elections). In this regard, it remains significant that in 1957
Franco himself confessed, in private, to his cousin and personal assistant that he
found great similarities between his regime and European totalitarianism, both

right-wing and left-wing: 'Communism, Hitlerism, fascism and Falangism are distinct political systems, but they all have something in common, such as the maintenance of the authority of the state, foundation for the order of a country, social and economic discipline, etc.'[34]

In essence, aside from its support and social goals specific to each case (and this is a crucial subject for many analysts), the typology of the totalitarian regime was characterized by the following defining features to varying degrees (historically more fully developed in the German case than in the others):

1 The presence of a centre of hegemonic power, personified and individualized in a charismatic leader, a *duce* or *führer*, exercising his absolute monopoly of authority with no upper restriction or appreciable autonomy for junior or intermediate commanders.

2 The existence of a single mass party which forms an integral part of the apparatus of the state (even becoming its controlling shadow) that responds to a precise and well-defined ideology, a messianic doctrine (a mode of 'political religion') of required knowledge and study by the population.

3 The claim of absolute control by the state and the party of all political and socio-cultural public activities with the private cultural and social life reduced to a minimum or simply suppressed.

4 The maintenance of a high degree of political mobilization of the population through channels of official regimentation of the one-party state: trade unions, youth organizations, women's groups, specific cultural associations, etc.

5 Systematic police control and intense and active repression of all latent or patent opposition and without any degree of freedom of press, speech, assembly, movement and communication.

6 The desire to control and centralize economic life through ultranationalist and autarkic policies as a vehicle for the military reinforcement of the state in the face of a potential test of superiority in a 'total war' against the enemy.

Without diminishing its hermeneutic consistency, the concept of 'totalitarianism' described has been subjected to fair historiographical criticism for its 'polymorphous, malleable, elastic and, ultimately, ambiguous character'.[35] The definition seems insufficient because it responds to a typology of rigid political traits and overlooks very real differences of social implementation or ideological projection between the systems classified as mostly 'totalitarian' (Nazism and Communism, basically).

On this point, particularly relevant are the recent words of Richard Overy in his comparative study of both systems and the method of exercise of power of the two dictators, Hitler and Stalin. According to him, it is clear that Stalinism and Nazism had great similarities in their political forms, popular and cultural control modes, strategies of economic management and utopian social and messianic aspirations. However, they also showed differences in ideology and socio-cultural objectives. Soviet power under Stalin was a totalitarian dictatorship to build the utopia of an international socialist paradise 'in which everyone would be equal and happy', regardless of its giant human cost. Nazi power conformed to totalitarianism with a utopian dream 'of creating an empire of the superior race' that involved the extermination of its enemies and a biological purification of mankind on a large scale (including the unprecedented genocide of almost 6 million Jews). This key difference in their basic social, political and ideological worldviews 'explains the war for hegemony between both dictatorships'.[36] It could be added, following Enzo Traverso, that such differences also explain their various historical developments: 'certainly it is not by chance that the Fascist and Nazi regimes were born and died with their leaders, while the Soviet system survived Stalin's death for nearly 40 years.'[37]

In any case, with regard to Francoism, we have seen that during the Civil War and in the postwar period, many observers and political analysts particularly known for their anti-fascist commitment noted the existence of some or all of those factors that defined the concept of 'totalitarianism' at some stage of the regime's history (especially at the beginning). Therefore, they advocated that Franquismo should be regarded as a specifically Spanish variant of European fascism originating in the interwar period. They believed that a full definition of fascism should consider the counter-revolutionary and violently repressive social function exercised in each national case by different coalitions of right-wing forces that created their own fascist solution to address their respective crises and protect the interests of the ruling classes.

However, the definition of Franquismo as a specific Spanish variant of fascism ('clerical fascism', 'fascism of the military barracks', 'clerical-military fascism') ceased to be shared by all political scientists, sociologists and historians interested in the theme from the 1960s, once the survival of the regime had been proven despite international condemnation by the Western world during the Cold War (Spain joined the UN in 1955). In the context of the great socio-economic and cultural changes experienced by Spain in that decade of development, and in view of the transformations inside the regime and in its international political activity, many analysts began to see the invalidity of this identification or, at the very least, its problematic consistency with the fascist totalitarian model (especially given that all had been defeated in 1945). We should not forget that by then the regime was remarkable in its similarities to other political models in full force in the postwar period (from Salazar's Portugal to Latin American *caudillista* and military dictatorships and similar regimes in recently decolonized Arab and Asian countries).

It was in 1964 when a different and alternative definition of the nature of the Franco regime emerged in the academic (and political) world. Its main author was a Spanish sociologist based in the United States, Juan José Linz, who formulated the concept of 'authoritarian regime', taking as his reference and counterpart the previous concept of 'totalitarianism'.[38]

According to Linz's analysis, the Franco regime was a prime example of 'authoritarianism' because the five defining basic features of that category of political analysis would be clearly different from those of a totalitarian system.

1 The regime would enjoy a degree of 'limited political pluralism' within its own internal ranks (the political game between the so-called 'Francoist families': Falangists, Carlists, Catholics, monarchists, etc.).

2 The regime lacked 'an elaborate and leading ideology' of messianic features that required knowledge and study by the population, while maintaining 'a peculiar mentality' (an archaic Catholic conservatism).

3 The regime would eliminate the need for 'intensive or extensive political mobilization' framed by the state bodies in favour of the promotion of 'apathy', the demobilization and the passive conformism of the population.

4 The official single party would have subordinate functions and its claim of absolute dominance of the state would be halted by the effective resistance of other institutions equal to or greater in power and influence (such as the army and the Church).

5 The authoritarian dictator, in contrast to the totalitarian, 'exercises his power within badly defined but actually fairly predictable formal limits', which therefore are not unlimited.

This attempt to define a concept expressly applied to the regime of General Franco had many supporters in the field of sociology (Amando de Miguel) and political science (Guy Hermet) and among historians (Stanley G. Payne, Juan Pablo Fusi and Javier Tusell). But it also caused much academic debate with undeniable political overtones. Some critics felt that this conceptual revision could be understood as a form of acquittal of the Franco regime as it focused on the more benevolent character of the regime in its developmental phase (forgetting the first philo-totalitarian phase of civil and world war). Similarly, certain inaccuracies that weakened the scope and rigour of the concept were noted: the questionable comparison between a fascist 'ideology' (precise, defined and closed) and an authoritarian 'mentality' (broad, blurred and open to many ideological components); the relative nature of the 'limited political pluralism', which only affected the ruling classes and obscured the fundamental political agreement in that group; and the possible confusion between 'demobilization' (such as apathy induced by the authorities) and the lack of rejection or opposition from the masses, forgetting the existence of a non-conformity drowned out by the fear of repression.

However, the fundamental criticism of the authoritarian model focused on the lack of references to classes and social groups that supported the regime or benefited from it (or, vice versa, classes and groups that suffered the effects of the regime and were excluded from its benefits). In other words, it censured the strictly political-formalist character of the definition and its lack of attention to the social and class dimensions of political regimes.

One of the first and most refined proposals to overcome Linz's thesis was the work of sociologists Salvador Giner and Eduardo Sevilla-Guzmán. In 1975, trying to combine the social aspects (content) with the formal political aspects (container), both authors formulated the concept of 'modern despotism' as a political system distinct from totalitarianism and traditional autocratic regimes. In their view, the Franco dictatorship fulfilled all the characteristic features of the model:

A typical case of modern despotism was Franco's Spanish state, as well as the Portuguese regime of Salazar, which lasted until 1974, and a good number of contemporary African or South American dictatorships. In all cases of modern despotism we find: (a) a mode of domination of the class in which power is exercised for the ruling class and, on its behalf, by a despot or a reduced elite; (b) a series of service communities – police, civil servants, members of a single party, clergy – who always obey the leader or leaders; (c) a restricted political pluralism to that class within these service communities; (d) a political formula of government that includes an ideological façade and the tolerance of a certain degree of ideological pluralism among the factions that make up the coalition's dominant forces; and (e) a popular majority from which is required passive obedience, and which is economically exploited by the dominant classes.

While the concept of 'modern despotism' gathered and expanded in a social sense the features embedded in an 'authoritarian regime', other criticisms of this notion were much more radical in their rejection of the original political formalism. In essence, returning to and renewing the Marxian interpretative tradition, these criticisms insisted that the definition of Franquismo could not omit its social function to constitute a historic solution to a grave capitalist crisis through a reaction of counter-reformist and counter-revolutionary forces to tackle the threat of workers' mobilization. In this sense, according to the argument of the Italian sociologist Gino Germani in 1969, the following should be considered: 'Both the basic objectives and the historical significance of the Franco regime are typically fascist. That its policy formulation can be characterized as authoritarian is, surely, important, but not least its fascist substance.'[39]

Following these lines of reasoning, British Hispanist Paul Preston also repeatedly called attention to the risks of exclusively identifying fascism with the squalid Falange of prewar Spain, since it 'obviates the need for examination

of the fascist features of other rightist groups and of the Franco regime itself'
and there is the potential 'to forget both the trappings and Axis alliances of
Francoism and the activities of its repressive machinery between 1937 and 1945'.[40]
Probably one of the most accredited representatives of this interpretative line is
the historian Julián Casanova in one of his first works on Francoist repression,
originally published in 1992. His reasoning in favour of seeing the fascist nature
of the Franco regime for social reasons rather than political criteria deserves to
be quoted extensively:

> The social function of fascism thus becomes the fundamental criterion for
> identification and understanding. [...] the counter-revolutionary coalition
> which took up arms in Spain in July 1936 to bring down the Republic,
> fulfilled the historic mission, pursued the same purpose and, above all, fought
> for the same 'benefits' as the fascist regimes of Italy and Germany. [...] Thus
> understood, fascism is for the historian something more than a style of
> politics, with a distinctive ideology, that knows how to mobilize the middle
> classes and appeal to the feelings of the community – with the consequent
> rejection of the concept of 'class' as an organizing principle of society – in
> a crisis situation. We, rather, have a counter-revolutionary process, a violent
> and extreme expression of a movement of reaction, which emerged in almost
> all European countries in the interwar period to deal with the advance of
> the left and labour parliamentary conquests, the fear of the revolution and
> the crisis of the liberal state. [...] A substantial difference, however (between
> the Spanish case and the Italian and German cases), resided in the nature
> of the executing arm of that reaction. In a society where the army had shown
> its capacity on multiple occasions to protect the interests of these classes
> by force, there was no need to invent another procedure. [...] A primary
> ingredient, therefore, of the historical mission of the Franco regime, which
> emerged from the victory in the war and inextricably linked to memories and
> consequences of it, was the aim of eradicating social conflicts endangering
> the very existence of the industrial bourgeoisie and the landowning classes.
> The reform project of the Republic, and all that that form of government
> meant, was wiped out and spilled over the graves of thousands of citizens.
> [...] In all three cases (Italy, Germany and Spain), the social function of

fascism was to stabilize and strengthen capitalist property and ensure the social and economic domain of the capitalist class.[41]

However, in the opinion of a wide range of historians from different ideological leanings, the 'social function' or 'historical mission' of the Franco regime does not in any way justify its consideration as fascist. One reason is that the stabilization of the 'capitalist property relations' ('function') and strengthening of the 'social and economic domain of the capitalist class' can be and historically has been performed under very different political forms ('developmentalist' or traditional military dictatorships, conservative or progressive democratic regimes, liberal or authoritarian oligarchies, fascism, etc.). In other words, the reproduction and continuity of a model of bourgeois social domination and capitalist economic accumulation is always exercised and developed under different and diverse means and political formulas (systems of relationship of power between classes and groups, rulers and ruled) – institutions, furthermore, that, due to the relative autonomy of the sphere of political power, have an impact on the specific evolution of this model of social domination and its economic basis.

In this regard, it is worth noting that even the most orthodox Marxist tendencies of the 1930s appreciated the qualitative political differences of fascism with other more or less dictatorial and repressive bourgeois regimes. In 1932, the then communist Spanish theorist Santiago Montero Díaz (he turned to fascism later) underlined the contrast and 'antithesis' between triumphant Italian Fascism and the traditional capitalist political systems, aside from their common class regimes:

Fascism means a new conception of the bourgeois state to maintain its class domination over the proletariat. [...] Essentially different from a parliamentary liberal state, distinct also from a simple absolute power, fascism has meant simply the most brilliant attempt to give bourgeois society a political structure that will preclude the existence of any revolutionary organization. [...] The fact was that [since 1922 in Italy], a new power was going to embark, with sails unfurled, in a new direction in history; absolutely new methods to defend old absolute objectives. The laborious, violent gestation of the seizure of power, fighting the revolution day by day and factory by factory, that plan for the conquest of the state, full of bullet-riddled flags, of illustrious demagogues and patriotic hymns, mobilizing masses and winning factions, did not resemble anything, absolutely nothing of the rotten government, nor the low palace coups such as that of [Miguel] Primo de Rivera (in 1923), that only the ineffable ignorance of some sectors can compare to the Mussolini conquest, heroic and criminal, nourished by arrogance and betrayal. [...] There is no actual difference; there is antithesis. The arrests, tactics, and the field of operations are different. [...] With regard to various European dictatorships, either they have, behind the screen of a Primo de Rivera, the will of an absolute king, the personal powers of a Pilsudski or a Carmona [Portuguese general in charge of the dictatorship in 1926], they do not have, as refers to the seizure of power or the state, any essential contact with fascism. They will perhaps have some of the features of violence, some of its shock troops or some of its ways of addressing and cutting the knot of social problems.[42]

In response to this set of reasons, the definition of fascism on the exclusive basis of social (or historical) functions and regardless of the specific political format seems to be an example of *reductio ad extremum*, ineffective and confusing for its all-inclusiveness and absence of content to discriminate different cases of political regimes historically crystallized and socially similar in its function. Precisely that 'inflationary use' that invalidated the scientific-social potential of the concept is also the cause of the devaluation of the 'fascist' voice as a mere label of denigratory political denunciation.[43] Thus, starting a long time ago, in everyday language and even the media, to be fascist meant total opposition to the democratic system or the demands of workers' trade unions, acceptance of the use of violence as a political instrument and the suppression of dissent as an expeditious method of government, including all cultural action considered displeasing. In July 2008 the singer Iggy Pop attained widespread press coverage with his resounding statement: 'Rock should be fun; without that, it becomes fascist.' It was a perverted and 'inflationary use' of the word that simply serves to relativize and minimize the significance of a truly fascist and totalitarian dictatorship (such as Nazi Germany, for example), equating it to any regime with a capitalist base (or other imaginable) to some degree prone to the use of force against its internal dissidents and real or potential enemies.

In view of these conceptual difficulties in the interpretation of fascism, the latest trend in historiography on Franquismo consists of shading the fascist character (*stricto sensu*) of the regime without neglecting its social and class meaning. The fascist component of the reactionary coalition forged during the Civil War under the leadership of Franco was clear and evident, but it had no majority nor decision-making capability at the end of the war. In the words of Ricardo Chueca and José Ramón Montero, 'Spanish society in the 1930s was fascist, as much as it could or needed to be.'[44] That was true largely because, as had already been appreciated by President Azaña, the basic social structure of Spain in the 1930s was too archaic and backward to produce forms of an unequivocally 'modern' political organization and practice associated with Italian and German fascism, which were emerging in much more developed and diversified societies. This was no obstacle to the reactionary coalition's taking advantage of fascism's most novel and appropriate features for the Spanish war situation: violent, repressive and coercive civil functionality, attractive organic corporate and anti-democratic rhetoric, and its illusory imitation of inclusive participation of the masses in the politics of the regenerated nation.

In this innovative interpretative line are several historians of different orientations, such as Santos Juliá ('fascism under a canopy, in military uniform'), Manuel Pérez Ledesma ('a dictatorship by the grace of God'), or Antonio Elorza. The latter is also the author of a definitive synthesis that is worth quoting for its conciseness:

> Franco's regime would have been a personal dictatorship, a Caesarism, with a military base, with a counter-revolutionary and archaic orientation, and a strictly fascist content in its 'permanent state of exception', in the politics of repression of opponents and dissidents, and until 1966, in the politics of information and elimination of freedom of thought. [...] One should place Franquismo amongst military dictatorships (like Caesarism, not like praetorianism), and different to the civilian dictatorships of Hitler or Mussolini. [...] Fascism was there, in the symbols and in the repressive methods, but the regime was above all else a military dictatorship.[45]

Also included in this school should be the neo-Marxist historian Julio Aróstegui, who in 1986 recovered the classification of authoritarian political regime and leader as part of a reactionary and restorative social project:

> The military insurrection corresponded to the characterization that Arno J. Mayer gave to the violent movements of extreme social reaction in the twentieth century as 'a bayonet in search of an ideology'. [...] [On the pro-Franco side] the primitive and absolute social reaction was giving way to a 'social-national' discourse, with anti-bourgeois and anti-capitalist rhetoric, whose components show such a degree of amalgamation hidden behind the programme of the Falange that it can be defined as a mere fascist formalism which, moreover, was being eroded gradually in the postwar regime and which covers the real plan of preserving the social structures of the Spain of the Restoration, with a new framework for the regimentation of the masses. [...] The model of the authoritarian 'caudillista' regime was established before the design of the state itself. Franco assumed the four leaderships: state, party, government and army. [...] The political connotations were such that in this area, as in the social, it is impossible to speak of a true fascist regime and state, if it is not as a mere matter of formal mimicry. The party was not the owner of the state, nor did the state rest on the party, if we are talking about both with its strict significance within the fascist regimes.[46]

Some of the latest and most recent contributions to the subject of the relationship between fascism and Franquismo stress the protean character of the military regime built during the Civil War and its potential either to evolve in a full fascist and totalitarian sense or to come back to a mere reactionary stance given its military origin. As had been perceived by Mussolini from the beginning of the Spanish conflict, the Francoist state, despite its reactionary and autocratic original nature, by virtue of the imposed war and international mobilization, 'can be used tomorrow as a base for the totalitarian state'. It was expected, therefore, that Franco would lead the process of the fascistization of Spain. The process would mean the penetration by the single party of the administrative public services (including, if possible, the army and police), with the creation of new social agencies (the *sindicatos verticales* and similar organizations) and the formation of party structures parallel to those of the state and, as far as possible, superior to them. That is to say, 'a complex, dynamic hybridization' which entailed 'a vast field of interaction and entanglement – from the circulation of new ideas to the selective adaptation of institutional, political and stylistic experiments'.[47]

Under this analytical perspective, focusing on the historical-evolutionary dynamic, Franquismo would have been a reactionary military regime that suffered a remarkable but unfinished process of fascistization, eventually truncated and watered down by the outcome of World War II and the defeat of Italy and Germany. The nature of 'fascistized dictatorship' could be appreciated, in the words of Ismael Saz, for its peculiar 'ability to combine certain elements of the rigidity peculiar to fascism with the versatility and manoeuvrability of the non-fascists'.[48] One of the features of the fascistized regimes was that they could revert to their initial state of authoritarian dictatorial regime. To a great degree, that process of fascistization undertaken, truncated and then reversed is the reason for the difficulties in conceptualizing the Franco regime and is key to its evolutionary and adaptive capacity.

Ismael Saz has rigorously exposed this interpretation of Francoism as a fascistized regime, potentially equidistant between the fascist totalitarian model and the mere authoritarian dictatorship and able to evolve or stand still in one sense or another. His argument deserves to be quoted fully to appreciate its meaning:

> Franco's dictatorship rested on the same undemocratic and counter-revolutionary alliance as the Italian or the German, it was as repressive – and in a sense even more – than those; it was structured on the basis of a single party and on the principle of leadership (*caudillaje*); it had the same centralized and uniform design of the state; it copied much of the essential institutions of the Italian fascist regime; it adopted something like an official ideology; it created structures, allegedly classless and corporative and took refuge in economic autarky; it announced, as did the fascist dictatorships, its purpose to *last*. However, in each and every one of the cases mentioned, one can find essential differences: the correlation of forces within the counter-revolutionary alliance was never favourable to the fascist sector; its repressive

policy annihilating the democratic and labour opposition was only partially accompanied by an effort of remobilization or articulation of consensus; there was some populist politics but far more of the jail, Church and barracks; the single party was really a party unified from above and from outside; the Caudillo was not the expression, depiction or concretion of some form of so-called popular will, but of the divine will – *by the grace of God* – and the military; the official ideology may or may not be an ideology but it was certainly not a fascist ideology; the Francoist state was less interventionist and more *respectful* of civil society than the fascist, but it was also better structured; it lacked the anarchic *Darwinist* connotations, characteristic in greater or lesser degree, of the fascist regimes; no one ever believed in the trade unionism of the Sindicato Vertical, and autarky, more than obeying the internal logic of the fascist regimes, even, eventually, went against the interests of key sectors of the *great capital*, connected perfectly with autarkic, defensive, tendencies of capitalism that rather than being expansionist sought internal protection.[49]

The consideration of the Franco regime as a military *caudillista* regime subjected to an intense process of fascistization during the Civil War has also been developed by Ferran Gallego in his more recent works, particularly in *El Evangelio Fascista (The Fascist Gospel)*.[50] According to his accurate analysis, the fascistization of the conservative Spanish right had been very deep in the years prior to the Civil War as it had assumed and integrated a good deal of the ideas, projects, rituals and symbols of Spanish fascism-Falangism. That dynamic would reach its culmination with the Civil War, when the novelty provided by Falangism became a key element of the 'new Francoist political culture': the palingenetic organic nationalism, the modern renewal of tradition, elitism combined with the mobilization of masses, the defence of order coupled with the demand for social justice, the fascination with technocracy and social Darwinist vitalism and extremely charismatic *caudillismo*. For this reason, in his view, fascism penetrated the depths of Francoism not only as a 'social function' but also as a project for the construction of a 'national-syndicalist state', even if it was led by a military leader. In any case, that process was truncated from 1943 for reasons of internal attrition as much as by the loss of external opportunities linked to the world war. In the consequent pragmatic reflux, the original fascist component was displaced and eclipsed in favour of others equally present in the Francoist cultural synthesis (particularly National Catholicism) and without serious ruptures (neither ideological, nor in political staff, nor in forms of the exercise of personal power). In the words of Ferran Gallego: 'Fascism was not abandoned, but overcome in the regime's own evolution as an ideological means to integrate all its elements.'[51]

By virtue of these considerations, it is now increasingly rare to define Francoism as a truly fascist and totalitarian regime. The dominant perception now that it was a military dictatorship first fascistized and then transformed into an essentially authoritarian regime, despite the fascistic features, which remained until the end.

For example, at the end of the 1990s, a fruitful comparative analysis of the interwar European regimes by Gregory M. Luebbert still considered that the Franco regime showed 'the more diluted character of Spanish fascism'.[52] However, more recently, a leading expert in the history of European fascism, Emilio Gentile, wrote that, in Franquismo, 'the Falangist movement was reduced to being a support of a military authoritarian regime, which confined it to a subordinate and marginal position'.[53] In 2004, in his comparison between Italian Fascism and Spanish Francoism, Gentile advanced conclusions that lowered the so-called 'affinity' between the two regimes and criticized the tendency to 'exaggerate the similarities rather than the differences', with express reference to the charismatic leadership of both leaders:

The analogy between the figures of both 'leaders' is, in fact, superficial, since it does not consider the substantial differences between the Duce – a professional politician, with training and a revolutionary mentality, an enemy of the traditional *establishment*, who came to power as head of a mass movement organized in a *party militia* which was always the main pillar of his personal power – and the Caudillo – a professional soldier, with a conservative mentality and training when not directly reactionary, integrated within the traditional establishment, who came to power as a general in the army, and whose political power rested on the armed forces.[54]

The judgement of Gentile was confirmed at the same time by another leading specialist in the phenomenon of interwar European fascism, Robert O. Paxton, who pointed out that the crisis of the 1930s in Spain 'led to Franco's military dictatorship rather than to power for the leader of the fascist Falange, José Antonio Primo de Rivera'.[55] A few years ago, in 2013, Enzo Traverso also discounted the applicability of the category of totalitarian fascism to the Francoist regime for similar motives:

> Francoist repression, during the Spanish Civil War, was particularly fierce and widespread, but the ideology of the regime, founded on Catholicism and the myth of the eternal Spain, was too traditionalist and its social base, in which the clergy and large property owners played a fundamental role, too conservative to build a totalitarian project. Francoism appears, then, against Italian Fascism and Nazism, as the authoritarian and violent variant (particularly in its origins) of a classic military dictatorship, without official ideology (outside of Catholicism and nationalism), with neither revolutionary pretensions nor millenarian aspirations.[56]

In the same vein, one could include the assessment of Julián Sanz Hoya in 2013, one of the last Spanish historians to have reflected on the role of fascism in the shaping and duration of Franquismo. In his view, similar to that of Emilio Gentile, Robert O. Paxton or Enzo Traverso and not too far from that of Ismael Saz or Ferran Gallego, if the fascistization of the regime had its clear boundaries, the defascistization was not complete even in the final stages of the dictatorship:

> The new FET-JONS (created in April 1937) was subordinate to Franco and was based on a fusion of political and ideological Falangism and traditionalism, fascism and National Catholicism, but that did not prevent the Falangist component from always being hegemonic in the party. Its control was the base from which the Falangists boosted their offensives in the struggle for power, in the pursuit of their longed-for acquisition of a totalitarian hegemony or to expand or sustain specific plots for power and influence. These conflicts were solved with apparent defeats as with undeniable achievements, ambiguous

victories and, above all, frequent compromises. [...] Franco knew well that he needed the party of which he was national leader to perpetuate himself in power, to counter the other right-wing tendencies and sustain the efforts of social legitimation of the dictatorship. And on the other hand, the successive losses of Falangist political weight did not prevent the leaders of the movement from retaining until the very end a relevant power share, supported by a strong political and clientelist network.[57]

It is highly unlikely that the lively debate about the nature of the Franco regime has finished with these contributions, which although not exhaustive are some of the most relevant. There is no doubt that the controversy has been very fruitful and has contributed to the critical rethinking of the nature and defining features of the peculiar political system headed by General Franco and the reasons for its undoubted social foundations and its lengthy historical duration. If that political regime had to be defined in a concise and brief way, one could resort to Franco's own words in a speech in Seville on 16 April 1953: 'In short: we are the counterpart of the Republic.'[58]

Indeed, the regime moulded by Franco to his image and likeness was the outright denial of Republican democracy and the political institutionalization of his military victory over reformism and the revolutionary spectre believed to be behind it which prevailed in Spain between 1931 and 1936. The anti-democratic, counter-revolutionary and dictatorial character did not suffer during the long evolution of the regime and the ongoing biography of its titular head, despite pragmatic changes in tune with the evolution of the international context. As the Caudillo acknowledged in his message of the end of 1964, celebrating the 25 years of existence of his regime: 'During the long period of time we have governed, adapting the standards to the times in which we had to live, faithful to the principles that justified our intervention in public life.'[59]

For this reason, one would reiterate that probably the only defining constant feature of Franquismo as a political regime was the presence of General Franco as caudillo and dictator with sovereign powers, 'lifetime ruler' and only responsible 'before God and history'. Perhaps the imperviousness of the unperturbed Caudillo lay in his desire to cling on to absolute power. This was appreciated very early by 'Pacón', his loyal cousin and military assistant, who related it in his private diary:

> I have always believed (and I know him very well) that he cannot make way for another person as head of state. I repeat that Franco is Franquista one hundred per cent, and that he will not give power to any other person voluntarily.[60]

The Times of Francoism and its Modulations

The different stages of Francoism – its periodization – provide a good basic framework for the study of the regime. As should already be obvious, the long duration of the Franco regime, along with its evident correlative evolution, mean it is essential to pay special attention to the chronological dimensions as a basis for its study and rigorous historical understanding. As Javier Tusell remarked in 1988: 'To a large extent, the peculiarity of Franco resides in his long-lasting rule.'[61] Tusell was not alone in that regard, as evidenced by the judgement of Stanley G. Payne, just one year before, in his canonical book:

> The definition and classification of the regime became, obviously, increasingly complex as it extended in time. This is due in part to the same phenomenon of its persistence [...]. The system of Franco had a longer history and suffered more historical changes than the majority of non-Marxist dictatorships.[62]

Much more recently, in 2014, a global study of the dictatorship by Miguel Ángel Giménez Martínez began with a crucial starting premise:

> It is difficult to provide a clear conceptualization of a regime that lasted for more than three decades and which was transformed to the beat of the political, economic and social circumstances. So, the Franco regime arose at the time of development of European fascisms, subsequently coincided with the so-called 'developmental dictatorships' of the 1960s, and finally disappeared in the context of a generalized crisis of dictatorships.[63]

The shared warning of Tusell, Payne and Giménez Martínez is relevant because, quite simply, historical analysis is based on a simultaneous consideration of the spatial and temporal axes of any human phenomenon. As the classic aphorism states, the Muse named Clio had two equally beautiful eyes: one saw chronology and the other geography. The discipline of history, in essence, is nothing more than a human science that tries to study social phenomena in time and space in order to understand and explain the processes of evolutionary forms of human society. By virtue of the inescapable spatial–temporal nature of historical phenomena, one cannot embark upon a historiographical work without due consideration of the chronology. This requires the hard work of 'periodization': to categorize the past, which is continuous and ungeneralizable, into discrete blocks of time, however imprecise. In fact, without such 'named periods', the past would be nothing more than scattered events lacking a framework through which to understand them. In Thomas Mann's classic phrase, 'Time has no divisions to mark its passage.' However, historians (and human beings in general) do need to mark such passages of time to try to understand the past, as Henri Berr and Lucien Febvre remarked in 1932: 'There is no methodological problem of greater importance within the field of history than that of periodization.'[64] Half a century ago, in a text published posthumously in 1956, José Ortega y Gasset tellingly expressed this same principle:

> We began to persuade ourselves that in history the chronology is not, as often believed, a *denominatio extrinseca* but, on the contrary, the more substantive. The date of a human reality, whatever it is, is its most constitutive attribute. It transforms the figure which refers to the date from a purely arithmetic or astronomical meaning, into the name and notion of a historical reality. [...] Each historical date is the technical name and conceptual abbreviation – in short, the definition – of a general form of life constituted by the repertoire of experiences, verbal, intellectual, moral, etc., which 'reign' in a given society.[65]

In view of the long duration of Franquismo, the introduction of its chronological boundaries implies, in turn, the determination of stages, phases or significant periods within the contemporary history of Spain. Here, for the first time, appears the need to describe Francoism with temporary denotations such as 'first Franquismo', 'final Franquismo'. It seems clear that from a historiographic perspective it is not possible to consider the period of the initial configuration of the system, in the context of the Civil War in Spain and of the pre-world war, with Franco in the fullness of his life and physical and mental faculties, in the same way as we consider the end of the regime, in the context of international détente, deep Spanish internal socio-economic transformations and the Caudillo suffering a serious deterioration of his mental faculties and physical decline. In other words, the historian is obliged to break up, to periodize, the time of Franco to find 'spaces of intelligibility' within its global evolution. That is to say, to identify spatial–temporal fractions of a historical phenomenon defined by a particular combination of factors (whether social, economic, political or cultural) that create a uniquely stable situation, without prejudice to the whole.

The consequential and necessary work of historical periodization requires, of course, a determination of the existence of stages, phases or periods differentiated by that combination of relevant significant and substantive factors of social, political, cultural or economic order. The historiography on Franquismo has confronted this task of periodization in meaningful temporary fragments, although the results are not always consistent.

Among the historians and other analysts of Franquismo, there is near unanimity that the whole stage of the dictatorship can be divided, at least roughly, into two distinct periods – articulating a periodization based on a binary scheme. The year 1959, with the adoption of the economic measures of the Plan de Estabilización, is often considered the crucial milestone between the two phases. In fact, almost no one denies that economic decisions taken in that year (required by the previous political and statutory measures and their given immediate social and economic consequences) were a crucial watershed in the evolution of the Franco regime. These measures represented the end of the first stage (still characterized by the political and material effects of the Civil War, with its sequels of repression, misery, autarky and isolation) and the start of a second phase (defined by rapid economic development, profound social change, incipient material well-being and international openness).[66]

In short, a *first*, 'backward', Franquismo existed, with socio-economic stagnation, political rigidity and international isolation, replaced by a *second*, 'modernizing', Franquismo, devoted to social and economic development, political easing and foreign openness. It is still debated among specialists whether 1959 is the date best suited to discriminate between the two stages, or if it is more appropriate to set the year at 1957 (with the resolution of a serious political crisis through a new government) or even 1960 (with the first tangible and positive effects of that stabilization and liberalization) as key milestones in this transformation. In any case, what is not subject to discussion is the relevance of the years 1957–60 as decisive 'hinge years' between these two great stages of the historical evolution of the dictatorship.

A brief review of the historiographical debate bears out the general acceptance of the binary division of Francoism taking as its axis the year 1959. For example, Javier Tusell, a staunch supporter of that binary schema, used four criteria for highlighting two stages defined by 1959:

If I had to point out a cardinal date in Spanish history during the Franco period, without a doubt, with all the reservations of the case, that date would be 1959. Firstly, this year witnessed a fundamental change in economic policy through the Plan de Estabilización, which, in turn, made it possible for further economic development. [...] In domestic policy, this is a moment when the institutionalization of the regime had definitely abandoned the Falangist proposals [...]. As for the opposition, formed only by the vanquished, it had touched its lowest point of activity [...]. Foreign policy had abandoned any attempts at imperialism and had already confronted with flexibility the first problems of decolonization (Morocco) or those even more serious (Ifni).[67]

That is why, in 1993, the first major international conference on Franquismo organized in Spain, directed among others by Javier Tusell and titled 'El Régimen de Franco (1936–75)', took a historiographically far-reaching organizational decision. Its session was divided into two different parts for the purpose of presentation of papers and communications. The first part, under the heading 'Primer Franquismo' ('First Franquismo'), collected all the work relating to the years ranging from 1936 to 1959. The second part, under the heading 'Tecnocracia y crisis' ('Technocracy and Crisis'), collected all works whose scope went from 1959 to 1975. Of course, the corresponding proceedings were divided into two volumes dedicated to the two phases of Franquismo.[68]

Another influential author, the economist Gabriel Tortella, could also be considered an ardent defender of this binary scheme, taking into account, where appropriate, economic factors of socio-political impact. In his often-reprinted 1994 economic history textbook *El desarrollo de la España contemporánea*, Tortella argued for the binary periodization with these compelling reasons:

> From an economic point of view, Francoism divides into two clearly distinct periods: the first 15 years [1939–55] of economic stagnation and slow recovery; the two following decades, [1955–75] of rapid economic growth, intense industrialization and profound social change. The first period saw radically interventionist and autarkic economic policy; the second, a lukewarm liberalization. [...] The history of Franco's economy can be divided into two major periods: until 1959, a fascist-autarky economy; from 1959 until its end in 1975, an economy with open and liberal connotations. It was the dismal failure of the first stage which determined the second step.[69]

One might say that the influence of this binary periodization on the historiography of the Franco regime was formalized by the reputed *Historia de España Menéndez Pidal*, the huge collection started in the 1930s by the historian Menéndez Pidal and revised during the past decade under the general direction of José María Jover Zamora. The volumes dedicated to Franquismo were published in 1996 in Madrid. For example, volume 41/1, edited by the British Hispanist Raymond Carr, under the title 'La época de Franco, 1939–1975' divided its political analysis of the Francoist regime into two major stages defined precisely by the crucial year of 1959: a first stage initially called 'De la posguerra a la tecnocracia' (From postwar to technocracy); and a second stage that culminated with the death of the Caudillo.[70]

Significantly, a few years later, one of the first general studies on the opposition to the Franco regime also adopted this binary criterion. It was a work written by Encarna Nicolás and Alicia Alted Vigil and titled *Disidencias en el Franquismo*.[71] According to its analysis, that book considers the year 1960 as a landmark division. The authors established a binary timeline under the following headings: '1. 1939–1960. Repression, clandestinity, exile' and '2. 1960–1975. Old and new disagreements in the second age of Francoism'.

As a demonstration of the historical survival of this binary scheme, two further influential works that have dealt with the study of 'El Primer Franquismo' (1939–59) should be noted. The first is the book edited by the economic historian Carlos Barciela with the title *Autarquía y mercado negro. El fracaso económico del Primer Franquismo* (*Autarky and Black Market: The Economic Failure of First Francoism*).[72] In its preface, the prominent economist Luis Ángel Rojo (governor of the Bank of Spain between 1992 and 2000) gave the following definition of what is to be understood by 'first Franquismo': 'Historians say that students today show great curiosity in the Spanish economic reality during the "first Francoism", i.e. the period ranging from the Civil War up to the Plan de Estabilización of 1959.' The second book which proves the widespread dissemination of this binary scheme is a work that does not belong to the field of economic history, but to socio-political history: the special issue of the respected Madrid journal *Ayer*, organ of the Asociación de Historia Contemporánea, edited by the historian Glicerio Sánchez Recio, which appeared in 1999 and carried the significant title: 'El Primer franquismo (1939–1959)'. The abstract is revealing: 'it deals with the phase in which the regime was imposed by force, was shaped, and links were established between the state, the single party and society to create the instruments to ensure its existence.'[73]

It does not seem necessary to put more emphasis on this issue. It is evident that the Franco regime as a historical stage divided into two distinct phases defined by the caesura of 1959 is a general historiographic and almost undisputed fact. It is also a timely and convenient teaching resource, at least in the first instance of a general overview.

However, if the lens of analysis zooms in, the generic binary periodization described in no way exhausts the need to define more precisely and rigorously the time of Franquismo – particularly if one looks at the chronological demarcation of political, socio-political and cultural criteria over other economic criteria. In this respect, the opinions and available alternatives are much more varied and controversial because the criteria and factors are more heterogeneous or, at a minimum, debatable.

Thus, for example, one must begin by pointing out that a minority of authors considered that the nearly three years of civil war were not properly part of the period of the Franco dictatorship, but a previous and different stage (of the Civil War). Javier Tusell, in his canonical study *La dictadura de Franco*, defended this thesis with great aplomb:

> In the opinion of the author of this book, it would not make sense to include, as the first of these stages [of Franco's regime], the Spanish Civil War: it would be something like including the Russian Civil War in a history of Stalinism. Not only at the time was it not clear what would be the final result of the contest, but also that if anything characterized Franco's regime it was the almost exclusive, precise focus on the conduct of the war in a way that the few institutional measures taken during the war period followed most of all a propaganda purpose.[74]

Following this advice by Tusell, many historical accounts of Francoism begin in 1939 and not 1936. However, this position is not unanimously accepted. A large majority of researchers believe that the war was decisive in the configuration and the establishment of Franco's dictatorship. Thus, for example, Stanley G. Payne in his 1987 study on Franquismo, started in 1936 with the Civil War as the first stage of the history of the regime, as did the organizers of the already mentioned conference of 1993, in their title 'El Régimen de Franco (1936–1975)'. And much more recently, Giuliana Di Febo and Santos Juliá, aforementioned authors of one of the latest and best introductory textbooks on the subject, restated the case:

> Undoubtedly, the fundamental peculiarity of Franco's regime lies in the fact that it had been structured during the Civil War, that occurred by the attempts of some generals to overthrow the Republican government which had won the elections of 1936. This beginning and *incipit* for a long time marked the institutions, political orientations and the very conception and management of power.[75]

Aside from the inclusion or exclusion of the war phase in the chronology of the Franco regime, the remaining alternatives of periodization of the regime basically rest on a structure that ranges from the use of three stages to a preference for six, passing through four and five as intermediate options.

One scheme of six is, for example, the analysis of Franquismo by two authors, Carme Molinero and Pere Ysàs, an influential 'political history' of the dictatorship that is part of a famous collection of 'Historia de España'.[76] According to them, the history of the regime might be ordered through the following periodization:

1 1939–45: First Franquismo.
2 1945–50: Franquismo surviving.
3 1950–60: Franquismo forgiven.
4 1961–9: Franquismo exultant.
5 1969–73: Franquismo retreating.
6 1973–5: Franquismo in crisis.

A good example of the alternative scheme of five stages is the periodization offered by this author in a global study of the regime (including the period of the Civil War):

1 1936–9: Initial configuration of the regime during the Civil War.
2 1939–45: Stage of national-syndicalist hegemony in the course of World War II.
3 1945–59: Stage of National Catholic predominance in the context of isolation and subsequent subordinate reintegration in the Western arena.
4 1959–69: Stage of authoritarian technocratic development, economic expansion and attempts at political opening up.
5 1969–75: Stage of late Francoism defined by the crisis and terminal agony of the regime.[77]

The scheme of periodization in four stages has a unique example in Manuel Tuñón de Lara's contribution to a general history of Spain with Julio Valdeón and Antonio Domínguez Ortiz.[78] This four-phase scheme again combines political, social, cultural and economic criteria (excluding the three years of the Civil War):

1 1939–50: The years of the 'first Francoismo' or 'blue' stage of 'penchant for fascism', dominated by the impact of the war and its consequences.
2 1951–60: The decade of external consolidation of the regime and the first flare-up of internal rebellion.
3 1961–73: The stage of economic development and growing worker and university conflict.
4 1973–5: The 'epilogue' – the two years characterized by the world economic crisis and internal political crisis.

A slightly different version of this four-part scheme has been suggested by the British Hispanist Paul Preston in different works on the Franco regime. For example, in his 1995 book on fascism and militarism in twentieth-century Spain, Preston points out the existence of four basic stages in the evolution of the dictatorship:

1 1939–45: The so-called 'blue era' of apparent Falangist dominance.
2 1946–57: The period of 'dour Christian democrat rule'.
3 1957–69: The burst of economic modernization presided over by the technocrats associated with Opus Dei.
4 1969–75: The break-up of the regime coalition.[79]

Also attached to the quartet model is the notable manual on Francoism produced by Giuliana Di Febo and Santos Juliá, already quoted. This version has the virtue of incorporating the Civil War as a crucial constituent part of the regime. According to this study, the periodization of Franquismo should follow these four stages:

1 1936–45: The new state.
2 1945–57: Catholic hegemony.
3 1957–69: Authoritarian state and social change.
4 1969–75: The crisis of the regime.

Finally, one of the authors that have better defined the tri-part structure of periodization of the dictatorship is Stanley G. Payne.[80] According to his 1987 introductory study, the story of the Franco regime can be divided into three distinct eras:

1 1936–45: The semi-fascist phase, potentially imperialist.
2 1945–57: The decade of National Catholic corporatism that witnessed the hopeless and final subjugation of the fascist component.
3 1957/9–75: The developmental phase of the so-called technocrats and a kind of bureaucratic authoritarianism.

It should be emphasized that this preference for tri-partition by Payne had a notable precedent in the work of the historian Juan Pablo Fusi in his 1985 biographical essay on Franco.[81] In it, Fusi said that the socio-political evolution of the dictatorship should be studied under the premise of three distinct stages:

1 1939–45: A stage of certain Falangist hegemony.
2 1945–57: A stage of the ascendency of political Catholicism.
3 1957–73 (expandable to 1975): A stage of strong Opus Dei and technocratic presence.

Everything seems to indicate that the tri-part option is still very much alive and even that it is experiencing a noticeable resurgence in recent times. This can be proved by an examination of two very significant and recent cases. First, the new studies of economic history are eclipsing the less accurate binary scheme that saw 1959 as the central dividing point. By way of example, José Luis García Delgado and Juan Carlos Jiménez, in a famous book on Spanish economic history published in 1999, challenged the idea that there had been only two historical stages in Francoism. According to García Delgado and his collaborator, 'three stages are easily distinguishable.' They propose a first stage, defined as 'the first Franquismo', from 1939 until 1950, characterized by 'the harshness of the postwar'. Their second stage is 'the hinge decade', from 1951 until 1959, characterized by 'the zigzaging of economic autarky'. The third and final stage is called 'the years of development', from 1960 until 1975. To justify this tri-part periodization, García Delgado and Jiménez wrote:

The distinction of these three fundamental stages has, however, unquestionable advantages for the study of Spanish economic evolution during Francoism. First, it singles out the 1950s, avoiding therefore the excessive simplification that is sometimes incurred in distinguishing just two great periods in the Francoist economy, divided by the crossroads of 1959: first, autarky; later, economic openness and development. It also has in its favour the facility to make meaningful comparisons at an international level, adjusting to chronological compartmentalization which, broadly speaking, can be seen in the evolution of Western European economies: war and recovery in the 1940s; openness, cooperation and growth in the decade of 1950, and integration and continuity of development in the 1960s until, at the end, unmistakable signs of exhaustion of the prolonged previous expansion cycle are evident. Tri-partition simplifies, in the end, the selection of the determining factors of the route of the Spanish economy in the Franco regime.[82]

It is not only new economic histories of Francoism that have unveiled the 1950s as an age of notorious growth, installed as a kind of hinge between the autarky and misery of the 1940s and the development and well-being of the 1960s. For example, the three-part structure is also the one adopted by a renowned study on the cultural and everyday life of Franquismo written by Jordi Gracia and Miguel Ángel Ruiz Carnicer.[83] In the opinion of these authors, the evolution of Spanish society and culture under the Franco regime should be studied according to three basic phases which mainly take into account cultural factors and daily life:

1 Postwar Spain: Terror and gasifiers.
2 1950s: From desolation to hope.
3 1960–75: Social control and articulation of protest.

In short, this summary of the varied and divergent attempts at periodizing the Franco dictatorship suggests something notorious and relevant: the difficulty of establishing definitive historiographic agreement on the precise phases that were outlined in the chronological evolution of the Franco dictatorship. Above all, regardless of the type of analysis exercised (political, social, economic or cultural), it is clear that none of the alternatives raised is fully satisfactory – all lack nuance and generate difficulties.

In any case, one needs to remember that the proposed hypothetical evolutionary stages correspond to the development of a political regime defined from beginning to end by a common and persistent factor: the huge concentration of almost absolute and unlimited political power in the hands of a single man, General Franco, in his capacity as Caudillo of Spain by the grace of God. This is already a common and accredited thesis, confirmed by an opinion as little suspected of being anti-Francoist as that of Stanley G. Payne in his contribution to the corresponding volume of the accredited *Historia de España Menéndez Pidal*, published in 1996: 'In 1939, Franco had concentrated in his hands much more power than any previous Spanish ruler, since no medieval or early modern monarch enjoyed an authority as absolute as his.'[84]

For this reason we could reiterate that perhaps the only defining and configurative constant of the Franco regime was the presence of General Franco as an absolute Bonapartist military dictator of unappealable judgement and sovereign 'lifetime power', only responsible 'before God and history'. Thus it was appreciated and described long ago by the fine and insightful observer, the historian Salvador de Madariaga:

> Franco's political strategy is as simple as a spear. There is no action of his that is not directed towards his consolidation in power. Under the appearance of varied and even contradictory tactics (peace, neutrality, bellicosity; amnesty, persecution; monarchy, regency), the only thing that Franco believes in is Franco himself.[85]

This judgement by Madariaga must be always present when it comes to understanding the long times of Francoism and its political modulations. It was reiterated in 2010 by the historian Borja de Riquer in what is probably the most up-to-date global research on the Franco regime. His words may serve as the climax to this section and the whole of this work:

> Franco was a chameleon-like character who, without ever renouncing his fierce authoritarianism, knew how to exercise it in successive forms of fascist

caudillo, devoted national Catholic and modern technocrat. But the permanent and decisive fact was, that above all else, Franco acted always as a soldier. His main political ace consisted of keeping the army united, disciplined and loyal to himself. Although his regime was not strictly a military dictatorship, the armed forces always enjoyed a decisive role: they had won the war, raised Franco to head of state and accepted his dictatorship at the same time that they emerged as the main guarantor of his lifelong and unlimited power. The fascist and national Catholic components, which were always present in the regime, had a relative and temporary importance. At the end, Franco finished shaping the regime in his image and at his convenience.[86]

Notes

Introduction: Franco: An Uncomfortable Spectre from the Past

1 These were titles used in official publications. See, for example, the decree of the Junta de Defensa Nacional published in *Boletín Oficial del Estado* (30 September 1936); the article 'Caudillo de España' in *Extremadura. Diario católico* (1 April 1944); and the book by Luis de Galinsoga and Francisco Franco Salgado-Araujo, *Centinela de Occidente. Semblanza biográfica de Francisco Franco* (Barcelona: AHR, 1956).

2 José María Pemán, *La historia de España contada con sencillez para los niños ... y para muchos que no lo son* (Cádiz: Cerón y Librería Cervantes, 1939), vol. 2, p. 213.

3 Antonio Muñoz Molina, 'La cara que veía en todas partes', *El País*, 19 November 2000.

4 Vicente Sánchez-Biosca, 'Introducción. Los iconos de Franco: imágenes en la memoria', in V. Sánchez-Biosca (coordinator), *Materiales para una iconografía de Francisco Franco*, double issue of the journal *Archivos de la Filmoteca* (Valencia) 42–3/1 (2002–3), pp. 16–17.

5 The reluctance to call Franco a dictator or to address him by his official titles (Caudillo and Generalissimo) is systematic. For an example, see the text of the photographic exhibition sponsored by the Fundación Telefónica, *25 años después. Memoria gráfica de una transición*, exhibited in Madrid between 16 November 2000 and 10 January 2001: 'En noviembre de 2000 se cumplen veinticinco años de la muerte del anterior Jefe del Estado'.

6 Juan José Linz (ed.), *Informe sociológico sobre el cambio político en España 1975–1981* (Madrid: Euramérica, 1981), p. 588.

7 The findings of the survey were published in *El País*, 19 November 1985.

8   Survey carried out by the Servicio de Estudios of *El País*. The fieldwork was completed between 6 and 11 November 1985. *El País*, 20 November 1985.

9   Jesús Rodríguez, 'Ese fantasma de la historia', *El País*, 19 November 2000.

10 Survey carried out by Demoscopia and published in *El País*, 19 November 2000.

11 Survey carried out by Sigma-Dos. *El Mundo*, 20 November 2000.

12 *Estudio 2.401. 25 años después* (Madrid: CIS, 2000), pp. 1–2.

13 Survey conducted by Sigma-Dos, *El Mundo*, 19 November 2005.

14 *El Mundo*, 18 July 2006.

15 *Estudio CIS número 2.760. Memorias de la guerra civil y el franquismo* (Madrid: CIS, 2008). For the debate opened up by this law in Spain, see the contributions of Sebastian Balfour, Julián Casanova, Ángela Cenarro, Enrique Moradiellos and Antonio Cazorla in *International Journal of Iberian Studies* 21/3 (2008) (Themed Issue: Historical Memory and Revisionism: The Spanish Civil War and the Franco Dictatorship).

16 Antonio Cazorla, *Franco. Biografía del mito* (Madrid: Aguilar, 2015), p. 320. English edition: *Franco: The Biography of the Myth* (New York: Routledge, 2014).

17 Both cited by Paloma Aguilar Fernández, *Memoria y olvido de la guerra civil española* (Madrid: Alianza, 1996), pp. 31 and 48. On this topic, see the reflections of Alberto Reig Tapia, *Memoria de la guerra civil. Los mitos de la tribu* (Madrid: Alianza, 1999). A review of the topic is in Helen Graham, *The War and its Shadows: Spain's Civil War in Europe's Long Twentieth Century* (Brighton: Sussex Academic Press, 2012) and Gonzalo Pasamar (ed.), *Ha estallado la memoria. Las huellas de la guerra civil en la Transición a la democracia* (Madrid: Biblioteca Nueva, 2014).

18 Real Decreto-Ley nº 10/76 of 30 July 1976. *Boletín Oficial del Estado*, 3 and 4 August 1976. My emphasis.

19 '18 de julio' (editorial article), *El País*, 17 July 1977.

20 *El País*, 15 October 1977.

21 Both quotations in *El País*, 24 May 1993 and 29 March 2001.

22 See in this respect the contributions gathered by Josefina Cuesta (ed.), *Memorias históricas de España. Siglo XX* (Madrid: Fundación Largo Caballero, 2007).

23 Francisco Ayala, 'El sentido de una pregunta', *El País*, 18 July 1996.

24 Santos Juliá was editor of the first serious study on this subject: *Víctimas de*

la guerra civil (Madrid: Temas de Hoy, 1999). The latest and most up-to-date analysis, which validates these figures in general terms, is in Paul Preston, *The Spanish Holocaust: Inquisition and Extermination in Twentieth Century Spain* (London: Harper, 2012).

25 Jon Elster, *Closing the Books: Transitional Justice in Historical Experience* (Cambridge: Cambridge University Press, 2004). Stathis N. Kalyvas, *The Logic of Violence in Civil War* (Cambridge: Cambridge University Press, 2006).

26 Santos Juliá, 'Echar al olvido: memoria y amnistía', in Santos Juliá, *Hoy no es ayer. Ensayos sobre la España del siglo XX* (Barcelona: RBA, 2010), ch. 12, p. 313.

27 Fragment of the first speech by King Juan Carlos before the Cortes, 22 November 1975, reproduced in Laureano López Rodó, *La larga marcha hacia la monarquía* (Barcelona: Noguer, 1977), p. 497.

28 Anonymous report entitled 'Vestigios mudos del pasado', *El País*, 18 July 1986; and news on 'la estatua del dictador' in *El País*, 4 July 2008 and *Abc*, 19 September 2013. Pieter Leenknegt, 'El Franco ecuestre de Capuz: una estatua, tres destinos', in *Archivos de la Filmoteca* 42–3/2 (2002-3), vol. 2, pp. 13–29 (in the case of Valencia, pp. 26–9). The three equestrian statues in Valencia, Madrid and Santander are works by the same sculptor: the Valencian José Capuz.

29 José L. Lobo, 'Así que pasen otros 25 años', *El Mundo*, 20 November 2000. See Manuel Darriba, 'Ferrol, huérfano', *El Periódico de Extremadura*, 19 November 2000. News of the fate of the statue was in *El Mundo*, 18 March 2010.

30 Rafael Fraguas, 'Franco, aún presente', *El País*, 18 November 2000. Pieter Leenknegt, 'El Franco ecuestre de Capuz: una estatua, tres destinos', pp. 16–19. News on the withdrawal in *El País*, 17 March 2005. Jesús de Andrés, 'Las estatuas de Franco, la memoria del franquismo y la transición política española', *Historia y Política* 12 (2004), pp. 161–86.

31 Alberto Reig Tapia, *Memoria y olvido de la guerra civil*, p. 27.

32 Jesús Delgado, 'El franquismo sigue vivo en el callejero', *El País*, 18 February 2001. The study, commissioned by the city of Santander, was completed by Carlos Dardé (University of Cantabria), Miguel Ángel Sánchez (UNED) and Benito Madariaga (official chronicler of the city). See Leenknegt, 'El Franco ecuestre de Capuz', pp. 23–6; and the news of the withdrawal in *El País*, 18 December 2008.

33   Santos Juliá's statements included in the collection by Javier Valenzuela, 'El despertar tras la amnesia', *El País*, 2 November 2002.

34   See the reflections of Fernando Savater, 'Lo que queda de franquismo', *El País*, 20 November 1992; Javier Pradera, 'Las huellas del franquismo. Los vestigios en la cultura política española de una dictadura de casi cuarenta años', *El País*, 3 December 1992; and Tereixa Constela, 'El franquismo. 40 años después', *El País*, 28 March 2015. See Enrique González Duro, *La sombra del general* (Madrid: Debate, 2005).

35   Julián Casanova (ed.), *40 años con Franco* (Barcelona: Crítica, 2014), p. 13.

36   Statements collected in *El Mundo*, 20 November 2000.

37   'Los papeles de Franco', *La aventura de la historia* 38 (December 2001), p. 12. 'Archivo de la dictadura', *El Mundo*, 22 September 2002.

38   Rafael Fraguas, 'Una sepultura para Franco en Mingorrubio', *El País*, 16 October 2010. See Jeremy Treglown, *La cripta de Franco. Viaje por la memoria y la cultura del franquismo* (Barcelona: Ariel, 2014), pp. 63–73, published in English as *Franco's Crypt: Spanish Culture and Memory since 1936* (London: Chatto and Windus, 2014).

39   Quoted in David Lowenthal, *The Past is a Foreign Country* (Cambridge: Cambridge University Press, 2003), p. 68: Lord Acton, 'Inaugural Lecture on the Study of History', delivered in Cambridge in June 1895.

40   Ian Kershaw, 'Introduction: Reflecting on Hitler', in Ian Kershaw, *Hitler, 1889–1936: Hubris* (London: Penguin Books, 2001).

1: The Man: A Brief Biography

1   J. Arrarás Iribarren, *Franco* (Valladolid: Santarén, 1939), pp. 303 and 314.

2   Luis de Galinsoga and Francisco Franco Salgado-Araujo, *Centinela de Occidente. Semblanza biográfica de Francisco Franco* (Barcelona: Editorial AHR, 1956).

3   José María Sánchez Silva and José Luis Sáenz de Heredia, *Franco, ese hombre* (Madrid: Lidisa, 1975), pp. 150–1 and 154.

4   Ricardo de la Cierva, *Francisco Franco: un siglo de España*, 2 vols (Madrid: Editora Nacional, 1973).

5   Luis Suárez Fernández, *Francisco Franco y su tiempo*, 8 vols (Madrid: Fundación F. Franco, 1984).

6   Salvador de Madariaga, *General, márchese usted* (New York: Ediciones Ibéricas, 1959), pp. 10–11. The title is a play on words as in Spanish 'sentinel' and 'leech' are pronounced in a similar way.

7   Luis Ramírez, *Francisco Franco: historia de un mesianismo* (París: Ruedo Ibérico, 1964).

8   Amando de Miguel, *Franco, Franco, Franco* (Madrid: Ediciones 99, 1976).

9   Francisco Umbral, *La leyenda del César visionario* (Barcelona: Seix Barral, 1991). Manuel Vázquez Montalbán, *Autobiografía del general Franco* (Barcelona: Mondadori, 1992). José Luis de Vilallonga, *El sable del Caudillo* (Barcelona: Plaza y Janés, 1997). Albert Boadella, *Franco y yo. Buen viaje, Excelencia* (Madrid: Espasa, 2003). Juan Luis Cebrián, *Francomoribundia* (Madrid: Alfaguara, 2003).

10 Juan Pablo Fusi Aizpurúa, *Franco: autoritarismo y poder personal* (Madrid: El País, 1985). Proof of the success of the book was its immediate translation into English with an introductory preface by the Hispanist Raymond Carr as *Franco: A Biography* (London: Unwin Hyman, 1987).

11 Stanley G. Payne, *Franco, el perfil de la historia* (Madrid: Espasa Calpe, 1992). Javier Tusell. *Franco en la guerra civil. Una biografía política* (Barcelona: Tusquets, 1992).

12 Paul Preston. *Franco: A Biography* (London: HarperCollins, 1993) pp. xx–xxi. Spanish translation published in Barcelona by Ediciones Grijalbo in 1994 as *Franco. Caudillo de España*.

13 A. Reig Tapia, *Franco, 'caudillo'. Mito y realidad* (Madrid: Tecnos, 1995). B. Bennassar, *Franco* (Madrid: Edaf, 1996). A. Bachoud, *Franco* (Barcelona: Crítica, 2000). F. García de Cortázar, *Fotobiografía de Franco* (Barcelona: Planeta, 2000). Stanley G. Payne and Jesús Palacios, *Franco: A Personal and Political Biography* (Madison: University of Wisconsin Press, 2014). I would also like to mention my own contribution: E. Moradiellos, *Francisco Franco. Crónica de un caudillo casi olvidado* (Madrid: Biblioteca Nueva, 2002).

14 Confession of Franco in October 1973 to Luis Moreno Nieto. Reproduced in the extremely hagiographic biography by the journalist Rogelio Baón, *La cara humana de un Caudillo* (Madrid: San Martín, 1975), p. 49.

15 Franco's response to a question in an interview published by a Madrid illustrated magazine: 'Are you political? I am a soldier, he affirmed outright and definitively.' *Estampa*, 29 May 1929.

16   Opinion in *Franco visto por sus ministros* (Barcelona: Planeta, 1981), p. 195. The previous quote is in Pedro Sainz Rodríguez, *Testimonio y recuerdo* (Barcelona: Planeta, 1978), p. 324.

17   M. Menéndez y Pelayo, *Historia de España seleccionada en la obra del maestro* (Madrid: Gráfica Universal, 1934), pp. 352 and 354. The book, a compilation of writings edited by General Jorge Vigón, was widely circulated in military and right-wing circles. On the impact of Menéndez y Pelayo see Juan Pablo Fusi, *España. La evolución de la identidad nacional* (Madrid: Temas de Hoy, 2000), pp. 188 and 241–2; and Jorge Novella, *El pensamiento reaccionario español, 1812–1975* (Madrid: Biblioteca Nueva, 2007), ch. 9.

18   Quoted by Stanley G. Payne, *Los militares y la política en la España contemporánea* (París: Ruedo Ibérico, 1968), p. 80, originally published as *Politics and the Military in Modern Spain* (Stanford: Stanford University Press, 1967). See Gabriel Cardona, *El poder militar en la España contemporánea hasta la guerra civil* (Madrid: Siglo XXI, 1983) and Geoffrey Jensen, *Irrational Triumph: Cultural Despair, Military Nationalism and the Ideological Origins of Franco's Spain* (Reno: University of Nevada Press, 2002).

19   José Ortega y Gasset, *España invertebrada* (Cáceres: Universidad de Extremadura, 1999), p. 43.

20   The first quote is from a speech at the town hall of Baracaldo (21 June 1950). The second is from his declarations in Paris journal *Le Figaro* (13 June 1958). Both are quoted in F. Franco, *Pensamiento político de Franco* (Madrid: Servicio Informativo Español, 1964), pp. 54 and 57.

21   Payne, *Los militares y la política en la España contemporánea*, chs 7 and 9, pp. 428–9. María Rosa de Madariaga, *España y el Rif. Crónica de una historia casi olvidada* (Melilla: UNED, 2000).

22   Esteban Carvallo de Cora, *Hoja de servicios del Caudillo de España* (Madrid: Biosca, 1967). Also see Juan Blázquez Miguel, *Franco. Trayectoria militar* (Madrid: Almena, 2009).

23   Francisco Franco, *Marruecos. Diario de una bandera* (Madrid: Pueyo, 1922), pp. 57–8 and 89–90. Later editions eliminated passages of the original text: F. Franco, *Papeles de la guerra de Marruecos* (Madrid: Fundación Nacional F. Franco, 1986).

24   Sebastian Balfour, *Deadly Embrace: Morocco and the Road to the Spanish Civil War* (Oxford: Oxford University Press, 2002). Gustau Nerín, *La guerra que vino de África* (Barcelona: Crítica, 2005).

25 Declarations of Franco, 31 December 1939 in *Palabras del Caudillo, 19 Abril 1937–31 Diciembre 1938* (Barcelona: Ediciones Fe, 1939).

26 Judgement expressed by the Falangist leader José María Fontana, *Franco. Radiografía del personaje para sus contemporáneos* (Barcelona: Acervo, 1979), p. 28. Also see Stanley G. Payne and Jesús Palacios, *Franco, mi padre. Testimonio de Carmen Franco* (Madrid: La esfera de los libros, 2008).

27 Notes on his private life in Baón, *La cara humana de un Caudillo*, pp. 30, 37, 52 and 126. Vicente Gil, *Cuarenta años junto a Franco* (Barcelona: Planeta, 1981). José María Fontana would write of Franco's friendships: 'Very few friends, one could say none' (Fontana, *Franco. Radiografía del personaje*, p. 28).

28 Good overviews of the period are in Francisco J. Romero Salvadó, *Twentieth-Century Spain: Politics and Society in Spain, 1898–1998* (London: Routledge, 1999); Mary Vincent, *Spain 1833–2002: People and State* (Oxford: Oxford University Press, 2007); and Julián Casanova and Carlos Gil-Andrés, *Twentieth-Century Spain: A History* (Cambridge: Cambridge University Press, 2009).

29 Francisco J. Romero Salvadó and Angel Smith (eds), *The Agony of Spanish Liberalism: From Revolution to Dictatorship, 1913–1923* (New York: Palgrave Macmillan, 2010). On the effects of World War I, see Arthur Marwick (ed.), *Total War and Historical Change in Europe, 1914–1945* (Buckingham: Open University Press, 2001).

30 Preston, *Franco*, p. 49.

31 Carlos Blanco Escolá, *La Academia General Militar de Zaragoza* (Barcelona: Labor, 1989). Carvallo de Cora, *Hoja de servicios del Caudillo*, p. 77. Ricardo de la Cierva, *Franco* (Barcelona: Planeta, 1986), p. 101.

32 José Antonio Ferrer Benimeli, 'Franco y la masonería', in Josep Fontana (ed.), *España bajo el franquismo* (Barcelona: Crítica, 1986), pp. 246–68. Herbert R. Southworth, *Conspiracy and the Spanish Civil War: The Brainwashing of Francisco Franco* (London: Routledge, 2000).

33 According to the judgement of Ricardo de la Cierva, *Historia del Franquismo* (Barcelona: Planeta, 1975), vol. 1, p. 102.

34 Confession of the minister of finance between 1957 and 1965, *Franco visto por sus ministros*, p. 88. The phrase about the arrogance of intellectuals is from José María Pemán and is reproduced in Baón, *La cara humana de un Caudillo*, p. 163.

35　The political crisis in the Republican period is analysed in Paul Preston, *The Coming of the Spanish Civil War: Reform, Reaction and Revolution in the Second Republic* (London: Routledge, 1994); Nigel Townson, *The Crisis of Democracy in Spain: Centrist Politics under the Second Republic, 1931–1936* (Eastbourne: Sussex Academic Press, 2000); and Manuel Álvarez Tardío and Fernando del Rey (eds), *The Spanish Second Republic Revisited: From Democratic Hopes to the Civil War* (Eastbourne: Sussex Academic Press, 2011).

36　F. Franco, *Apuntes personales sobre la República y la guerra civil* (Madrid: Fundación Nacional F. Franco, 1987), p. 7.

37　F. Franco Salgado-Araujo, *Mis conversaciones privadas con Franco* (Barcelona: Planeta, 1976), p. 425.

38　Ricardo de la Cierva, *Franco*, p. 121.

39　M. Azaña, *Memorias políticas y de guerra, 1931–1939* (Barcelona: Grijalbo-Mondadori, 1978), vol. 1, pp. 47 and 100. The first comment from Sanjurjo is in Preston, *Franco*, p. 119. The judgement of her brother in Pilar Franco, *Nosotros, los Franco* (Barcelona: Planeta, 1980), p. 73.

40　The impact of the Depression is well covered in Joseph Harrison, *An Economic History of Modern Spain* (Manchester: Manchester University Press, 1978), pp. 125–44. See Jordi Palafox, *Atraso económico y democracia: la Segunda República y la economía española* (Barcelona: Crítica, 1991).

41　Quoted in Preston, *Franco*, p. 105.

42　Ramón Serrano Suñer, *Entre el silencio y la propaganda, la Historia como fue. Memorias* (Barcelona: Planeta, 1977).

43　Raúl Morodo, *Los orígenes ideológicos del franquismo: Acción Española* (Madrid: Alianza, 1985).

44　Stanley G. Payne, *Franco y José Antonio. El extraño caso del fascismo español* (Barcelona: Planeta, 1997).

45　Arrarás, *Franco*, p. 226. Franco, *Apuntes personales*, pp. 25–31.

46　This version of the interview is quoted in Arrarás, *Franco*, pp. 228–9. See Preston, *Franco*, p. 121.

47　Note of 27 April 1968. Franco Salgado-Araujo, *Mis conversaciones privadas*, p. 526. The earlier comment on the lack of army unity was told by Franco to General Orgaz at the beginning of spring. Preston, *Franco*, p. 129.

48　Note of 27 April 1968. Franco Salgado-Araujo, *Mis conversaciones privadas*, p. 527. Suárez Fernández, *Francisco Franco*, vol. 2, pp. 24–5. Franco, *Apuntes personales*, pp. 33–4.

49 Radio broadcast of 13 September 1936. Emilio Mola, *Obras completas* (Valladolid: Santarén, 1940), p. 1184.

50 The text of the manifesto, published on 18 July, was reproduced in the Seville newspaper *Abc*, 23 July 1936.

51 Preston, *Franco*, pp. 151. De la Cierva, *Franco*, p. 164. Franco, *Nosotros, los Franco*, p. 89.

52 Updated overviews of the conflict are in Francisco J. Romero-Salvadó, *The Spanish Civil War* (New York: Palgrave Macmillan, 2005); Helen Graham, *The Spanish Civil War* (Oxford: Oxford University Press, 2005); Paul Preston, *The Spanish Civil War* (London: Norton & Co., 2007); and Julián Casanova, *The Spanish Republic and Civil War* (Cambridge: Cambridge University Press, 2010).

53 An overview of the international context of the war is in Enrique Moradiellos, 'The International Dimensions of the Spanish Civil War', in Frank McDonough (ed.), *The Origins of the Second World War* (London: Continuum, 2011), pp. 311–26. See Michael Alpert, *A New International History of the Spanish Civil War* (London: Macmillan, 1997) and Enrique Moradiellos, *El reñidero de Europa. Las dimensiones internacionales de la guerra civil española* (Barcelona: Península, 2001).

54 Confession made towards the end of his life, in 1974, to his doctor Vicente Pozuelo, *Los últimos 476 días de Franco* (Barcelona: Planeta, 1992), p. 46.

55 *Boletín Oficial del Estado*, 30 September 1936.

56 Alejandro Pizarroso (ed.), *Propaganda en guerra* (Salamanca: Consorcio, 2002).

57 Preston, *Franco*, p. 183.

58 F. Franco, *Discursos y escritos del Caudillo* (Madrid: n.p., 1939), p. 12.

59 On the profile of the military in the war see Gabriel Cardona, *Historia militar de una guerra civil* (Barcelona: Flor del Viento, 2006); Jorge Martínez Reverte, *El arte de matar. Cómo se hizo la guerra civil española* (Barcelona: RBA, 2009); and James Matthews, *Reluctant Warriors: Republican Popular Army and Nationalist Army Conscripts in the Spanish Civil War* (Oxford: Oxford University Press, 2012).

60 *Boletín Oficial del Estado*, 20 April 1937. Sheelagh M. Ellwood, *Spanish Fascism in the Franco Era: Falange Española de las JONS, 1936–76* (London: Macmillan, 1987). Ismael Saz, *Fascismo y franquismo* (Valencia: Universidad

de Valencia, 2004). Joan María Thomàs, *La Falange de Franco. El proyecto fascista del régimen* (Barcelona: Plaza y Janés, 2001).

61 Dispatch of 14 April 1937. *Documents on German Foreign Policy, 1918–1945*, Series D, vol. 3, *Germany and the Spanish Civil War* (London: His Majesty's Stationery Office, 1951), no. 243. Hereafter: *DGFP*, volume and document number.

62 In the words of R. Serrano Suñer, *Entre Hendaya y Gibraltar* (Madrid: Nauta, 1973), pp. 57, 59 and 117.

63 According to Tusell in *Franco en la guerra civil*, p. 139.

64 Azaña, *Memorias políticas y de guerra*, vol. 2, p. 313. Annotation of 6 October 1937.

65 Quoted in María Luisa Rodríguez Aisa, *El cardenal Gomá y la Guerra de España* (Madrid: CSIC, 1981), p. 23. Hilari Raguer, *Gunpowder and Incense: The Catholic Church and the Spanish Civil War* (London: Routledge, 2007). Alfonso Álvarez Bolado, *Para ganar la guerra, para ganar la paz. Iglesia y guerra civil* (Madrid: Universidad Pontificia de Comillas, 1995). See Mary Vincent, 'The Spanish Civil War as a War of Religion', in Martin Baumeister and Stefanie Schüler-Springorum (eds), *'If you tolerate this …': The Spanish Civil War in the Age of Total War* (Frankfurt: Campus, 2008), pp. 74–89.

66 Declarations of Father Bulart in Baón, *La cara humana de un Caudillo*, pp. 33–4; and María Mérida, *Testigos de Franco. Retablo íntimo de una dictadura* (Barcelona: Plaza y Janés, 1977), p. 33.

67 Giuliana Di Febo, *Ritos de guerra y de victoria en la España franquista* (Valencia: Universidad de Valencia, 2012), pp. 87–94.

68 The words of Martínez Reverte in his *El arte de matar*, pp. 263–4. See Michael Alpert, 'The Clash of Spanish Armies: Contrasting Ways of War in Spain, 1936–1939', *War in History* 6/3 (1999), pp. 331–51.

69 Herbert R. Southworth, *Guernica! Guernica! A Study of Journalism, Diplomacy, Propaganda and History* (Berkeley: University of California Press, 1977). José Luis de la Granja and J.A. Echániz (eds), *Gernika y la guerra civil* (Guernica: Gernikazarra Historia Taldea, 1998).

70 Dispatch of 10 December 1936. *DGFP*, vol. 3, no. 148.

71 Galeazzo Ciano, *Ciano's Hidden Diary, 1937–1938* (New York: Dutton, 1953), p. 46.

72 Quoted in Preston, *Franco*, pp. 221–2.

73 Preston, *Franco*. pp. 241–2.

74 Franco Salgado-Araujo, *Mis conversaciones privadas*, p. 78. Annotation of 5 February 1955.

75 Santos Juliá (ed.), *Víctimas de la guerra civil* (Madrid: Taurus, 1999), pp. 407–12. Paul Preston, *The Spanish Holocaust: Inquisition and Extermination in Twentieth Century Spain* (London: Harper, 2012). See Julius Ruiz, 'A Spanish Genocide? Reflections on the Francoist Repression after the Spanish Civil War', *Contemporary European History* 14/2 (2005), pp. 171–91.

76 Tusell, *Franco en la guerra civil*, pp. 228–33. See *Los 90 ministros de Franco* (Barcelona: Dopesa, 1970), pp. 19–67.

77 *Boletín Oficial del Estado*, 31 January 1938.

78 Franco, *Palabras del Caudillo*, p. 168.

79 *Boletín Oficial del Estado*, 10 March 1938.

80 *Abc*, 2 April 1939. Paul Preston, *El final de la guerra. La última puñalada a la República* (Madrid: Debate, 2014).

81 Jordi Catalán, *La economía española y la Segunda Guerra Mundial* (Barcelona: Ariel, 1995), pp. 40–59. José Ángel Sánchez Asiaín, *La financiación de la guerra civil española* (Barcelona: Crítica, 2012), ch. 22.

82 Di Febo, *Ritos de guerra y de victoria en la España franquista*, p. 115.

83 Memorandum by Count Torrellano, 20 May 1938, quoted in Enrique Moradiellos, *La perfidia de Albión. El gobierno británico y la guerra civil española* (Madrid: Siglo XXI, 1996), p. 306.

84 Elena Hernández Sandoica and Enrique Moradiellos, 'Spain and the Second World War', in Neville Wylie (ed.), *European Neutrals and Non-Belligerents During the Second World War* (Cambridge: Cambridge University Press, 2002), pp. 241–67. See contributions of Christian Leitz, Paul Preston and Denis Smith in Sebastian Balfour and Paul Preston (eds), *Spain and the Great Powers in the 20th Century* (Oxford: Routledge, 1999). There are three essential general studies on the theme: Javier Tusell, *Franco, España y la Segunda Guerra Mundial* (Madrid: Temas de Hoy, 1995). Luis Suárez Fernández, *España, Franco y la Segunda Guerra Mundial* (Madrid: Actas, 1997). Manuel Ros Agudo, *La guerra secreta de Franco, 1939–1945* (Barcelona: Crítica, 2002).

85 Quoted in Javier Tusell and Genoveva García, *Franco y Mussolini. La política española durante la Segunda Guerra Mundial* (Barcelona: Planeta, 1985), p. 97.

86 Letter published in *I Documenti Diplomatici Italiani* (hereafter *DDI*), 9th series (1939–43), vol. 4 (Rome: 1954), document no. 847.

87   Quoted in Enrique Moradiellos, *Franco frente a Churchill. España y Gran Bretaña en la Segunda Guerra Mundial* (Barcelona: Península, 2005), pp. 118–19. Ramón Serrano Suñer, *Entre el silencio y la propaganda, la Historia como fue* (Barcelona: Planeta, 1977), p. 288.

88   The minutes of the interview are in *DGFP*, vol. 9, no. 456. The letter to Hitler ended: 'I do not need to assure you how great my desire is not to remain aloof from your cares and how great is my satisfaction in rendering to you at all times services which you regard as most valuable.' The report to Mussolini, 18 June 1940 is in *DDI*, vol. 5, no. 54.

89   Stanley G. Payne, *Franco and Hitler: Spain, Germany and World War II* (New Haven: Yale University Press, 2008). David W. Pike, *Franco and the Axis Stigma* (New York: Palgrave Macmillan, 2008). See also the contributions of Christian Leitz ('Nazi Germany and Francoist Spain') and Paul Preston ('Italy and Spain in Civil War and World War') in Balfour and Preston (eds), *Spain and the Great Powers in the 20th Century*, chs 6 and 7.

90   Report from Canaris, 27 August 1940. Reproduced in the diary of General Franz Halder, chief of the general staff of the Army High Command, *The Halder War Diary, 1939–1942* (London: Greenhill Books, 1988), p. 252.

91   Moradiellos, *Franco frente a Churchill*, pp. 134–46. Richard Wigg, *Churchill and Spain: The Survival of the Franco Regime, 1940–45* (Oxford: Routledge, 2005).

92   Memorandum by A. Yencken (commercial attaché at the Madrid embassy), 5 January 1942. Foreign Office Records, series 'Political Correspondence' (371), vol. 31234, document no. C514. Hereafter FO 371/31234 C514. Professor Atkinson, 'Anglo-Spanish Relations since the Outbreak of the War', 3 June 1942, FO 371/31230 C5659. All British sources used are in The National Archives in Kew, Surrey.

93   The German minutes of the conversation in *DGFP*, vol. 11, nos 63, 66, 67, 97, 104 and 117. Serrano Suñer, *Entre el silencio y la propaganda*, pp. 329–48.

94   Notes by Ciano on an interview with Hitler (28 September) and conversation with Mussolini (1 October), *Ciano's Diary, 1939–1943* (London: Heinemann, 1947), pp. 294–5. The German minutes of the interview are in *DGFP*, vol. 11, no. 124. Minutes of meeting in *DGFP*, vol. 11, no. 149, and *DDI*, vol. 5, no. 677. *Ciano's Diplomatic Papers* (London: Odhams Press, 1948), pp. 395–8.

95   P. Preston, 'Franco and Hitler: The Myth of Hendaye 1940', *Contemporary*

European History 1/1 (1992), pp. 1–16. The German minutes of the interview are in *DGFP*, vol. 11, nos 220 and 221. Serrano Suñer's version in *Entre el silencio y la propaganda*, pp. 283–308. See Manuel Ros, *Franco/Hitler, 1940. De la Gran Tentación al Gran Engaño* (Madrid: Arco Libro, 2009).

96   *Ciano's Diplomatic Papers*, p. 404.

97   The report by Canaris in *DGFP*, vol. 11, no. 476. Maximum pressure was exerted on 21 January 1941. *DGFP*, vol. 11, nos 682 and 692.

98   The congratulations and offer in *DGFP*, vol. 12, no. 671, and vol. 13, no. 12. Xavier Moreno Juliá, *The Blue Division: Spanish Blood in Russia, 1941–1945* (Eastbourne: Sussex Academic Press, 2015). Gerald R. Kleinfeld and Lewis A. Tambs, *Hitler's Spanish Legion: The Blue Division* (Carbondale: Southern Illinois University Press, 1979).

99   R. Serrano Suñer, *Entre Hendaya y Gibraltar* (Barcelona: Nauta, 1973), p. 209.

100 The speech was reproduced in the Spanish press on 18 July and had great international repercussions. See as an example the Cáceres paper *Extremadura*, 18 July 1941.

101 The British ambassador, Sir Samuel Hoare, repeatedly heard such explanations: Samuel Hoare, *Ambassador on Special Mission* (London: Collins, 1946), p. 139; and also the adviser to the US embassy in Madrid, Willard L. Beaulac, *Franco: Silent Ally in World War II* (Carbondale: Southern Illinois University Press, 1986), pp. 177–82.

102 Report entitled 'Consideraciones sobre la situación internacional actual en orden a la actitud de España', 12 December 1941, Archivo General de la Universidad de Navarra, Fondo Carrero Blanco, series 'Política Internacional'. On the growing importance of Carrero Blanco see Javier Tusell, *Carrero. La eminencia gris del régimen de Franco* (Madrid: Temas de Hoy, 1993).

103 Manuel Loff, *Salazarismo e franquismo na Época de Hitler* (Oporto: Campo das Letras, 1996). Juan Carlos Jiménez Redondo, 'La política del Bloque Ibérico. Las relaciones hispano-portuguesas (1936–1949)', *Mèlanges de la Casa de Velázquez* 29/3 (1993), pp. 175–201.

104 Denis Smyth, 'Screening "Torch": Allied Counter-Intelligence and the Spanish Threat to the Secrecy of the Allied Invasion of French North Africa in November, 1942', *Intelligence and National Security* 4/2 (1989), pp. 335–56. C.J.H. Hayes, *Wartime Mission in Spain, 1942–1945* (New York: Macmillan, 1945).

105 Letter from Gómez-Jordana to the ambassador in London, the Duke of Alba,

17 November 1942. Archivo del Ministerio de Asuntos Exteriores (Madrid), series 'Renovado', file 1371, record 3B. Hereafter: AMAE R1371/3B.

106 Tusell and García Queipo de Llano, *Franco y Mussolini*, p. 193.

107 Memorandum by Sir Samuel Hoare, 1 May 1944. FO 371/49612 Z7075. Text of the agreement in the Archivo de la Presidencia del Gobierno (Madrid), series 'Jefatura del Estado', file 38. See Joan Maria Thomàs, *La batalla del wolframio. Estados Unidos y España de Pearl Harbor a la Guerra Fría, 1941–1947* (Madrid: Cátedra, 2010).

108 Telegram of Sir Samuel Hoare on his interview with Franco, 12 December 1944. FO 371/39672 C17266. Reproduced in Moradiellos, *Franco frente a Churchill*, p. 399.

109 Good analyses of the period in the classic works of Florentino Portero, *Franco aislado. La cuestión española, 1945–1950* (Madrid: Aguilar, 1989); Qasim Ahmad, *Britain, Franco Spain and the Cold War, 1945–1950* (Kuala Lumpur: Noordeen, 1995); and Jill Edwards, *Anglo-American Relations and the Franco Question, 1945–1955* (Oxford: Oxford University Press, 1999).

110 E. Moradiellos, 'The Potsdam Conference and the Spanish Problem', *Contemporary European History* 10/1 (2001), pp. 73–90.

111 'España ante la situación actual del mundo' and 'Notas sobre nuestra situación actual en el Mundo', 12 April 1945, Archivo General de la Universidad de Navarra, fondo Carrero Blanco, series 'Política Internacional'.

112 'Notas sobre la situación política', 29 July 1945, Archivo General de la Universidad de Navarra, fondo Carrero Blanco, series 'Política Internacional'.

113 As it was expressed before the Cortes on 14 May 1946. Franco, *Pensamiento político de Franco*, p. 248. The original text of the speech in F. Franco, *Manuscritos de Franco* (Madrid: Otero, 1990), document 17, p. 102.

114 Franco in 1945 reproduced in Javier Tusell, *Franco y los católicos. La política interior española entre 1945 y 1957* (Madrid: Alianza, 1984), pp. 55 and 101.

115 Franco, *Pensamiento político de Franco*, p. 395.

116 Alfredo Kindelán, *La verdad de mis relaciones con Franco* (Barcelona: Planeta, 1981), p. 287. Baón, *La cara humana de un Caudillo*, p. 171.

117 Tusell and García Queipo de Llano, *Franco y Mussolini*, p. 290.

118 Dispatch of Sir Victor Mallet, 8 March 1946. FO 371/60352 Z2295.

119 Speech in Seville on 1 May 1956. Franco, *Pensamiento político de Franco*, p. 406.

120 Suárez Fernández, *Francisco Franco y su tiempo*, vol. 4, p. 29.

121 Telegram from the British ambassador in Washington to the Foreign Office, 17 May 1945. FO 371/49611 Z6002.

122 Minute of Oliver Harvey for Ernest Bevin (Foreign Secretary), 7 June 1946. The previous quotations are from a letter from the British ambassador in Madrid and from some minutes from high-ranking officials in the Foreign Office, 6 and 10 August and 3 September 1945. Reproduced in Moradiellos, *Franco frente a Churchill*, pp. 440 and 443.

123 The original text of the speech in Franco, *Manuscritos de Franco*, document 17, pp. 101–10.

124 *Boletín Oficial del Estado*, 27 June 1947.

125 Enrique Moradiellos, *La España de Franco. Política y Sociedad* (Madrid: Síntesis, 2000) pp. 107–9. Stanley G. Payne, *El régimen de Franco* (Madrid: Alianza, 1987) pp. 385–6.

126 Kindelán, *La verdad de mis relaciones con Franco*, p. 344.

127 An updated review of relations between Franco and the future king in Paul Preston, *Juan Carlos: A People's King* (London: HarperCollins, 2003).

128 José Luis de Vilallonga, *El Rey. Conversaciones con D. Juan Carlos I de España* (Barcelona: Salvat, 1995), pp. 47–8 and 82.

129 Commentary of Manuel Lora Tamayo, minister of education between 1962 and 1968. Collected in *Franco visto por sus ministros*, p. 128.

130 Annotation in Pemán's diary on 1 January 1955. Reproduced by Tusell, *Franco y los católicos*, p. 442.

131 Preston, *Franco*, pp. 595–6. De la Cierva, *Franco*, p. 402. Suárez Fernández, *Francisco Franco*, vol. 4, p. 426. Palacios and Payne, *Franco, mi padre*, p. 552.

132 The comments of Father Bulart (9 August 1955) recorded in Franco-Salgado Araujo, *Mis conversaciones privadas*, p. 131. His own comments (25 July 1955) are on p. 126. The comments on Franco's indifference to his son-in-law in de la Cierva, *Franco*, p. 402.

133 Report by Paul Culberston, 20 June 1950. *Foreign Relations of the United States, 1950. Vol. III: Western Europe* (Washington: United States Printing Office, 1977), pp. 1563–5.

134 Ángel Viñas, *Los pactos secretos de Franco con Estados Unidos* (Barcelona: Grijalbo, 1981). Boris N. Liedtke, *Embracing a Dictatorship: US Relations with Spain, 1945–1953* (New York: Palgrave Macmillan, 1997). Rafael Gómez Pérez, *El franquismo y la Iglesia* (Madrid: Rialp, 1986) and Tusell, *Franco y los católicos*, ch. 3.

135 Message to the Cortes, *Abc*, 1 October 1953. Declaration of Alberto Martín Artajo in Mérida, *Testigos de Franco*, pp. 200–1.

136 Quoted by George Hills, *Franco. El hombre y su nación* (Madrid: San Martín, 1968), p. 430.

137 Recapitulation of María Mérida on the interviews with supporters of Franco in *Testigos de Franco*, pp. 24–5.

138 Pilar Franco Bahamonde, *Nosotros, los Franco*, p. 78.

139 Notes on this in Baón, *La cara humana de un Caudillo*, pp. 30, 37, 47 and 72–3.

140 José Luis García Delgado and Juan Carlos Jiménez, 'La economía', in Raymond Carr (ed.), *Historia de España Menéndez Pidal. La España de Franco* (Madrid: Espasa Calpe, 1996), vol. 41, pp. 446–511 (figures on p. 450). Albert Carreras (ed.), *Estadísticas históricas de España. Siglos XIX y XX* (Madrid: Fundación Banco Exterior, 1989), p. 193. Jordi Nadal (ed.), *La economía española en el siglo XX* (Barcelona: Ariel, 1987).

141 Private report of 13 January 1951. Quoted in Antonio Cazorla, *Las políticas de la victoria. La consolidación del Nuevo Estado franquista* (Madrid: Marcial Pons, 2000), p. 148.

142 Tusell, *Carrero*, p. 204.

143 Tusell, *Franco y los católicos*, pp. 55 and 57–8.

144 Sheelagh M. Ellwood, *Spanish Fascism in the Franco Era: Falange Española de las JONS, 1936–1976* (London: Macmillan, 1987), p. 101.

145 Baón, *La cara humana de un Caudillo*, p. 146.

146 Joan Clavera et al., *Capitalismo español: de la autarquía a la estabilización* (Madrid: Cuadernos para el Diálogo, 1978), p. 219.

147 García Delgado and Jiménez, 'La economía', p. 450. Carreras, *Estadísticas históricas de España*, p. 193.

148 Clavero et al., *Capitalismo español*, pp. 331 and 345. Gabriel Tortella, *El desarrollo económico de la España contemporánea* (Madrid: Alianza, 1994), pp. 273–80.

149 Amando de Miguel, *Sociología del franquismo. Análisis ideológico de los ministros de Franco* (Madrid: Euros, 1975), p. 224. See Equipo Mundo, *Los 90 ministros de Franco*, pp. 255–314.

150 Franco Salgado-Araujo, *Mis conversaciones privadas*, p. 280. Annotation of 24 March 1960. The preference for the Prince in Franco Salgado-Araujo, *Mis conversaciones privadas*, p. 240 (conversation of 23 June 1958).

151   Details of Franco's reservations in Tusell, *Carrero*, p. 258; Fusi, *Franco*, p.145; and Suárez Fernández, *Francisco Franco y su tiempo*, vol. 6, p. 88–91.

152   Preston, *Franco*, p. 677. Laureano López Rodó, *Memorias* (Barcelona: Plaza y Janés, 1990), vol. 1, p. 184.

153   Nigel Townson, *Spain Transformed: The Franco Dictatorship, 1959–1975* (New York: Palgrave Macmillan, 2010). José Luis García Delgado et al., *Economía española, 1960–1980. Crecimiento y cambio estructural* (Barcelona: Blume, 1982), pp. 26–7. Jacinto Ros Hombravella, *Política económica española, 1959–1973* (Barcelona: Blume, 1979).

154   Edmund Stillman (ed.), *El resurgir económico de España. Informe del Hudson Institute Europe* (Madrid: Instituto de Estudios de Planificación, 1975), pp. 90, 94 and 189. Payne, *El régimen de Franco*, pp. 489–90. Jacinto Rodríguez Osuna, *Población y desarrollo en España* (Madrid: Cupsa, 1978), pp. 40–1 and 44–5.

155   Data collected by Fundación Foessa, *Informe sociológico sobre la situación social de España. 1970* (Madrid: Euroamérica, 1971), p. 169; Gabriel Tortella, *El desarrollo económico de la España contemporánea* (Madrid: Alianza, 1995), p. 227; and Moradiellos, *La España de Franco*, pp. 263–5.

156   Adrian Shubert, *A Social History of Modern Spain* (London: Unwin Hyman, 1990), ch. 5. Sebastian Balfour, 'The *Desarrollo* Years, 1955–1975', in José Álvarez Junco and Adrian Shubert (eds), *Spanish History since 1808* (London: Arnold, 2000), ch. 17. Santos Juliá, *Historia económica y social moderna y contemporánea de España. Siglo XX* (Madrid: UNED, 1993), pp. 192–6. Carmen Molinero y Pere Ysàs, *Productores disciplinados y minorías subversivas. Clase obrera y conflictividad laboral en la España franquista* (Madrid: Siglo XXI, 1998), p. 96.

157   Fundación Foessa, *Informe sociológico sobre la situación social de España*, pp. 351, 956, 963 and 987.

158   Baón, *La cara humana de un Caudillo*, pp. 34, 37 and 68–9. Laureano López Rodó, *La larga marcha hacia la monarquía* (Barcelona: Noguer, 1977), pp. 195–7. The memoirs of Dr Vicente Gil confirm Franco's good state of health until the start of the 1960s: *40 años junto a Franco*, pp. 37–8.

159   Manuel Fraga Iribarne, *Horizonte español* (Madrid: Editora Nacional, 1968), pp. 2–25.

160   Franco, *Pensamiento político* (1964 edition), p. 391.

161   Comment of 4 February 1963. Franco Salgado-Araujo, *Mis conversaciones privadas con Franco*, p. 369.

162 Speech before a gathering of excombatants in Garabitas (Madrid) and before the FET National Council, 27 May 1962 and 9 March 1963. Franco, *Pensamiento político*, pp. 242–3 and 440.

163 Speech of 3 June 1961. The earlier quote on the compromise in the speech of 13 July 1960 in homage to Calvo Sotelo. F. Franco, *Pensamiento político*, pp. 212 and 254.

164 Quoted from the text published in Cáceres newspaper *Extremadura*, 13 December 1966. The official results were published in the newspaper on 15 December 1966.

165 'Consideraciones sobre la aplicación del artículo 6º de la Ley de Sucesión', 21 October 1968, Archivo General de la Universidad de Navarra, fondo Carrero Blanco, series 'Leyes Fundamentales'. López Rodó, *La larga marcha hacia la monarquía*, p. 279.

166 De Vilallonga, *El Rey*, pp. 80–1.

167 De Vilallonga, *El Rey*, pp. 18, 85 and 98. P. Sainz Rodríguez, *Un reinado en la sombra* (Barcelona: Planeta, 1981), pp. 342–4. Pilar and Alfonso Fernández-Miranda, *Lo que el rey me ha pedido. Torcuato Fernández-Miranda y la reforma política* (Madrid: Plaza y Janés, 1995), pp. 52–5. On the conduct of the future king in this period see Charles T. Powell, *El piloto del cambio: el rey, la monarquía y la transición a la democracia* (Barcelona: Planeta, 1991), ch. 1.

168 López Rodó, *La larga marcha hacia la monarquía*, pp. 331–2.

169 The speech is in F. Franco, *Pensamiento político de Franco* (Madrid: Ediciones del Movimiento, 1975), vol. 2, pp. 755–8. Sainz Rodríguez, *Un reinado en la sombra*, pp. 264–5 and 344; and López Rodó, *La larga marcha hacia la monarquía*, p. 371.

170 See the chapter corresponding to the *desarrollista* (development) decade in José María García Escudero, *Historia política de la época de Franco* (Madrid: Rialp, 1987) and Álvaro Soto Carmona, *¿Atado y bien atado? Institucionalización y crisis del franquismo* (Madrid: Biblioteca Nueva, 2005). See de Miguel, *Sociología del franquismo*, pp. 352–4.

171 'Consideraciones sobre la conveniencia de proceder a un reajuste ministerial', 15 October 1969, Archivo General de la Universidad de Navarra, Fondo Carrero Blanco, series 'Gobierno'. Tusell, *Carrero*, pp. 355–64. López Rodó, *La larga marcha hacia la monarquía*, pp. 654–9.

172 Equipo Mundo, *Los 90 ministros de Franco*, pp. 419–500.

173 The quote from Fraga Iribane in de la Cierva, *Franco*, p. 472. The recollection

of López Rodó is in *Franco visto por sus ministros*, pp. 166–7. On this crisis and the formation of the reformist front against the Franco regime see Cristina Palomares, *The Quest for Survival after Franco: Moderate Francoism and the Slow Journey to the Polls, 1964–1977* (Eastbourne: Sussex Academic Press, 2006).

174 A good analysis of this final period is in Pere Ysàs Solanes, *Disidencia y subversión. La lucha del régimen franquista por su supervivencia, 1960–1975* (Barcelona: Crítica, 2004); and Javier Fernández López, *El Rey y otros militares. Los militares en el cambio de régimen político en España, 1969–1982* (Madrid: Trotta, 1998).

175 Reproduced in López Rodó, *La larga marcha hacia la monarquía*, pp. 440–1.

176 Judgement of de la Cierva, *Franco*, p. 478.

177 Tusell, *Carrero*, pp. 433–41. Ismael Fuente, Javier García and Joaquín Prieto, *Golpe mortal. Asesinato de Carrero y agonía del franquismo* (Madrid: El País, 1983). De la Cierva (*Franco*, p. 480) suggests the hypothesis of foreign help to the terrorists. A good and measured account is in Soto Carmona, *¿Atado y bien atado? Institucionalización y crisis del franquismo*, pp. 130–5.

178 López Rodó, *La larga marcha hacia la monarquía*, p. 458. Suárez Fernández, *Francisco Franco*, vol. 8, p. 357.

179 The snub was from the minister of education, Julio Rodríguez Martínez, who wrote his version in *Impresiones de un ministro de Carrero Blanco* (Barcelona: Planeta, 1974). Palacios and Payne, *Franco, mi padre*, p. 122. Preston, *Franco*, pp. 761–2.

180 Javier Tusell, 'El tardofranquismo', in Carr (ed.), *Historia de España Menéndez Pidal*, p. 164. Javier Tusell and Genoveva García Queipo de Llano, *Tiempo de incertidumbre: Carlos Arias Navarro entre el franquismo y la transición* (Barcelona: Crítica, 2006). Luis de Llera, *España actual. El régimen de Franco* (Madrid: Gredos, 1994), pp. 607–14.

181 Quoted by Raymond Carr and Juan Pablo Fusi, *España, de la dictadura a la democracia* (Barcelona: Planeta, 1979), p. 236.

182 Josep Sánchez Cervelló, *La revolución portuguesa y su influencia en la transición española* (Madrid: Nerea, 1995).

183 Dr Gil's version is in his memoirs, *Cuarenta años junto a Franco*, ch. 12. A softened overview is in Baón, *La cara humana de un Caudillo*, pp. 219–21.

184 Vicente Pozuelo, *Los últimos 476 días de Franco* (Barcelona: Planeta, 1980), p. 29.

185   According to Dr Pozuelo: 'Contrary to what might be expected, my main problem, in all seriousness, was not the thrombophlebitis, but raising the low psychological state of Franco' (*Los últimos 476 días de Franco*, p. 38).

186   Paul Preston, *The Triumph of Democracy in Spain, 1969–1982* (Oxford: Routledge, 1987), ch. 3. Charles T. Powell, 'Crisis del franquismo, reformismo y transición a la democracia', in Javier Tusell (ed.), *Las derechas en la España contemporánea* (Madrid: UNED, 1997), pp. 247–70.

187   Quoted in Carr and Fusi, *España, de la dictadura a la democracia*, p. 266.

188   Molinero and Ysàs, *Productores disciplinados*, p. 96.

189   In Spanish: 'No queremos apertura, queremos mano dura'. Payne, *El régimen de Franco.*, pp. 644–5. López Rodó, *La larga marcha hacia la monarquía*, p. 483.

190   Reproduced in *Extremadura* (Cáceres), 1 October 1975. Franco, *Pensamiento político*, vol. 2, p. 869.

191   Rafael López Pintor, *La opinión pública española: del Franquismo a la democracia* (Madrid: Centro de Investigaciones Sociológicas, 1982), pp. 84, 86 and 97.

192   Pozuelo, *Los últimos 476 días de Franco*, p. 210.

193   Pozuelo, *Los últimos 476 días de Franco*, p. 221.

194   *Extremadura*, 22 October 1975. On the suffering and death of Franco, other than the testimony of his personal doctor, see also: Yale [Felipe Navarro], *Los últimos cien días. Crónica de una agonía* (Madrid: Prensa Económica, 1975); Baón, *La cara humana de un Caudillo*, pp. 226–49; de la Cierva, *Franco*, pp. 492–503; and Preston, *Franco*, pp. 776–8.

195   Evidence of Carmen Franco in Palacios and Payne, *Franco, mi padre*, p. 130.

196   Testimony collected in Rafael Abella et al., *España diez años después de Franco, 1975–1985* (Barcelona: Planeta, 1985).

2: The Caudillo: A Charismatic Dictator

1   *Boletín Oficial del Estado*, 19 December 1946.

2   Quoted in Miguel Martorell, *Historia de la peseta* (Barcelona: Planeta, 2002), p. 219. See José María de Francis Olmos, 'Estudio de la tipología monetaria como documento propagandístico de la evolución política española', *Revista general de información y documentación* 15/2 (2005), pp. 5–38.

3   Declarations to the Lisbon newspaper *O Século*, 13 August 1936, reproduced

in José García Mercadal, *Ideario del Generalísimo* (Zaragoza: Tipografía La Académica, 1937) pp. 42–3. The earlier mentioned decree of 24 July 1936 was published in *Boletín Oficial de la Junta de Defensa Nacional*, 25 July 1936.

4 Decree of 29 September 1936, *Boletín Oficial de la Junta de Defensa Nacional*, 30 September 1936.

5 Franco's speech was reproduced in all the Spanish press of the insurgent zone with slight differences. That reproduced here appears in Seville's *Abc*, 2 October 1936. Franco's speeches in later collections reflect a text identical in background but more elaborate in form: *Palabras de Franco* (Bilbao: Editora Nacional, 1937), pp. 9–10. However, in later years the press would quote the abbreviated speech, as can be verified in the tribute published in the journal *Extremadura* (Cáceres) on 1 October 1946.

6 *Boletín Oficial del Estado*, 4 August 1939.

7 *Boletín Oficial del Estado*, 22 May 1941.

8 *Boletín Oficial del Estado*, 27 July 1947. The extreme importance of this law in the confirmation of Franco's supreme leadership was well appreciated by many analysts. Worth special mention is the Italian jurist Giovanni Mammucari in his study *Il Caudillo di Spagna e la sua successione* (Rome: Edizioni dell'Ateneo, 1955).

9 *Boletín Oficial del Estado*, 20 November 1975.

10 Apart from the relevant section in the canonical biography of Paul Preston (*Franco: A Biography*, London: HarperCollins, 1993), very good analyses of this process of promotional propaganda can be found in the works of Alberto Reig Tapia, *Franco. El César superlativo*, (Madrid: Tecnos, 2005); Francisco Sevillano Calero, *Franco, Caudillo por la Gracia de Dios* (Madrid: Alianza, 2010); Laura Zenobi, *La construcción del mito de Franco* (Madrid: Cátedra, 2011); and Antonio Cazorla, *Franco. Biografía de un mito* (Madrid: Alianza, 2015 - published in English as *Franco: The Biography of the Myth* (New York: Routledge, 2014).

11 Falangist propaganda always made extensive use of the slogan. See the monthly *FE. Doctrina Nacional-Sindicalista*, published in Zaragoza by the Jefatura Nacional de Prensa y Propaganda from January 1937. A general review of the role of propaganda in the conflict is in Alejandro Pizarroso (ed.), *Propaganda en guerra* (Salamanca: Consorcio, 2002).

12 Examples of each of these variations can be seen on the front covers of different newspapers: *Extremadura* (Cáceres), 18 July 1940, 1 April 1959

and 31 March 1962; *Arriba* (Madrid), 7 September 1943 and 8 May 1945; *El Alcázar* (Toledo), 22 October 1937; *Abc* (Seville), 1 October 1937; *El Heraldo de Aragón* (Zaragoza), 20 April 1937.

13 Quoted in Julio Rodríguez Puértolas, *Literatura fascista española. Antología* (Madrid: Akal, 1987), p. 568.

14 Padre González Menéndez-Reigada, *Catecismo patriótico español* (Salamanca: Establecimiento Tipográfico Calatrava, 1939), pp. 33 and 70. There is a new edition of this book with commentary by Father Hilari Raguer (Barcelona: Península, 2003).

15 Antonio J. Onieva and Federico Torres, *Enciclopedia Hernando. Grado Medio* (Madrid: Librería y Casa Editorial Hernando, 1953), p. 32.

16 Antonio Álvarez Pérez, *Enciclopedia Álvarez. Primer Grado* (Valladolid: Miñón, 1964), p. 264.

17 Quoted in Ferran Gallego, *El Evangelio Fascista. La formación de la cultura política del franquismo, 1930–1950* (Barcelona: Crítica, 2014), p. 492.

18 Mammucari, *Il Caudillo di Spagna*, pp. 17–18 and 26–7.

19 Juan Ferrando Badía, *El régimen de Franco. Un enfoque político-jurídico* (Madrid: Tecnos, 1984), p. 54.

20 José Zafra Valverde, *El sistema político en las décadas de Franco* (Baracaldo: Grafite, 2004), p. 15.

21 Speech of 29 October 1960. Francisco Franco, *Pensamiento político de Franco. Antología* (Madrid, Servicio Informativo Español, 1964), p. 79.

22 *Abc*, 30 December 1960. The speech was broadcast on radio and television at 10 p.m. on 29 December.

23 Maurilio Pérez González, *El latín de la cancillería castellana, 1158–1214* (Salamanca: Universidad de Salamanca, 1985), p. 193. Mammucari, *Il Caudillo di Spagna*, pp. 19–20.

24 Laureano Vallenilla Lanz, *Cesarismo democrático* (Caracas: Monte Ávila Editores, 1990), p. 165; the first edition of this work was published in 1919.

25 Domingo Irwin and Ingrid Micett, *Caudillos, militares y poder. Una historia del pretorianismo en Venezuela* (Caracas: Universidad Católica, 2008), p. 18.

26 Hugh M. Hamill (ed.), *Caudillos: Dictators in Spanish America* (Norman: University of Oklahoma, 1992). John Lynch, *Caudillos en Hispanoamérica, 1800–1850* (Madrid: Mapfre, 1993). Paul H. Lewis, *Authoritarian Regimes in Latin America: Dictators, Despots and Tyrants* (Lanham: Rowman & Littlefield, 2006).

27 Cited in Stanley G. Payne, *Los militares y la política en la España contemporánea* (Paris: Ruedo Ibérico, 1968), p. 32, first published as *Politics and the Military in Modern Spain* (Stanford: Stanford University Press, 1967). See Manuel Ballbé, *Orden público y militarismo en la España contemporánea* (Madrid: Alianza, 1983).

28 'Dictatorship' and 'party' definitions in Javier Fernández Sebastián and Juan Francisco Fuentes (eds), *Diccionario político y social del siglo XIX español* (Madrid: Alianza, 2002). See José Álvarez Junco, *The Emergence of Mass Politics in Spain: Populist Demagoguery and Republican Culture, 1890–1910* (Eastbourne: Sussex Academic Press, 2003); and the contributions of Álvarez Junco and Martin Baumeister in Ludger Mees and José Manuel Núñez Seixas (eds), *Nacidos para mandar. Liderazgo, política y poder* (Madrid: Tecnos, 2012).

29 Gustau Nerín, *La guerra que vino de África* (Barcelona: Crítica, 2005), pp. 37, 45–6 and 64. On the formation of the Africanista army see also Sebastian Balfour, *Deadly Embrace: Morocco and the Road to the Spanish Civil War* (Oxford: Oxford University Press, 2002).

30 Pablo La Porte, *La atracción del imán. El Desastre de Annual y sus repercusiones en la política europea, 1921–1923* (Madrid: Biblioteca Nueva, 2001).

31 Text reproduced in Joaquín Arrarás, *Franco* (Valladolid: Santarén, 1939), p. 140. Zenobi (*La construcción del mito de Franco*, pp. 62–4) rightly stresses the context of this honour.

32 Alejandro Quiroga Fernández de Soto, 'Cirujano de Hierro. La construcción carismática del general Primo de Rivera', *Ayer* 91/3 (2013), pp. 147–68. By the same author, 'Miguel Primo de Rivera: Overture to Franco', in A. Quiroga and M.Á. del Arco Blanco (eds), *Right-Wing Spain in the Civil War Era: Soldiers of God and Apostles of the Fatherland, 1914–1945* (London: Continuum, 2012), ch. 2.

33 Juan F. García Santos, *Léxico y política de la Segunda República* (Salamanca: Universidad de Salamanca, 1980), pp. 99–102.

34 Declaration of October 1933 reproduced in Valverde, *El sistema político en las décadas de Franco*, p. 13.

35 The conclusions expressed by García Santos have been previously pointed out by Miguel Ángel Rebollo Torío: 'Both Jefe and Caudillo are positive terms in the language of the right', in *El lenguaje de la derecha en la II República* (Valencia: Fernando Torres, 1975), p. 83.

36   Indalecio Prieto, *Discursos fundamentales* (Madrid: Turner, 1975), pp. 257–8.

37   On the outbreak of the conflict and its military profile, apart from the classic works of Ramón Salas Larrazábal, Michael Alpert and others, there are the updated works by Gabriel Cardona, *Historia militar de una guerra civil* (Barcelona: Flor del Viento, 2006); Jorge Martínez Reverte, *El arte de matar. Cómo se hizo la guerra civil española* (Barcelona: RBA, 2009) and James Matthews, *Reluctant Warriors: Republican Popular Army and Nationalist Army Conscripts in the Spanish Civil War* (Oxford: Oxford University Press, 2012).

38   *Boletín Oficial de la Junta de Defensa Nacional*, 25 July 1936.

39   A valid overview of the global vision of the insurgent military is in Juan Carlos Losada Malvárez, *Ideología del Ejército Franquista, 1939–1959* (Madrid: Istmo, 1990) and Geoffrey Jensen, *Irrational Triumph: Cultural Despair, Military Nationalism and the Ideological Origins of Franco's Spain* (Reno: University of Nevada Press, 2002). Its previous gestation among the troops in Africa is amply discussed in the works already mentioned by Gustau Nerín and Sebastian Balfour.

40   *Boletín de la Junta de Defensa Nacional*, 30 July 1936. On the performance of these courts generally see Peter Anderson, *The Francoist Military Trials: Terror and Complicity* (London: Routledge, 2010).

41   *Boletín de la Junta de Defensa Nacional*, 9 and 25 August 1936.

42   Nerín, *La guerra que vino de África*, pp. 133–41. On this fruitful source see Juan José López Barranco, *El Rif en armas. La narrativa española sobre la guerra de Marruecos, 1859–2005* (Madrid: Mare Nostrum, 2006).

43   A revealing description of this first information policy of the rebels can be found in Paul Preston, *We Saw Spain Die: Foreign Correspondents in the Spanish Civil War* (London: Constable, 2008), ch. 4; Hugo García, *The Truth about Spain: Mobilizing British Public Opinion, 1936–1939* (Eastbourne, Sussex Academic Press, 2010), ch. 2; and Antonio Cazorla, *Franco. Biografía del mito* (Madrid: Alianza, 2015), ch. 2. On Giménez Caballero, see Mario Martín Gijón, *Los (anti)intelectuales de la derecha española* (Barcelona: RBA, 2011), ch. 2.

44   The words of Concha Langa, '*Abc* de Sevilla, el diario de mayor circulación de la España nacional', in Antonio Checa, Carmen Espejo and María José Ruiz (eds), *Abc de Sevilla. Un diario y una ciudad* (Seville: Universidad de Sevilla, 2007), pp. 85–102.

45   Examples of both attributions of *caudillaje* in the issue of 31 July (Queipo: 'our

brave Caudillo') and 5 August 1936 (Sanjurjo: 'The remains of the Caudillo were brought to Estoril').

46   *Abc* (Seville), 30 July 1936.

47   Rafael Fernández de Castro Pedrera, *Vidas de soldados ilustres de la Nueva España* (Melilla: Gráficas Postal Exprés, 1937), p. 88. The author was the official chronicler of Melilla and he had known personally all of the Africanist commanders.

48   So pronounced J. García Mercadal in his *Ideario del Generalísimo*, pp. 42 and 43, which at the height of March 1937 had already had two editions and had been 'endorsed by censorship'.

49   Manuel García-Pelayo, *Los mitos políticos* (Madrid: Alianza, 1981), p. 12.

50   A classic selection of those authors and works is in Lewis A. Coser and Bernard Rosenberg, *Sociological Theory: A Book of Readings* (London: Collier Macmillan, 1976).

51   Gallego, *El Evangelio Fascista*; Ismael Saz, *España contra España. Los nacionalismos franquistas* (Madrid: Marcial Pons, 2003). To these one could add, from perspectives more reduced but interesting, the earlier work of José Andrés-Gallego, *¿Fascismo o Estado Católico? Ideología, religión y censura en la España de Franco, 1937–1941* (Madrid: Encuentro, 1978).

52   For a successful exhibition of this panoramic see Paul Preston, *Las derechas españolas en el siglo XX* (Madrid: Sistema, 1986); José Luis Rodríguez Jiménez, *La extrema derecha española en el siglo XX* (Madrid: Alianza, 1997); Pedro Carlos González Cuevas, *El pensamiento político de la derecha española en el siglo XX* (Madrid: Tecnos, 2005); Jorge Novella Suárez, *El pensamiento reaccionario español, 1812–1975. Tradición y contrarrevolución* (Madrid: Biblioteca Nueva, 2007); and Eduardo González Calleja, *Contrarrevolucionarios. La radicalización violenta de las derechas en la Segunda República* (Madrid: Alianza, 2011).

53   Javier Tusell, *Historia de la democracia cristiana en España* (Madrid: Cuadernos para el Diálogo, 1974), vol. 1. José R. Montero, *La CEDA. El catolicismo social y político en la Segunda República* (Madrid: Revista de Trabajo, 1977), 2 vols. Alfonso Álvarez Bolado, *Para ganar la guerra, para ganar la paz. Iglesia y guerra civil* (Madrid: Universidad Pontificia de Comillas, 1995). Giuliana Di Febo, *Ritos de guerra y de victoria en la España franquista* (Valencia: Universidad de Valencia, 2012). Feliciano Montero, *La Acción Católica en la Segunda República* (Alcalá: Universidad de Alcalá, 2008). José Manuel Cuenca

Toribio, *Nacionalismo, franquismo y nacional-catolicismo* (Madrid: Actas, 2008). A brilliant local study of this movement is Mary Vincent, *Catholicism in the Second Spanish Republic: Religion and Politics in Salamanca, 1930–1936* (Oxford: Clarendon, 1996).

54 Raúl Morodo, *Los orígenes ideológicos del Franquismo. Acción Española* (Madrid: Alianza, 1985). Julio Gil Pecharromán, *Conservadores subversivos. La derecha autoritaria Alfonsina, 1913–1936* (Madrid: Eudema, 1994). Pedro Carlos González Cuevas, *Acción Española. Teología política y nacionalismo autoritario en España* (Madrid: Tecnos, 1998).

55 Martin Blinkhorn, *Carlism and Crisis in Spain, 1931–1939* (Cambridge: Cambridge University Press, 1975). José Carlos Clemente, *El carlismo en el novecientos español, 1876–1936* (Madrid: Huerga y Fierro, 1999). Jordi Canal, *Banderas blancas, boinas rojas. Una historia política del carlismo, 1876–1939* (Madrid: Marcial Pons, 2006).

56 Joan María Thòmas, *Lo que fue la Falange* (Barcelona: Plaza y Janés, 1999) and *Los fascismos españoles* (Barcelona: Planeta, 2011). Ferran Gallego and Francisco Morente (eds), *Fascismo en España* (Barcelona: El Viejo Topo, 2005). Ferran Gallego, *Ramiro Ledesma Ramos y el fascismo español* (Madrid: Síntesis, 2005). Ismael Saz, *Fascismo y Franquismo* (Valencia: Universidad de Valencia, 2004). Miguel Ángel Ruiz Carnicer (ed.), *Falange. Las culturas políticas del fascismo en la España de Franco* (Zaragoza: Institución Cultural Fernando el Católico, 2013). In English the basic text is that of Sheelagh Ellwood, *Spanish Fascism in the Franco Era* (London: Macmillan, 1987).

57 The first two quotes are in Gallego, *El Evangelio Fascista*, pp. 125 and 137. For Pedro Sainz Rodríguez, see Julio Rodríguez Puértolas, *Literatura fascista española* (Madrid: Akal, 1987), p. 119.

58 Words spoken on 12 January 1936, quoted in Joaquín Arrarás, *Historia de la Segunda República* (Madrid: Editora Nacional, 1968), vol. 4, p. 13.

59 José Antonio Primo de Rivera, *Textos de doctrina política* (Madrid: FET de las JONS, 1966), p. 929. Declarations of Gil-Robles on 15 April 1936 reproduced in Manuel Álvarez Tardío, 'La CEDA y la democracia republicana', in Fernando del Rey (ed.), *Palabras como puños. La intransigencia política en la Segunda República Española* (Madrid: Tecnos, 2011), p. 416.

60 Emilio Mola, *Obras completas* (Valladolid: Santarén, 1940), p. 1184. The decree of 25 September prohibiting political activities is in *Boletín de la Junta de Defensa Nacional*, 28 September 1936. The acceptance of this

military demand for civil subordinate support is related well in José Luis Orella, *La formación del Estado Nacional durante la guerra civil* (Madrid: Actas, 2001).

61 Gabriel Cardona, *Historia militar de una guerra civil* (Barcelona: Flor del Viento, 2006). Jorge Martínez Reverte, *El arte de matar. Cómo se hizo la guerra civil española* (Barcelona: RBA, 2009). Michael Seidman, *The Victorious Counterrevolution: The Nationalist Effort in the Spanish Civil War* (Madison: University of Wisconsin Press, 2011). James Matthews, *Reluctant Warriors: Republican Popular Army and Nationalist Army Conscripts in the Spanish Civil War* (Oxford: Oxford University Press, 2012), published in Spanish as *Soldados a la fuerza* (Madrid: Alianza, 2013).

62 The words of Juan Carlos Losada in *Ideología del Ejército Franquista, 1939–1959* (Madrid: Istmo, 1990), p. 25; Gabriel Cardona, *El poder militar en el franquismo* (Barcelona: Flor del Viento, 2008), p. 18; and Di Febo in *Ritos de guerra y de victoria en la España Franquista*, pp. 17, 31 and 56. The previous quotation from Menéndez y Pelayo (1882) formed part of his book *Historia de los heterodoxos españoles* and was widely disseminated in all formats. One of its great communicators in the 1930s was a prestigious general, Jorge Vigón, who published a synthesis of that work under the title of *Historia de España* (Madrid: Fax, 1934), quoted on p. 354.

63 Matthews, *Soldados a la fuerza*, pp. 140 and 144.

64 Thorough analyses of this process of charismatic construction are in Alberto Reig Tapia, *Franco. El César superlativo* (Madrid: Tecnos, 2005); Francisco Sevillano, *Franco. Caudillo por la Gracia de Dios* (Madrid, Alianza, 2010); Zira Box, *España, año cero. La construcción simbólica del Franquismo* (Madrid: Alianza, 2010); Laura Zenobi, *La construcción del mito de Franco* (Madrid: Cátedra, 2011); and Antonio Cazorla, *Franco. Biografía del mito* (Madrid, Alianza, 2015).

65 Thus Paul Preston showed in his classic biography *Franco*, ch. 7.

66 The words of the professor of law, Luis Jordana de Pozas, former collaborator of the Primo de Rivera dictatorship and an advocate of political Catholicism, in 'El principio de unidad y sus consecuencias políticas y administrativas', *Revista de Estudios Políticos* 3–4 (1941), pp. 621–40 and 33–53.

67 Decree of 19 May 1939, reproduced in the newspaper *Abc*, 20 May 1939. An analysis of the parade and its preparations are in Di Febo, *Ritos de guerra y de victoria*, pp. 97–113. Miguel Platón, *Hablan los militares. Testimonios para la historia* (Barcelona: Planeta, 2001), pp. 12 and 15, remembered that the display

was 'one of the largest of its kind held in the world during this century' and constituted 'the apotheosis of the army which had taken for itself the designation of national' and of its 'young Generalissimo'.

68 The statement of Gomá in his confidential reports to the Vatican on 24 October and 9 November 1936. María Luisa Rodríguez Aisa, *El cardenal Gomá y la guerra de España* (Madrid: CSIC, 1981), pp. 32 and 36. On the traumatic experience of the Church with secular modernity and the Republican era, see Frances Lannon, *Privilege, Persecution and Prophecy: The Catholic Church in Spain, 1875–1975* (Oxford: Oxford University Press, 1987).

69 The prayer and ceremony context is analysed in Di Febo, *Ritos de guerra y de victoria*, pp. 109–18 (prayer on p. 113). The canonical sources of this Christian concept of public authority were well exposed by the classical work of Walter Ullmann, *A History of Political Thought: The Middle Ages* (London: Pelican Books, 1965). Its contemporary adaptation in Spain can be seen in the aforementioned work by Jorge Novella.

70 A recent analysis of that complex process is in Joan María Thòmas, *El gran golpe. El 'caso Hedilla' o cómo Franco se quedó con la Falange* (Barcelona: Debate, 2014).

71 Dionisio Ridruejo, 'La Falange y su Caudillo', *FE. Revista mensual de doctrina Nacional-Sindicalista* 4–5 (1938), pp. 35–8.

72 Ernesto Giménez Caballero, *España y Franco* (San Sebastián: Ediciones Los Combatientes, 1938), pp. 14–15 and 29.

73 Speech before the Cortes and before the FET National Council, 17 March and 17 July 1943. Francisco Franco, *Franco ha dicho. Recopilación de las más importantes declaraciones del Caudillo desde la iniciación del Alzamiento Nacional* (Madrid: Editorial Carlos Jaime, 1947), pp. 53 and 57.

74 Speech of 16 October 1945. Franco, *Franco ha dicho*, p. 109.

75 Speech of 5 November 1957 in the Alcázar of Toledo to celebrate the golden anniversary of the XIV Infantry cohort. Reproduced in *La Vanguardia Española* (Barcelona), 6 November 1957. On the importance of the Alcázar in Francoist symbology, see Vicente Sánchez-Biosca, 'Imágenes, relatos y mitos de un lugar de memoria: el Alcázar de Toledo', *Archivos de la Filmoteca* 35 (2000), pp. 45–59.

76 Franco, *Pensamiento político de Franco* (1975 edition), vol. 2, p. 863.

77 Roger Eatwell, 'Introduction: New Styles of Dictatorship and Leadership in Interwar Europe', *Totalitarian Movements and Political Religions* 7/2 (2006),

pp. 127–37. See also Gerhard Besier and Katarzyna Stoklosa, *European Dictatorships: A Comparative History of the Twentieth Century* (Newcastle: Cambridge Scholars Publishing, 2013); and António Costa Pinto and Aristotle Kallis (eds), *Rethinking Fascism and Dictatorship in Europe* (New York: Palgrave Macmillan, 2014).

78 The context of the intellectual process is described in the classical analysis of Henry Stuart Hughes, *Consciousness and Society: The Reorientation of Social Thought, 1890–1930* (Brighton: Harvester Press, 1979); Karl Dietrich Bracher, *The Age of Ideologies: A History of Political Thought in the Twentieth Century* (London: Methuen, 1984); George L. Mosse, *Fallen Soldiers: Reshaping the Memory of the Two World Wars* (Oxford: Oxford University Press, 1990); and Mark Mazower, *Dark Continent: Europe's Twentieth Century* (London: Allen Lane, 1998). A useful compendium of classic texts on 'power and authority' appears in Lewis A. Coser and Bernard Rosenberg (eds), *Sociological Theory; A Book of Readings* (London: Collier Macmillan, 1976), ch. 5.

79 Words of Luciano Cavalli, *Carisma. La qualitá straordinaria del leader* (Rome: Laterza, 1995), pp. 6–7 and 83–4. In the same sense see Charles Lindholm, *Charisma* (Oxford: Blackwell, 1990); and Roger Eatwell, 'The Concept and Theory of Charismatic Leadership', *Totalitarian Movements and Political Religions* 7/2 (2006), pp. 141–56.

80 A Spanish version of the study by Weber, translated and annotated by Joaquín Abellán, was published under the title *Sociología del poder. Los tipos de dominación* (Madrid: Alianza, 2007), quotations from p. 75. It corresponds to ch. 3 of his great study *Economy and Society* (Oakland: University of California Press, 2013).

81 Carl Schmitt, *Dictatorship* (Cambridge: Polity, 2013). The first German edition of the text is from 1921, the same year as Weber's formulation of the concept of 'charismatic authority'. The concept of 'personal power' by Burdeau (reformulated after 1945) is exposed in Juan Ferrando Badía, 'Las formas históricas de poder político y sus legitimidades', *Revista de Estudios Políticos* 138 (1964), pp. 85–121.

82 Words of Cavalli, *Carisma*, pp. 84–5.

83 Ian Kershaw, *The Hitler Myth: Image and Reality in the Third Reich* (Oxford: Oxford University Press, 2001). Luisa Passerini, *Mussolini immaginario. Storia di una biografia, 1915–1939* (Bari: Laterza, 1991). Sarah Davis and

James Harris (eds), *Stalin: A New History* (Cambridge: Cambridge University Press, 2005). Richard Overy, *Dictators: Hitler's Germany and Stalin's Russia* (London: Allen Lane, 2004).

84 Reproduced in Emilio Gentile, *El culto del Littorio. La sacralización de la política en la Italia fascista* (Buenos Aires: Siglo XXI, 2007), pp. 219–20. See Piero Melograni, 'The Cult of the Duce in Mussolini's Italy', *Journal of Contemporary History* 11 (1976), pp. 221–37; and Renzo de Felice and Luigi Goglia, *Mussolini. Il Mito* (Rome: Laterza, 1983).

85 Franz Neumann, *Behemoth. Pensamiento y acción en el nacional-socialismo* (Mexico: Fondo de Cultura Económica, 1983), pp. 108–9 and 121, published in English as *Behemoth* (New York: Octagon Press, 1983).

86 *Abc*, 17 July 1938, p. 23. See Langa, '*Abc* de Sevilla, el diario de mayor circulación de la España nacional'.

87 Speech before Cardinal Cicognani, 28 January 1964. *Abc*, 29 January 1964.

88 Instructions reproduced in Zenobi, *La construcción del mito de Franco*, pp. 126–7. Marta Bizcarrondo, 'Imágenes para un Salvador', *Bulletin d'histoire contemporaine de l'Espagne* 24 (1996), pp. 229–44.

89 Zenobi, *La construcción del mito de Franco*, p. 141.

90 Nicolás Sesma Landrín, *Antología de la Revista de Estudios Políticos* (Madrid: Centro de Estudios Políticos y Constitucionales, 2010). Benjamín Rivaya, *Filosofía del Derecho y primer franquismo* (Madrid: Centro de Estudios Políticos y Constitucionales, 1998). Matilde Eiroa San Francisco, 'Palabra de Franco. Lenguaje político e ideología en los textos doctrinales', in C. Navajas and D. Iturriaga (eds), *Coetánea. Actas del III congreso internacional de historia de nuestro tiempo* (Logroño: Universidad de la Rioja, 2012), pp. 71–88. Jaume Claret Miranda, *El atroz desmoche. La destrucción de la Universidad española por el franquismo, 1936–1945* (Barcelona: Crítica, 2006). According to this author (pp. 352–3), the numbers of professors in 1935 dropped by perhaps half as a result of deaths, expulsions and departures into exile. In law faculties, the reduction affected 27 professors and 28 lecturers.

91 Francisco Elías de Tejada, *La figura del Caudillo. Contribución al derecho público nacionalsindicalista* (Seville: Ateneo de Sevilla-Tipografía Andaluza, 1939).

92 Juan Beneyto Pérez, *El Nuevo Estado Español. El régimen nacional-sindicalista ante la tradición y los demás sistemas totalitarios* (Madrid: Biblioteca Nueva, 1939), pp. 113, 115–16, 165 and 168. In the accurate view of Gallego, the work was 'one of the most important texts of the time' (*El Evangelio Fascista*,

p. 595). The speech of Fernández Cuesta is in *18 de julio. Tres discursos* (Madrid: Arriba, 1938), p. 37.

93 Juan Beneyto and José M. Costa Serrano, *El Partido. Estructura e historia del derecho público totalitario* (Zaragoza: Hispania, 1939), p. 153.

94 Luis Jordana de Pozas, 'El principio de unidad y sus consecuencias políticas y administrativas', *Revista de Estudios Políticos* 4 (1941), pp. 41–4.

95 Alberto Reig Tapia, *Franco. El césar superlativo*, p. 191. Gallego, *El Evangelio Fascista*, pp. 553 and 617.

96 Francisco Javier Conde, *Contribución a la doctrina del Caudillaje* (Madrid: Vicesecretaría de Educación Popular, 1942), pp. 17, 23, 30, 31 and 34. The previous articles were published by *Arriba* between 4 and 8 February 1942.

97 Francisco Moret Messerli, *Conmemoraciones y fechas de la España nacional-sindicalista* (Madrid: Delegación Nacional de Prensa y Propaganda de FET, 1942), pp. 71–2.

98 Luis del Valle Pascual, *Democracia y Jerarquía* (Zaragoza: Atheneum, 1942), pp. 9, 162–4, 218 and 239 (first published 1938).

99 They all appear and are discussed, to a greater or lesser degree, in the already mentioned works of Ferran Gallego, Ismael Saz, Alberto Reig Tapia, Benjamín Rivaya and José Manuel Cuenca Toribio.

100 An updated analysis of the institutional evolution is in Miguel Ángel Giménez Martínez, *El Estado franquista. Fundamentos ideológicos, bases legales y sistema institucional* (Madrid: Centro de Estudios Políticos y Constitucionales, 2014). An instruction to the debate on 'the nature of the Franco regime' is in Enrique Moradiellos, 'Franco y el franquismo en tinta sobre papel: narrativas sobre el régimen y su caudillo', in Julián Casanova (ed.), *40 años con Franco* (Barcelona: Crítica, 2015), ch. 9. Jorge Novella Suárez analyses well the transition of Francoist ideology since the days of Conde to the final formulations of Gonzalo Fernández de la Mora in *El pensamiento reaccionario español*, chs 12 and 13.

101 Manuel Fraga Iribarne, *Así se gobierna España* (Madrid: Oficina de Información Diplomática, 1951), pp. 36–7 and 54.

102 Torcuato Fernández-Miranda, *El hombre y la sociedad* (Madrid: Ediciones Doncel-Delegación Nacional de Juventudes, 1963, fourth edition), p. 190.

103 José Zafra Valverde, *Régimen político de España* (Pamplona: Universidad de Navarra, 1973), pp. 164–7, 195 and 200.

104 Ismael Saz, 'Franco, ¿Caudillo fascista? Sobre las sucesivas y contradictorias

concepciones falangistas del Caudillaje franquista', in I. Saz, *Las caras del franquismo* (Granada, Comares, 2013), ch. 7, pp. 113–33.

105   Quoted in Badía, 'Las formas históricas de poder político y sus legitimidades', pp. 97 and 112.

106   Luis Sánchez Agesta expressly mentioned it in his well-known manual *Lecciones de Derecho Político* (Granada: Librería Prieto, 1959), p. 471. The political context of this crucial debate arises in Álvaro Soto Carmona, *¿Atado y bien atado? Institucionalización y crisis del franquismo,* (Madrid: Biblioteca Nueva, 2005); Cristina Palomares, *The Quest for Survival after Franco: Moderate Francoism and the Slow Journey to the Polls, 1964–1977* (Eastbourne: Sussex Academic Press, 2004); and Carme Molinero and Pere Ysàs, *La anatomía del franquismo. De la supervivencia a la agonía, 1945–1977* (Barcelona: Crítica, 2008).

107   Declarations of Franco to the editor of the newspaper *Arriba*, 23 January 1955, quoted in Valverde, *El sistema político en las décadas de Franco*, p. 395. The formula of Fueyo was published in the journal *Pueblo*, organ of the Organización Sindical franquista. It is reproduced in Raymond Carr and Juan Pablo Fusi, *España, de la dictadura a la democracia* (Barcelona: Planeta, 1979), p. 236.

108   The ideas of Fernández-Miranda (in 1973) is in Pilar and Alfonso Fernández-Miranda, *Lo que el rey me ha pedido. Torcuato Fernández-Miranda y la Reforma Política* (Barcelona: Plaza y Janés, 1995), pp. 17 and 55–6. The earlier declaration by Fraga Iribane reproduced in Carr and Fusi, *España, de la dictadura a la democracia,* p. 266.

109   Statement of one of the members of the last government of Franco in 1976, reproduced in Carr and Fusi, *España, de la dictadura a la democracia,* p. 236.

110   Words of a confidential report of Guy de la Tournelle in October 1959, reproduced in Álvaro Fleites Marcos, *De Gaulle y España* (Avilés: Azucel, 2009), p. 152.

111   Salvador de Madariaga, *General, márchese usted* (New York: Ediciones Ibéricas, 1959), p. 10.

112   Juan Pablo Fusi, *Franco. Autoritarismo y poder personal* (Madrid: El País, 1985), p. 15.

3: The Regime: A Complex Dictatorship

1   Javier Tusell, *La dictadura de Franco* (Madrid: Alianza, 1988), p. 111.

2   Raymond Carr and Juan Pablo Fusi, *España, de la dictadura a la democracia* (Barcelona: Planeta, 1979), p. 11.

3   Borja de Riquer, *La dictadura de Franco* (Barcelona: Crítica, 2010), pp. xv–xvi.

4   Tusell, *La dictadura de Franco*, p. 263.

5   Stanley G. Payne, *El régimen de Franco* (Madrid: Alianza, 1987), p. 651, published in English as *The Franco Regime* (Madison: University of Wisconsin Press, 1987).

6   Robert O. Paxton, 'Franco's Spain in Comparative Perspective', in Miguel Ángel Ruiz Carnicer (ed.), *Falange. Las culturas políticas del fascismo en la España de Franco. 1936–1975* (Zaragoza: Institución Cultural Fernando el Católico, 2013), pp. 13–23 (quotation on pp. 22–3).

7   A general overview of such diverse regimes is in Gerhard Besier and Katarzyna Stoklosa, *European Dictatorships: A Comparative History of the Twentieth Century* (Newcastle: Cambridge Scholars Publishing, 2013).

8   Quoted in Josue Derman, *Max Weber in Politics and Social Thought: From Charisma to Canonization* (Cambridge: Cambridge University Press, 2012), p. 156.

9   Carl Schmitt, *Dictatorship* (Cambridge: Polity, 2013).

10 Manuela Azaña, *Memorias políticas y de guerra, 1931–1939* (Barcelona: Grijalbo-Mondadori, 1978), pp. 313 and 330.

11 Ricardo Chueca Rodríguez and José Ramón Montero Gibert, 'El fascismo en España: elementos para una identificación', *Historia Contemporánea* 8 (1992), pp. 215–47 (quote on p. 219).

12 Stanley G. Payne, *Falange. Historia del Fascismo español* (Paris: Ruedo Ibérico, 1965), p. 110.

13 Francisco Franco Salgado-Araujo, *Mis conversaciones privadas con Franco* (Barcelona: Planeta, 1976), p. 142.

14 Jesús Palacios and Stanley G. Payne, *Franco, mi padre* (Madrid: Esfera de los Libros, 2008), pp. 74–5.

15 Quoted in Paul Preston, *Leviatán. Antología* (Madrid: Turner, 1976), pp. 295–6 and 302–3.

16 Both quotes in Walter Laqueur (ed.), *Fascism: A Reader's Guide* (Aldershot: Wildwood House, 1988), pp. 420 and 430; and David Beetham, *Marxists in*

Face of Fascism (Manchester: Manchester University Press, 1983), pp. 22 and 295.

17 Dolores Ibárruri (ed.), *Guerra y revolución en España* (Moscow: Progreso, 1966), vol. 1, p. 305.

18 Quoted in Enrique Moradiellos, *La perfidia de Albión. El gobierno británico y la guerra civil española* (Madrid: Siglo XXI, 1996), p. 217.

19 'Notas sobre la situación internacional', 11 November 1942, Archivo General de la Universidad de Navarra, Fondo Carrero Blanco, Serie 'Política Internacional'. Salvador de Madariaga, *General, Márchese usted* (New York: Ibérica, 1959), p. 15.

21 Text of the final communiqué of the Potsdam Conference. Quoted in Enrique Moradiellos, 'The Potsdam Conference and the Spanish Problem', *Contemporary European History* 10/1 (2001), pp. 73–90 (quotation on p. 73).

22 Giuliana Di Febo and Santos Juliá, *El Franquismo. Una introducción* (Barcelona: Crítica, 2012), p. 7.

23 Law of 29 November 1878, quoted in José Antonio Olmeda Gómez, *Las Fuerzas Armadas en el Estado Franquista* (Madrid: El Arquero, 1988), p. 94.

24 Emilio Mola, *Obras completas* (Valladolid: Santarén, 1940), p. 1184.

25 Confession of Franco to the writer José María Pemán in the middle of August 1936, quoted in Paul Preston, *Franco: A Biography* (London: HarperCollins, 1993), p. 176. Franco's statement to the Portuguese journal *O Seculo*, mid-August 1936 in José Emilio Díez, *Colección de proclamas y arengas del Excmo. Sr. General D. Francisco Franco* (Seville: M. Carmona, 1937), p. 92.

26 Quoted in Julio Rodríguez Puértolas, *Literatura fascista española. Antología* (Madrid: Akal, 1987), pp. 520–1.

27 Quoted by Javier Tusell, *Franco en la guerra civil. Una biografía política* (Barcelona: Tusquets, 1992), p. 302.

28 *Boletín Oficial del Estado*, 31 January 1938.

29 Roger Eatwell, 'Introduction: New Styles of Dictatorship and Leadership in Interwar Europe', *Totalitarian Movements and Political Religions* 7/2 (2006), pp. 127–37. Roberto Cavalli, *Carisma. La qualitá straordinaria del leader* (Rome: Laterza, 1995).

30 Torcuato Fernández-Miranda, *El hombre y la sociedad* (Madrid: Delegación Nacional de Juventudes, 1960), pp. 188–90, with original emphasis

31 Enzo Traverso, *El totalitarismo. Historia de un debate* (Buenos Aires: Eudeba,

2013). Karl Dietrich Bracher, *The Age of Ideologies: A History of Political Thought in the Twentieth Century* (London: Methuen, 1985), pp. 81–6.

32 Emilio Gentile, *El Fascismo. Historia e interpretación* (Madrid: Alianza, 2004), pp. 99–101 and ch. 11. The aphorism of Mussolini, formulated in 1925, is in Traverso, *El totalitarismo*, p. 25.

33 Quoted in Franz Neumann, *Behemoth. Pensamiento y acción en el nacional-socialismo* (Mexico: Fondo de Cultura Económica, 1983), p. 69, published in English as *Behemoth* (New York: Octagon Press, 1983).

34 Annotation of 28 November 1957. Franco Salgado-Araujo, *Mis conversaciones privadas con Franco*, p. 220.

35 Traverso, *El totalitarismo*, p. 162.

36 Richard Overy, *Dictadores. La Alemania de Hitler y la Unión Soviética de Stalin* (Madrid: Tusquets, 2010), pp. 719–20; first published in English as *Dictators: Hitler's Germany and Stalin's Russia* (London: Allen Lane, 2004).

37 Traverso, *El totalitarismo*, p. 145.

38 Juan J. Linz, 'An Authoritarian Regime: The Case of Spain', in Erik Nard and Yrjo Littunen (eds), *Cleavages, Ideologies, and Party Systems* (Helsinki: Westermarck Society, 1964). Their theses were reworked and expanded in *Totalitarian and Authoritarian Regimes* (London: Lynne Rienner, 2000).

39 Quoted in José Félix Tezanos, 'Notas para una interpretación sociológica del Franquismo', *Sistema. Revista de Ciencias Sociales* 23 (1978), pp. 47–99 (the quote from Germani is on p. 61). The original work by Germani is *Authoritarianism, Fascism and National Populism* (New Brunswick: Transaction Books, 1978).

40 Paul Preston, *The Politics of Revenge: Fascism and the Military in Twentieth Century Spain* (London: Routledge, 1995), p. 11.

41 Julián Casanova, *El pasado oculto. Fascismo y violencia en Aragón, 1936–1939* (Madrid: Siglo XXI, 1992), pp. 3–25.

42 Santiago Montero Díaz, *Fascismo* (Valencia: Cuadernos de Cultura, 1932).

43 The words of Karl Dietrich Bracher, *Controversias de historia contemporánea sobre fascismo, totalitarismo y democracia* (Barcelona: Alfa, 1983), p. 33.

44 Ricardo Chueca and José Ramón Montero, 'El fascismo en España: elementos para una interpretación', *Historia Contemporánea* 8 (1992), p. 246.

45 Antonio Elorza 'Mitos y símbolos de una dictadura', *Bulletin d'Histoire Contemporaine de l'Espagne* 24 (1996), p. 49; Antonio Elorza, 'Las raíces

ideológicas del franquismo', in Antonio Elorza, *La modernización política de España* (Madrid: Endymion, 1990), p. 442.

46 Julio Aróstegui, 'Los componentes sociales y políticos', in Manuel Tuñón de Lara (ed.), *La guerra civil española. 50 años después* (Barcelona: Labor, 1986), pp. 61, 97 and 102.

47 Aristotle Kallis and António Costa Pinto, 'Conclusion', in Aristotle Kallis and António Costa Pinto (eds), *Rethinking Fascism and Dictatorship in Europe* (New York: Palgrave Macnillan, 2014), p. 275. See also Aristotle Kallis, 'Fascism, Para-Fascism and Fascistization: On the Similarities of Three Conceptual Categories', *European History Quarterly* 33/2 (2003), pp. 219–49.

48 The words of Ismael Saz, *Fascismo y Franquismo* (Valencia: Publicaciones de la Universidad de Valencia, 2004), p. 86.

49 Saz, *Fascismo y Franquismo*, pp. 88–9.

50 Ferran Gallego, *El Evangelio Fascista. La formación de la cultura política del franquismo* (Barcelona: Crítica, 2014).

51 Gallego, *El Evangelio Fascista*, p. 913.

52 Gregory M. Luebert, *Liberalism, Fascism or Social Democracy: Social Classes and the Political Origins of Regimes in Interwar Europe* (Oxford: Oxford University Press, 1991), p. 276.

53 Gentile, *Fascismo*, p. 59.

54 Emilio Gentile, 'Introducción al fascismo', in Javier Tusell, Emilio Gentile, Giuliana Di Febo and Susana Sueiro (eds), *Fascismo y Franquismo. Cara a cara. Una perspectiva histórica* (Madrid: Biblioteca Nueva, 2004), p. 18.

55 Robert O. Paxton, *Anatomía del fascismo* (Barcelona: Península, 2005), p. 98; first published in English as *The Anatomy of Fascism* (London: Penguin, 2004).

56 Traverso, *El totalitarismo*, p. 27.

57 Julián Sanz Hoya, 'Falangismo y dictadura. Una revisión de la historiografía sobre el fascismo español', in Ruiz Carnicer (ed.), *Falange*, pp. 25–60 (quote on pp. 58–9).

58 Francisco Franco, *Discursos y Mensajes del Jefe del Estado, 1951–1954* (Madrid: Publicaciones Españolas, 1955), p. 306. Reproduced in *Abc*, 17 April 1953.

59 Speech reproduced in the newspaper *Abc*, 31 December 1964.

60 Franco Salgado-Araujo, *Mis conversaciones privadas con Franco*, p. 156. Annotation of 31 December 1955.

61 Tusell, *La dictadura franquista*, p. 263.

62 Payne, *El régimen de Franco*, p. 651.

63 Miguel Ángel Giménez Martínez, *El Estado Franquista. Fundamentos ideológicos, bases legales y sistema institucional* (Madrid: Centro de Estudios Políticos y Sociales, 2014), p. 29.

64 The quotations by Mann, Berr and Febvre are in Donald R. Kelley, 'Ideas of Periodization in the West', in Q. Edward Wang and Franz L. Fillafer (eds), *The Many Faces of Clio: Cross-Cultural Approaches to Historiography* (Oxford: Berghahn, 2007), p. 19.

65 José Ortega y Gasset, 'Prólogo', in Wilhelm Dilthey, *Introducción a las ciencias del espíritu* (Madrid: Revista de Occidente, 1966), p. 15.

66 A recent example in English of this consensus can be seen in the title and work of Nigel Townson: *Spain Transformed: The Franco Dictatorship, 1959–1975* (New York: Palgrave Macmillan, 2010).

67 Tusell, *La dictadura de Franco*, pp. 249–50.

68 The proceedings of the conference were published as Javier Tusell (coord.), *El Régimen de Franco, 1936–1975. Política y Relaciones Exteriores* (Madrid: UNED, 1993).

69 Gabriel Tortella, *El desarrollo de la España contemporánea. Historia económica de los siglos XIX y XX* (Madrid: Alianza, 1994), pp. 204 and 385.

70 Raymond Carr (ed.), *La época de Franco, 1939–1975. I: Política, Ejército, Iglesia, Economía*, vol. 41/1 (Madrid: Espasa Calpe, 1996).

71 Encarna Nicolás and Alicia Alted Vigil, *Disidencias en el Franquismo, 1939–1975* (Murcia: Diego Marín Editor, 1999).

72 Carlos Barciela, *Autarquía y mercado negro. El fracaso económico del Primer Franquismo (1939–1959)* (Barcelona: Crítica, 2003).

73 Special issue of the journal *Ayer*, 33 (1999).

74 Tusell, *La dictadura de Franco*, p. 250.

75 Giuliana Di Febo and Santos Juliá, *El Franquismo* (Barcelona: Crítica, 2012), p. 7.

76 Carme Molinero and Pere Ysàs, *Historia de España. Historia política, 1939–2000* (Madrid: Istmo, 2001).

77 Enrique Moradiellos, *El Franquismo. Política y sociedad* (Madrid: Síntesis, 2000).

78 Manuel Tuñón de Lara, *Historia de España* (Barcelona: Labor, 1991), pp. 577–8.

79 Preston, *The Politics of Revenge*, pp. 112–13.

80 Payne, *El régimen de Franco*, pp. 651–2.

81 Juan Pablo Fusi, *Franco. Autoritarismo y poder personal* (Madrid: El País, 1985), pp. 73–4.

82 José Luis García Delgado and Juan Carlos Jiménez, *Un siglo de España. La economía* (Madrid: Marcial Pons, 1999), p. 114.

83 Jordi Gracia and Miguel Ángel Ruiz Carnicer, *El Franquismo. Cultura y vida cotidiana* (Madrid: Síntesis, 2001).

84 Stanley G. Payne, in Raymond Carr (ed.), *Historia de España Menéndez Pidal, Vol. 41/1* (Madrid: Espasa Calpe, 1996), p. 6.

85 Salvador de Madariaga, *España. Ensayo de historia contemporánea* (Madrid: Espasa-Calpe, 1979), p. 511.

86 De Riquer, *La dictadura franquista*, p. xviii.

FURTHER READING

General Studies on the Franco Regime

First and foremost, it is worth mentioning the dictionaries and general histories of contemporary Spain that have come out in recent times and that address, usually with perception, the times of Francoism and some of its major facets. In order of publication, one might cite the following six works for their high interpretive quality: Francisco J. Romero Salvadó, *Twentieth-Century Spain: Politics and Society in Spain, 1898–1998* (London: Macmillan, 1999); Mary Vincent, *Spain, 1833–2002: People and State* (Oxford: Oxford University Press, 2007); Angel Smith, *Historical Dictionary of Spain* (Plymouth: Scarecrow Press, 2009); Stanley Black, *Spain since 1939* (New York: Palgrave Macmillan, 2010); Christopher J. Ross, *Spain since 1812* (Oxford: Routledge, 2014) and Julián Casanova and Carlos Gil-Andrés, *Twentieth-Century Spain: A History* (Cambridge: Cambridge University Press, 2014).

The first useful synthesis in English on the general history of the Franco regime was published by Paul Preston, which retains its analytical vigour: *Spain in Crisis: The Evolution and Decline of the Franco Regime* (London: Harvester Press, 1976). Three years later, Raymond Carr and Juan Pablo Fusi published a commendable synthesis of the Francoist and subsequent period for the English-speaking public: *Spain: Dictatorship to Democracy* (London: Allen & Unwin, 1979). Nearly a decade later, the North American Hispanist Stanley G. Payne completed one of the first detailed studies of the regime: *The Franco Regime* (Madison: University of Wisconsin Press, 1987). Another decade later appeared the joint work of Jean Grugel and Tim Rees: *Franco's Spain* (London: Arnold, 1997). And just another ten years later was the translation into English of a famous work by Javier Tusell: *Spain: From Dictatorship to Democracy* (Oxford: Blackwell, 2007). One of the more recent contributions in English on the history of Franco is the work of Nigel Townson: *Spain Transformed: The Franco Dictatorship, 1959–1975* (New York: Palgrave-Macmillan, 2010). A final work should be mentioned in this regard, the book edited by Helen Graham as a tribute to Professor Preston's outstanding research on the Francoist period: *Interrogating Francoism* (London: Bloomsbury, 2016).

Monographs on Particular Aspects of the Franco Regime

As a military dictatorship in its origin and until the end, Franquismo is well addressed in the famous works of Stanley G. Payne, *Politics and the Military in Modern Spain* (Stanford: Stanford University Press, 1967) and Paul Preston, *The Politics of Revenge: Fascism and the Military in Twentieth Century Spain* (London: Routledge, 1995). Also interesting are the contributions of Wayne H. Bowen and José E. Álvarez, *A Military History of Modern Spain* (Westport: Praeger, 2007).

The fascist side of the regime is addressed in the aforementioned work of Paul Preston and in another two contributions of great interest: Stanley G. Payne, *Fascism in Spain, 1923–1977* (Madison: University of Wisconsin Press, 1999), first published as *Falange: A History of Spanish Fascism* (Stanford: Stanford University Press, 1961); and Sheelagh M. Ellwood, *Spanish Fascism in the Franco Era* (London: Macmillan, 1987). An early but very influential contribution is by Juan José Linz, 'From Falange to Movimiento-Organización: The Spanish Single Party and the Franco Regime', in Samuel P. Huntington and C.H. Moore (eds), *Authoritarian Politics in Modern Societies* (New York: Basic Books, 1970). A recent comprehensive introduction is by Miguel Jerez Mir and Javier Luque, 'State and Regime in Early Francoism, 1936–1945: Power Structures, Main Actors and Repression Policy', in António Costa Pinto and Aristotle Kallis (eds), *Rethinking Fascism and Dictatorship in Europe* (London: Palgrave Macmillan, 2014).

The role of the Catholic Church, following its influence and then defection, can be found in these works: Norman B. Cooper, *Catholicism and the Franco*

Regime (London: Sage, 1975); Frances Lannon, *Privilege, Persecution and Prophecy: The Catholic Church in Spain, 1875–1975* (Oxford: Oxford University Press, 1987); and Hilari Raguer, *Gunpowder and Incense: The Catholic Church and the Spanish Civil War* (London: Routledge, 2007).

The international context in which the regime unfolded and evolved is described in Sebastian Balfour and Paul Preston (eds), *Spain and the Great Powers in the Twentieth Century* (London: Routledge, 1999); and Raanan Rein (ed.), *Spain and the Mediterranean since 1898* (London: Routledge, 2007).

An overview of the economic developments of the country under the dictatorship can be seen in the following recent works: Sima Lieberman, *Growth and Crisis in the Spanish Economy, 1940–93* (London: Routledge, 1995) and David Corkill and Joseph Harrison, *Spain: A Modern European Economy* (London: Ashgate, 2004).

A good introduction to the cultural evolution during Francoism is the book edited by David T. Gies, *The Cambridge Companion to Modern Spanish Culture* (Cambridge: Cambridge University Press, 2003). A recent and balanced essay on the subject is Jeremy Treglown, *Franco's Crypt: Spanish Culture and Memory since 1936* (New York: Farrar, Strauss and Giroux, 2013).

The relationship between Franco and the monarchists is analysed in detail in the biography of Franco's successor by Paul Preston, *Juan Carlos: Steering Spain from Dictatorship to Democracy* (London: Harper, 2004). The same author is responsible for the more intense work on Franco's repression of his enemies, in the Civil War and the long postwar period: *The Spanish Holocaust: Inquisition and Extermination in Twentieth Century Spain* (London: Harper, 2012).

The legacy of that war and its consequent dictatorship can be seen in several recent analyses: Paloma Aguilar, *Memory and Amnesia: The Role of the Spanish Civil War in the Transition to Democracy* (Oxford: Berghahn Books, 2002); Helen Graham, *The War and its Shadows: Spain's Civil War in Europe's Long Twentieth Century* (Eastbourne: Sussex Academic Press, 2012); and Antonio Cazorla, *Franco: The Biography of the Myth* (London: Routledge, 2014).

Biographies

General Franco already has a large volume of biographies that give accounts of both his personal and political life. Leaving aside the works published during his lifetime, to a greater or lesser extent weighted by their pro- or anti-Francoist militancy, one might cite a small number of studies in English that have high historiographic value.

First, the famous work of Hispanist Paul Preston must be singled out as the best and most exhaustive study on the theme: *Franco: A Biography* (London: HarperCollins, 1993). In the same line, but less extensive, two other equally valuable works should be mentioned: that of Juan Pablo Fusi, *Franco: A Biography* (London: Routledge, 1987) and that of Sheelagh Ellwood, *Franco* (London: Routledge, 1994). An interesting psychological approach to Franco's character is by Gabrielle Ashford Hodges, *Franco: A Concise Biography* (London: Weidenfeld & Nicolson, 2000). And perhaps the most recent re-evaluation of this historical figure is by Stanley G. Payne and Jesús Palacios, *Franco: A Personal and Political Biography* (Madison: University of Wisconsin Press, 2014).

INDEX